Project
Evaluation AND
Feasibilty
Analysis
FOR HOSPITALITY
OPERATIONS

Dedication

To Les and Madge Baker
Proprietors of the Central Tourist Hotel
Wellington
New Zealand
1957–63

Project Evaluation AND Feasibilty Analysis

FOR HOSPITALITY OPERATIONS

Kevin Baker

BEc, MEc (Hons), MTheol, PhD (Sydney)

PEARSON
Education
Australia

Pearson Education Australia
Unit 4, Level 3
14 Aquatic Drive
Frenchs Forest NSW 2086

www.pearsoned.com.au

Project Evaluation and Feasibility Analysis for Hospitality Operations
First published 2000

National Library of Australia
Cataloguing-in-publication data:

Baker, Kevin. 1949–
  Project evaluation and feasibility analysis for hospitality operations

  Bibliography.
  Includes index.
  ISBN 1 86250 489 X

  1. Hospitality industry – Economic aspects – Australia. 2. Hospitality industry –
  Research – Australia. 3. Marketing research – Australia. 4. Feasibility studies –
  Australia. I. Title.

338.476479494

Edited by Ross Gilham (Ginross Editorial Services)
Designed and typeset by Lauren Statham (Alice Graphics)
Printed by Pearson Australia Demand Print Centre
Published by Hospitality Press Pty Ltd (ACN 006 473 454)h

Contents

Acknowledgments

I acknowledge the assistance of Jeremy Huyton, Christina Flynn and Judy Lundy who generously gave their time and advice in the preparation of this manuscript. Thanks also to Charlie Panakera for comments on capital investment decision-making.

Special thanks to Paul Morrison of the Department of Hospitality, Tourism and Property Management of the University of Queensland for comments and advice on the text.

I also thank David and Jean Cunningham, Ross Gilham for his editorial expertise, and my wife, Jane.

Preface

Why write a book on feasibility analysis? The answer is twofold.

The *first* reason relates to general economic conditions. Whereas, in the past, a new hotel could be built with the expectation that the market was growing, and would continue to grow, the market today is tight, and is likely to remain so. The Asian currency crisis, followed by bleak economic forecasts for several world regions, have ensured that every investment decision has to be considered very carefully—especially since demands for bigger and better hotels and resorts mean that a hospitality venture requires the input of a larger slice of capital at greater risk.

The *second* reason relates to the nature of feasibility studies themselves.

> Recently, the trade press has been buzzing with articles addressing the topic of hotel feasibility studies and whether they accurately portray the future operating results of a proposed hotel.
>
> Rushmore (1996)[1]

Academic study indicates that some of the feasibility studies conducted for projects in the recent past have not been accurate. Projects recommended as being feasible have proved not to be so—resulting in serious financial loss for their backers.

So the time is right for a comprehensive review of what a project evaluation is, why it should be done, and how it should be done. This book discusses the issues with examples and case studies from Australia and various Pacific Rim countries.

Preface Note

[1] Rushmore, S. 1996, 'Feasibility Studies: Fact or Fiction', *Lodging Hospitality*, October 1996, p. 14.

CHAPTER 1

Introduction

Synopsis of Chapter

This chapter gives an overview of the hospitality industry, and some important recent developments and strategies. The chapter then details what must be covered in a project evaluation—considering the uses and users of the report.

The membership and range of expertise required of the study team is also discussed.

The accuracy of feasibility studies is outlined, and the structure of the report is described.

Background to Project Evaluation and Feasibility Analysis

This book describes the processes necessary to conduct a project evaluation/feasibility study of a new project, or an evaluation of an existing operation with a view to extending or changing its role. Most of the material in the book refers to hotel/motel projects (including restaurants), but it can be applied to related tourism/hospitality projects—such as resorts and caravan parks, or even a venture such as a crocodile farm, similar to the one described in Chapter 2.

The two terms 'project evaluation' and 'feasibility study' are very similar in meaning. A project evaluation has a wider scope than a feasibility study because it could include an existing operation. The author has a preference for 'project evaluation' because the term implies the ranking of values, whereas the term 'feasibility study' seems to imply only a yes/no answer to the question: 'Is the project feasible or not?'. However, to avoid a complication that is semantic only, the two terms are used interchangeably in the following pages.

An Overview of the Hospitality Industry

The hospitality industry is influenced by two main factors—a growing tourism industry (including overseas visitor arrivals) and an expanding economy (particularly in the services sector). Australia rates well in both these factors.

- The nation has an expanding tourism industry. The Bureau of Tourism Research estimated that tourism contributed close to 6% of Australia's Gross Domestic Product in 1999.
- Australia has an economy heavily reliant on the services sector. The services sector accounted for 63% of Australia's gross domestic product (GDP) in 1997.

Australians spent $32.8 billion on 73.8 million overnight trips during 1998.[1]

As compared with other manufactured products, the product offered to consumers by the tourism and hospitality industry has an unusual feature—if the service is not used immediately it becomes available, it is instantly perishable. Once the night has passed, the hotel cannot sell accommodation to a guest, nor can a restaurant provide extra meals next day for the seats that were empty the night before. The airline industry is comparable in this regard—in that, once the aircraft takes off, no more seats on the flight can be sold.

This perishability means that a knowledge of the market and correct pricing are very important. Hotel operators will discount their rates heavily if it means that they can increase the number of guests occupying rooms (the occupancy rate). In theory, operators can make a profit out of a very low room-rate (the price charged guests to occupy the room)—because otherwise the room could be empty and producing no revenue at all. However, the problem that then arises is that all their other guests would expect to pay the same amount, and overall revenue would fall.

Therefore, any prospective developer needs either an excellent knowledge of the industry, or they must employ expert knowledge. Either way, that knowledge needs to be carefully applied to specific circumstances, because the hospitality market is fragmented and imperfect. Every different situation needs to be considered on its own merits. Supply-and-demand factors vary from place to place, and from product to product.

In practice, the demand for hotel rooms is imperfect because it is not dependent upon last-minute discounting of rates. First, many travellers book well in advance. Secondly, most travellers do not freely choose the hotel at which to stay, but are constrained by their own company practice (for business travellers) or by agency arrangements (for leisure travellers who purchase package tours).

There are others factors which impact upon demand, making it imperfect in economic terms. These include seasonality factors, and unpredictable factors such as industrial action by key groups (for example, airline pilots).

Who are the people staying at hotels these days? The Worldwide Hotel Industry Study[2] indicates that, in 1997, 52.6% of hotel room-nights were sourced from foreign travellers, and 47.4% were domestic. Leisure travellers made up 34.1% of the market; business travellers 28.5%; tour groups 17.7% and conference participants 10.1%. These are worldwide averages, and individual countries showed large variations from these norms.

The supply of rooms is also a market factor that is imperfect in economic terms. It can take up to two to three years to build a hotel, and another year to have it running at peak capacity. During that period, the market can change, and the supply might no longer meet the perceived demand that existed at the time that the investment decision was made. Extra hotel rooms cannot quickly be generated to meet changes in demand. Similarly, the supply does not quickly decline—for it is not easy either to demolish properties or to convert them to other uses (such as private apartments).

The supply of hotel rooms in Australia remained stable in the early 1990s but, in the mid-to-late 1990s, there was an increasing number of hotel commencements—including serviced apartments (which now constitute 20% of the market). Australia-wide, room rates increased by 6% in 1996, with occupancy levels at their highest since 1981–82, and revenue from rooms sold exceeded $3 billion.[3]

Although the supply-and-demand factors of the market are imperfect due to the time lags in hotel construction, there is, nevertheless, extensive competition between those hospitality operators who offer a similar product to the same market segment. The competition can be through pricing, through strategies to obtain repeat business, or through attempts to differentiate the product (for example, by offering services such as free Internet connections in the hotel suite).

Because of the degree of competition, it is essential that new hospitality proposals carefully examine market factors and, because of the large capital investment and the fact that pricing is critical, such proposals should also analyse financial factors in detail. Those two broad headings—market factors and financial factors—will be followed at a later stage in this book, when the structure of the project evaluation is examined (p. 12).

Current Development Strategies in the Hospitality Industry

In this context (of considering the background to feasibility studies and the tourism/hospitality industry), development strategies of existing hospitality operators should be examined. The strategies of small-to-medium hotels are, for obvious reasons, not publicised, but an examination of the development strategies of the larger hotel chains shows that there are some common factors underpinning current growth in hospitality operations.

There is a greater emphasis on 'branding' and market segmentation, providing a range of service categories—even within the same hotel group. A trend towards mergers and consolidations continues, as chains seek to cover geographical or segment gaps in their target markets. There is also a growth in franchising and linkages—such as referral chains and marketing chains—particularly at the lower levels of service, rather than at the four-star and five-star end of the range.

Although there was an oversupply of hotel rooms in many countries, including Australia, during the 1990s (with attendant problems of low occupancies and low room rates), there has been a recovery in some segments of the market. One of those is the mid-market accommodation segment which is experiencing strong growth in North America and Europe, driven by the preferences of business travellers. There is also a distinction being made between key cities of a region (where there is a larger demand for four-star and five-star accommodation), and so-called 'secondary' cities and smaller centres (where mid-market hotels are in demand, and chains such as Hampton Inn and Travelodge are expanding). 'Timeshare' accommodation has also shown good growth—with the participation of major brands such as Marriott, Hilton and Hyatt.[4]

Global distribution systems, or linked reservation systems, which were developed by airlines, have become indispensable for large hotel operators. There is also a tendency for large hotels to set up marketing consortia to handle advertising and marketing to global customers—in parallel with the complex worldwide reservations systems. It remains to be seen whether the exponential growth of the Internet—with its possibilities for online booking and information—will challenge global distribution and marketing systems. In 1997, travel had become the second-largest sector of online marketing, obtaining approximately a quarter of the United States' market.[5]

These development strategies of the larger chains have implications for smaller operators—who will probably be forced into 'niche' markets (with more specialised products), or be restricted to lower-market and mid-market products.

Key Features of Successful Business Investments

An organisation's ability to succeed in an increasingly hostile environment depends to a great extent on its ability to grow through wealth creation and strategically compatible capital investment.[6] In the tourism and hospitality industry, there is a range of ventures and avenues of investment—from small restaurant or merchandising operations, to hotels, motels and resorts.

In the tourism and hospitality industry, in economic terms, the 'barriers to entry' are low for a project such as a restaurant, although high for a project involving accommodation, such as a motel. A new developer can enter the industry with a relatively small investment. 'Barriers to entry' is an economic term referring to:

> . . . industry characteristics that limit the rate of entry [to an industry] in such a way that above-normal profits . . . are earned.
>
> Lewis, Morkel & Hubbard (1993)[7]

Low barriers to entry mean there are many players in the tourism/hospitality market place. This, in turn, means that competition is extensive. Although the tourism/hospitality market place is such a hazardous and competitive business, the committing of resources to long-term capital projects (in anticipation of an acceptable return) is essential for corporate vitality and wellbeing.

Decisions concerning investment in capital items or projects are clearly crucial to all businesses—because they affect the productive capacity of the business, and because the funding of the investment impacts upon returns and cash flow. Large enterprises have the professional expertise to evaluate capital projects, and to prepare formal feasibility studies where these are appropriate. Small-to-medium enterprises have limited management and professional resources, and decision-making might be subject to flawed information or process, with adverse implications for the firm.

A survey of a sample of small-to-medium hospitality operations—seeking data on how management uses information in financial management—was conducted in 1999 by Martin, Panakera and the present author.[8] Restaurants and small owner-operated motels were surveyed—because they are typically small-to-medium businesses, and because site owners and management have decision-making control. More than 90% had made significant investment decisions within the previous three years, but none had conducted formal feasibility studies. Moreover, two-thirds of those small businesses surveyed had been trading for less than three years.[8]

One key feature of business investment decisions is that they are linked to the long-term strategic goals of the organisation. The allocation of resources is a complex and crucial matter—which makes the whole sphere of capital investment and control central to the success of an enterprise. In the words of Horngren et al.:

> The decisions for the purchase of . . . non-current assets often require long-range planning and large risks.
>
> Horngren et al. (1997)[9]

Theories of capital investment decision-making have received considerable attention in the management accounting literature. Many definitions of capital investment/budgeting have been proposed—for example, in Drury (1992) and in Klammer (1994).[10,11] Horngren et al. define capital budgeting as follows:

> [Capital budgeting is] . . . formal means of making long-range decisions for investments such as non-current locations, equipment purchases, additions of product lines and territorial expansions.
>
> Horngren et al.[12]

In the main, these definitions from various authors have several common elements:

- the investment generally involves substantial financial outlay;
- the return from investment occurs over a number of years;

- there is generally some element of risk or uncertainty in predicting what the future return will be; and
- the expenditure typically includes the purchase or expansion of equipment or facilities which will directly impact upon an organisation's ability to meet its strategic and operating objectives.

There are other important features of capital investment not covered by these definitions. Capital investments often have implications for the behaviour and evaluation of organisational personnel.

Capital investment decision-making is not just the domain of accounting and finance personnel. Another key feature of successful investment decision-making is that many different players within an organisation are involved in the process.

Involving a range of people with appropriate skills, and good planning for investment decisions, are features that will minimise the risk of failure and loss of investment. There will always be a risk, for risk is inherent in investment and varies according to the type of operation, the quality of judgment and the accuracy of forecasts concerning future markets and conditions. Good planning requires an indepth analysis of all the factors that will contribute to success or failure. The input of people with appropriate skills and all the aspects of good planning and analysis should be packaged in the planning tool called a 'project evaluation'.

What is a 'Project Evaluation'?

A project evaluation (or a feasibility study) can be defined as:

> The systematic design, collection, analysis and reporting of data and findings relevant to a specific project being considered by a business.
>
> Based on Kotler (1994)[13]

Alternatively, a project evaluation is:

> . . . a careful consideration of the product being offered, the market it will be sold to, the physical, financial and operational requirements of creating it and the possibility of obtaining all the necessary approvals and finance to bring it into existence. It is, also, an assessment of the financial return which is likely to accrue to the developer.
>
> Tourism South Australia (1993)[14]

A project evaluation must provide the information and analysis that allows a reasoned decision. The study methodically covers all relevant factors and issues that will affect the new operation, and can have a wide scope—covering trends in national and international tourism, as well as regional or district factors. Such a study calls for an investment of funds—but a small investment in planning reduces the risk of losing a far larger amount.

Greene observes:

Many hotels and restaurants have gone bust because their owners have failed to carry out feasibility studies to determine long-term profits prior to acquisition . . . driven by a kind of mania where they cut corners.

Greene (1993)[15]

The project evaluation is of crucial importance. There are entrepreneurs who want to press ahead on the basis of their 'gut feeling'. But it should be noted that there is an old saying that warns, 'Beware a gut feeling—it's usually no more than wind'!

An operation that is a success in one area might not be a success in another for a number of reasons. An operation that has been a success in the past might not be the same success in the future—for in the tourism and hospitality industry, tastes and preferences change as often as people change their minds.

A project evaluation is not intended to be a justification for a decision already made. If construction has started, or approvals have been given and the project is about to start, it is too late for a balanced and independent study. A study must be conducted when the concept is a 'gleam in the eye'. When there is the gleam of money on the table, and the project is committed and already under way, there is limited benefit to be gained from conducting the project evaluation.

A formal study allows a decision to be made on a sound and reasoned basis before the commitment of substantial funds. It does not remove the risk but, if well done, a project evaluation does reduce risk of failure.

The Purposes of Evaluation

Evaluation can be applied to a new project to assess how it will operate, or to an existing operation to assess how well it is operating. Is it effective—that is, achieving or able to achieve its objectives? Is it efficient—that is, using resources in the best way to attain its output? The evaluation has to assess many factors in order to assess how effective and efficient a project will be once it is established and working to its peak operating capability.

CASE STUDY
Factors to Consider

The Coogee Bay Hotel in Sydney was a traditional hotel in an upmarket beachside area, but the hotel had been declining for a number of years. In 1991, new owners decided that the eastern suburbs of Sydney harboured a demand for upmarket accommodation, dining and entertainment venues. They proposed to renovate the property and provide a range of facilities to world-class standards. Among the new facilities are a 50-room boutique hotel catering for conference groups, a function room for 160, and a refurbished night-club. These are in addition to the beach bar, brasserie and bottle shops. The renovations cost $15 million and, in 1998, the Australian Hotels Association recognised the efforts of the new owners and awarded the Coogee Bay Hotel the title of 'Pub Hotel of 1998'. The hotel also won awards for its marketing, accommodation and retail outlets. The property has been transformed from its traditional (although declining) image because the new owners were prepared to consider a number of factors in their renovation plans, and prepared to provide extra services to which the market has clearly responded.

Rogers, *Daily Telegraph* (9 December 1998)[16]

A determination of the objectives of the operation is crucial to any discussion of evaluation. The developer/owner/entrepreneur should list those objectives—perhaps two or three major objectives and a number of minor objectives. These objectives can then be used as a benchmark against which to judge the subsequent achievements of the operation. In formulating objectives, the developer must give due attention to the nature of the operation, and the major factors affecting its activities. Present and future influences could affect the likelihood of the operation's achieving its objectives. For that reason, if the developer does not have access to timely and accurate information on the state of the market and the environment of the operation, he or she should seek advice from agencies or institutions which do have access to appropriate sources of data.

From this point, the developer might put together, and coordinate, a development team that possesses the range of expertise to formulate a reasonable and desirable set of objectives, and a timeline within which those objectives should be achieved.

Another benefit of establishing a development team, besides obtaining the necessary expertise, is that contact can be made with the consulting and financing institutions that will be necessary if the project is to get off the ground.

The objectives provide the benchmarks for the project. The setting of objectives is equivalent to deciding where you want to go before you get in the car or take a bus.

Uses of a Project Evaluation

Besides the purpose of determining how well the operation has (or can) meet the operator's objectives, the project evaluation/feasibility study has other uses as well:

■ to attract venture capital or finance;
■ to form the basis of ongoing plans for marketing and operations; and
■ to support applications to government and councils.

To Attract Venture Capital or Finance

Few projects are entirely owner-funded. The owner usually has to seek finance, or partners who can contribute funds to the operation. An evaluation study that includes market and financial research of good quality not only explains the essence of the project, but also can sell the project to potential investors. A good study invokes confidence in the expertise and professionalism of the developers.

An important element in raising finance, or building partnerships, is confidence, and confidence comes before trust. Even if they never use the words 'confidence' and 'trust', prospective investors/financiers will ask themselves something like: 'Would I buy a used car from this man or woman?'. A good evaluation—professionally presented in hard copy, that can be picked up and mused over after the owner has left—can be a silent salesperson. Feasibility studies are extremely important instruments in the borrowing of money (Szivas & Riley 1996).[17]

To Form the Basis of Ongoing Plans for Marketing and Operations

The study should have projections of external market factors (for, say, 3–5 years), and should also have projections on internal factors such as revenue/expenses and cash-flow budgets (for similar periods). These projections will have descriptive and statistical elements that can be brought into budgets and forward planning.

To Support Applications to Government and Councils

It is a fact of life that new developments require the approval of a range of authorities. Sometimes such approvals have to be argued. There is also the possibility that the federal or state governments will be involved—either for approvals, or to provide support of some kind. Again, a researched and documented study can be evidence of clear-headed decision-making.

Features of a Good Project Evaluation

Taking the above uses into account, a good project evaluation will:[18]

- define the development concept and its long-term viability;
- identify the market needs through indepth analysis;
- provide detailed documentation that investors can examine;
- enable the necessary finance and government approvals to be obtained with minimum delay; and
- define strategies for dealing with interested parties.

Solomon (1994)[19] relates the difficulty that he experienced in obtaining finance for a new restaurant. He notes that banks are particularly careful with all commercial loans, and especially so with loans for restaurants—because such small hospitality enterprises do not have a reputation for long-term success. In Solomon's view, preparing a good project evaluation is essential for establishing professional and financial credibility.

The Scope of the Project Evaluation

The scope and purpose of the project evaluation is the first decision which must be made. If the proposed project is a small restaurant, clearly the scope of the study would be different from, say, that relating to a mid-sized hotel. If there will be an international dimension to the operation, the research background must necessarily be extended.

The proposed development might have several operations. A hotel property will include restaurant facilities and there might be several food service venues—from a bistro for light meals and snacks, to an up-market restaurant. The hotel might also have dedicated conference areas. The project evaluation might have to include specialised market research on each of these facets of the operation.

The uses to which the study will be put must be borne in mind. If the study is to be used to support applications for financing, then it might have an emphasis on financial projections. Alternatively, if the venture is entirely new, and innovative, the emphasis might be upon testing of the local market and assessment of market demand for the service or product.

CASE STUDY
Taking a Critical Look at the Concept

The Crystal Group conducted a project evaluation of their proposal to build a new luxury hotel of 200 rooms at Deerfield Beach in Florida. The study found that there was insufficient demand in the prospective market to achieve a satisfactory occupancy rate for a luxury hotel of that size, but that there was a significant demand for mid-range accommodation. Crystal Group reviewed their plans and, instead, proposed two linked properties— the first a 100-room luxury hotel, and the other a 100-room economy hotel. This concept has been referred to as 'piggybacking'.[20] This means that one property is assisted by another to achieve greater economies of scale.

Accuracy and Necessity of Feasibility Studies

The American Hotel and Motel Association (AHMA) conducted a survey of developers and management companies to assess the use and accuracy of feasibility studies—and thereby started a debate on the necessity of such studies.

The survey found that the commonest reason for conducting a project evaluation was to prepare a submission to a lender. Two-thirds of feasibility studies were conducted by public accounting firms. Generally, developers found the studies accurate, but required more specific information instead of 'boilerplate material'.[21] 'Boilerplate material' is a term used to refer to general background information—that is, raw material that has to be shaped and cut before it can be useful for the finished product.

The debate on the accuracy of feasibility studies grew and, in 1990, Professor Tarras of Michigan State University was funded by the Hilton Corporation to report specifically on the 'Accuracy of Project Evaluation Projections'.[22] In his report, Tarras states that accuracy in a project evaluation is essential, but that:

> . . . over the years there have been discrepancies between forecasted results printed in certain feasibility studies and the actual operating results.
>
> Tarras (1990)[23]

His study found that only 29% of occupancy forecasts of his study group were within 5 percentage points of the actual occupancy rate, and that 60% of projected net income figures were inaccurate. The tendency was to overestimate occupancy and net income. The bright part of Tarras' study was that forecast figures appeared to be becoming more accurate.

Stephen Rushmore entered the debate with his observation that:

> Recently, the trade press has been buzzing with articles addressing the topic of hotel feasibility studies and whether they accurately portray the future operating results of a proposed hotel.
>
> Rushmore (1996)[24]

Rushmore argues that feasibility studies are necessary—because they provide third-party confirmation of factors related to a new proposal, and also because they provide credibility that is necessary to obtain funding. However, although feasibility studies might be accurate when they are conducted, the 'hotel markets are highly dynamic' (Rushmore[24]) and circumstances can change very quickly—through changes in transportation patterns or economic downturns. Essentially, a project evaluation is a snapshot of current conditions, and a developer must accept the risk that these conditions might change.

An alternative point of view is put by Stanley Turkel (1995), who claims that there is limited reality in the 'typical' project evaluation, and that he has never found a study which recommended against a project—despite his reading 'hundreds of hotel feasibility studies'. Turkel states that feasibility studies are used 'to protect lenders from criticism' and that they are 'not genuine business plans'.[25]

Payne (1996) takes issue with Turkel and suggests that there are few negative feasibility studies because those projects that are not feasible are discontinued at the initial assessment stage.[26]

Another experienced consultant, Frank Sikich (1995), believes that some feasibility studies are flawed because the people conducting the studies might have expertise in hotel or restaurant operations, but have limited expertise in real estate and property valuation.[27] Sikich goes on to state that errors he found in one particular study included failure to visit all the properties considered in the study, and failure to follow a predetermined work program.

The Structure of the Document

The structure of a project evaluation should be kept as simple as possible. However, it should include all that is necessary for the reader to follow the analysis, and it should refer to data that support all the assertions. The structure of feasibility studies has become fairly standard—to ensure that issues and material are covered in a logical and orderly fashion.

Worth Thinking About!

An old-time African-American preacher had a reputation for resounding and moving orations. He confided to others that his technique was very simple:
1 'First I tell 'em what I'm going to tell 'em;
2 then I tell 'em;
3 and then I tell 'em what I told 'em!'
A good study can borrow something from this—including an emphasis upon simplicity!

The structure of the study should be as follows:

1 a full *introduction*—explaining the reasons for the study, for whom it was conducted, any constraints upon its material, what property/facility was being evaluated, how the study was completed, when the study was done, and through whose agency;
2 an executive *summary*—describing the findings, the conclusions of the analysts, and the recommendations;
3 a description of the *methodology* of the study—if complex analytical tools are used;
4 the *body* of the study—dealing first with general market characteristics;
5 information on issues of *supply and demand*;
6 specific *market issues*;
7 a *description* of the project—including a site evaluation;
8 an *environmental impact study*;
9 *revenue and cost* projections;
10 *cash projections*;
11 *design characteristics*—as necessary;
12 *financing issues*;
13 *risk analysis*;
14 other *associated issues*—as necessary;
15 *recommendations*; and
16 supporting *schedules* and *documentation*.

The production of the report itself should be as professional as possible—bearing in mind its use as a tool in arranging finance, and in assisting the marketing of the project itself. The report should be compiled in an easily readable font, neatly bound, and reproduced clearly on quality paper.

Who Should Do a Project Evaluation?— The Analyst/Appraiser

A project evaluation will usually be compiled by a team—because the process requires input from several disciplines. It is important that a number of specialists is included, including:

■ people with experience of *hospitality* enterprises who understand the importance of guest services;
■ *marketing* specialists;
■ *architects* who understand design trends; and
■ *technology* specialists who understand the advances in communications and modes of travel.

The *team leader* has a crucial role in the project evaluation, as this person has the responsibility of integrating the input from these various specialists. Synergy—the art of making the whole greater than the sum of the parts—must be the goal of the team leader.

> Co-ordinating the efforts of all the resources and specialists who plan and design . . . services and facilities is critical to their talents blending together effectively.
>
> Petit (1985)[28]

The team must map out a plan for the study, and must be prepared to coordinate and review its own work—and the work of other consultants whose input is required at various stages of the study (such as the developer's accountant). The team must also be aware of the financial goals of the study. The team will have a schedule for its work, must be conscious of the need for communication among team members (and with the developers who have commissioned the study), and should have contingency plans for any problems and delays that might arise.

The person who will lead the team must be professional in his/her work. In this study context, the word 'professional' implies two general classes of attributes:

■ first, that the person will be capable and knowledgeable in the field—and thus able to make well-considered judgments; and
■ secondly, that the person will be personally ethical, independent and courageous enough to prepare a true and fair report (bearing in mind that there is also a legal obligation to do so to the best of one's ability).

Project XX Feasiblity Study Team

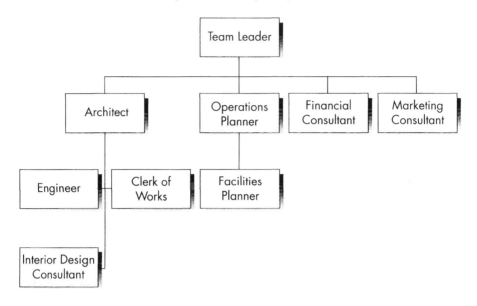

Figure 1.1 *Organisation Chart of Study Team*

Kevin Baker

The 'Unfeasibility Study'

Sometimes the analyst must present a negative report—even though this might disappoint and discourage the parties involved. Sometimes it is difficult to do this—to 'tell it like it is', rather than to report in optimistic terms.

> Why don't you see negative feasibility studies? . . . I have often advised prospective clients that a proposed project will not fly . . .
>
> Rushmore (1996)[29]

Renton (1992) has commented that, as uneconomic hotel construction in an area can threaten the viability of existing hotels, it would be in the interests of existing owners to conduct 'unfeasibility studies' to indicate to prospective developers that new projects would not be viable.[30]

A Last Word

Honesty is essential for an analyst preparing a project evaluation. Optimists are always popular, and pessimists are unpopular, but an appraisal is not an exercise in popularity. A negative report—a recommendation not to proceed with a project—might be a difficult conclusion to present to a developer, but it might be in the best long-term interests of the parties.

STUDY CHECKLIST #1
THE STUDY TEAM

- How extensive a report is required?

- Who will use the report?

- What aspects of the project must be covered?

- How big will the study team be?

- What expertise is required in the study team?

- What is the deadline for the report?

Chapter 1 ■ Review and Questions

1 Indicate whether the following statements are true or false and give a reason for your answer:

a There are high barriers to entry in the tourism and hospitality industry. (True/False? Why?)

b Because of their expense, feasibility studies are useful only for high-value projects. (True/False? Why?)

c The key aspect of the project evaluation is that it is a methodical analysis of all the relevant factors of a new project. (True/False? Why?)

d A project evaluation should be commissioned only after a decision to proceed has been made and investors are about to commit their funds. (True/False? Why?)

e A project evaluation takes all the risk out of an investment decision. (True/False? Why?)

f Feasibility studies are preferable to decisions made on 'gut feeling' alone. (True/False? Why?)

g Feasibility studies cannot cover all relevant aspects of an investment decision because a small group of people will not have the whole range of skills needed to properly assess a project. (True/False? Why?)

h The commissioning of a project evaluation means that the decision-makers must accept the recommendations of the report. (True/False? Why?)

2 Insert the word(s) that best completes each of the following, selecting your answers from the following possibilities:

overestimated; land development; global distribution systems; analyst; positive; supporting development applications; underestimated; team leader; simple; pooled resources; negative.

   a Besides determining how well the proposed operation can meet the owner's objectives, a project evaluation can be used for attracting venture finance, formulating ongoing plans and . . .

   b Large hotel operators use linked reservation systems that are also known as . . .

   c Recent surveys have generally found that projected occupancy and net income figures in feasibility studies are . . .

   d The crucial role in the project evaluation team is that of . . .

   e A . . . report in the project evaluation might be difficult to present but might be in the best long-term interests of the parties.

   f The structure of the project evaluation should be kept as . . . as possible.

3 Discuss the following in one or two sentences (for each statement).

   a It takes time to conduct a project evaluation and, during that time, an opportunity could be lost, so it will often be necessary to make a quick decision on instinct alone.

   b The evaluation report is no more and no less than a document an investor needs to tell finance authorities what they want to know before they lend money.

   c There is no one better qualified to research an issue than a prospective investor and project analysts can add only technical detail to what the investor already knows.

4 Analyse and discuss the following.

   If the decision-makers are to receive the full benefits of a study, the process of conducting a project evaluation must include several important factors. What are they and why are they important?

Chapter 1 Notes

[1] Bureau of Tourism Research (BTR) 1998, *Travel by Australians—Preliminary Results of the National Visitor Survey*, BTR: Canberra.

[2] Horwath International and Smith Travel Research, quoted by Bailey, M. 1998, *The International Hotel Industry—Corporate Strategies and Global Opportunities*, Travel and Tourism Intelligence Research Report, 2nd edn, p. 13.

[3] Macquarie Bank Group 1997, *Tourism Trends*, p.8, published: Sydney.

[4] This outline of development strategies based upon Travel and Tourism Intelligence 1998, *The International Hotel Industry*, pp 131–7.

[5] Forrester Research, quoted in Travel and Tourism Intelligence 1998, *The International Hotel Industry*, p.152.

[6] I am indebted to Charles Panakera for the substance of this section on the background and definitions of capital investment.

[7] Lewis, G., Morkel, A. & Hubbard, G. 1993, *Australian Strategic Management—Concepts, Context and Cases*, p. 85, Prentice Hall of Australia: Sydney.

[8] Martin, J., Panakera, C. & Baker, K. 1999, 'Financial Management Decision-Making and Control in Small-to-Medium Hospitality Enterprises', unpublished paper.

[9] Horngren, Harrison, Best, Fraser, & Izan (initials unavailable) 1997, *Accounting*, 2nd edn, p. 880, Prentice Hall Australia: Sydney.

[10] Drury, C. 1992, *Management and Cost Accounting*, Chapman & Hall: London.

[11] Klammer, T. 1994, *Managing Strategic and Capital Investment Decisions*, Irwin Professional Publishing: Burr Ridge, Illinois.

[12] Horngren et al. 1997, op. cit., p. 881.

[13] Based on the definition of 'marketing research' by Kotler, P. 1994, *Marketing Management—Analysis, Planning, Implementation and Control*, 8th edn, p. 130, Prentice-Hall International, Inc.: New Jersey.

[14] Tourism South Australia 1993, *Development Guide for the Preparation of Feasibility Studies for Tourism Projects*, p. 2, SA Government: Adelaide.

[15] Green, M. 1993, 'Let's be Feasible', *Caterer & Hotelkeeper*, 4 March 1993, p. 38.

[16] Reported in the *Daily Telegraph*, by Jo Rogers in the 'Food & Wine Notebook', 9 December 1998, p. 17.

[17] Szivas, E. & Riley, M. 1996 'The Role of the Hotel Project Evaluation in the Development Process: Putting Utility into Perspective', *International Journal of Contemporary Hospitality Management*, vol. 8, part 6, pp 29–30.

[18] Tourism South Australia 1993, op. cit., p. 3.

[19] Solomon, J. 1994, 'Let the Borrower Beware: A Game Plan for Getting the Dough You Need', *Restaurant USA*, September 1994, pp 14–17.

[20] Taylor, P. 1991, 'Piggybacking Properties for Profit', *Hotel and Resort Industry*, vol. 14, no. 5, May 1991, pp 34–5.

[21] American Hotel & Motel Association (AHMA) 1989, Committee on Market Research and Feasibility Studies, 'Project Evaluation Use', *Lodging*, June 1989, pp 5–14.

[22] Tarras, J. 1990, 'Accuracy of Project Evaluation Projections', *Hospitality Review*, Spring 1990, pp 53–9.

[23] Ibid., p. 53.

[24] Rushmore, S. 1996. 'Feasibility Studies: Fact or Fiction', *Lodging Hospitality*, October 1996, p. 14.

[25] Turkel, S. 1995, 'Executive Forum', *Hotel and Motel Management*, 6 November 1995, p. 42.

[26] Payne, K. 1996, 'Executive Forum', *Hotel and Motel Management*, 18 March 1996, p. 42.

[27] Sikich, F. 1995, 'Business Valuations: From the Accountant's Perspective', *Bottomline*, October 1995, p. 24.

[28] Petit, R. 1985, 'Integrated Planning: The Experts Interact', *Lodging*, November 1985, p. 31.

[29] Rushmore, S. 1996, op. cit., p. 14.

[30] Renton, D. 1992, 'Just Say No', *Lodging Hospitality*, May 1992, p. 17.

CHAPTER 2

The Concept Stage

Synopsis of Chapter

This chapter describes where the evaluation fits into the gestation of a new idea.

The chapter examines the background to business today, and major trends among consumers. An entrepreneur is defined, and then the process of turning an idea into a reality is discussed—including the place of the project evaluation in that process.

The necessity of strategic planning is considered, including such techniques as environmental scanning and dialectical inquiry.

Some common misjudgments that entrepreneurs make are enumerated.

The Genesis of Possibilities

> Successful companies are those that can recognise and respond profitably to unmet needs and trends in the macroenvironment.
>
> Kotler (1994)[1]

Unmet needs always exist. There are always new opportunities in the market place—it is simply a case of identifying them and having the resources and ability to do something about it.

We can find opportunities by identifying trends—a trend being a sequence of events that has some momentum and durability.[2] However, being able to identify trends accurately, and to forecast the consequences, demands critical skills. Some identifiable trends of international business today include:

- the increasing speed of international transportation and communications;
- the growth of global communication;
- the dissemination of global lifestyles;
- the opening of new markets in Asia, eastern Europe and the Arab countries;

- the increase in product and service branding; and
- the transcending of national characteristics by large multinational companies.

The above list is not exhaustive.

Ten Major Trends Among Today's Consumers

A marketing consultancy firm called 'Brainreserve' focuses on identifying market trends among consumers. This firm enumerates ten major trends that influence the behaviour of individuals in the marketplace:

1 **Cashing Out:** leaving a career for a slower pace
2 **Cocooning:** staying at home and ordering services in
3 **Down-ageing:** acting and feeling younger than one's age (and selecting adventurous holidays)
4 **Egonomics:** developing an individual personality
5 **Fantasy Adventure:** seeking an emotional escape to offset daily routines by going to theme parks or seeking fantasy adventures
6 **99 Lives:** juggling many responsibilities and roles
7 **Save Our Society:** seeking to make society more responsible and, in tourism terms, choosing ecotourism
8 **Small Indulgences:** consumers being stressed-out giving themselves 'rewards' (such as weekend skiing trips, or a weekend in another country) instead of longer holidays
9 **Staying Alive:** desiring to live longer and healthier lives (evidenced by the growing popularity of health resorts)
10 **The Vigilante Consumer:** consumers being on the alert for shoddy products or services, and seeking refunds if not satisfied

Based on Kotler (1994)[2]

Some people, contemplating these trends, can see the possibilities for new ventures to meet the changing tastes of consumers. The common word for such people is 'entrepreneur'.

Striking the Spark—the Entrepreneur

An entrepreneur is one who starts a business, or pursues opportunities, or who wants to undertake a venture. Adjectives often linked with entrepreneurs include 'adventurous', 'far-sighted', 'bold' and 'innovative'. An entrepreneur will walk along a wide ocean beach and, where other people see masses of driftwood scraped clean by salt water and bleached in the sunlight, the entrepreneur will see the biggest floral art accessory collection in the world!

Entrepreneurs have ideas and want to see them come to fruition. Many entrepreneurs will fail, but some will succeed, and most will try again. People who will never be entrepreneurs might have good ideas, but the ideas never come to reality. Such people can be likened to moviegoers—who sit in their seats eating popcorn while visions flash by on a screen.

The enthusiasm of entrepreneurs is also important to a new project. A marginal project can be made to succeed because of the enthusiasm of the people involved.

The entrepreneurial process can be illustrated as shown in Figure 2.1:

Figure 2.1 *The Entrepreneurial Process*

Based on: Robbins & Mukerji (1994)[3]

Note the importance of 'ability' in the first line of the above diagram. It doesn't matter how good an idea might be, or how great the demand in the market place might be, poor operational management can mean failure—even in the best-designed project.

CASE STUDY
An Innovative Tourism Idea

Don Weringa is a businessman in Fremantle, which is the port of Western Australia's capital, Perth. He noted that there were many visitors to the city, but that there were few attractions for the visitors.

In 1986, the film 'Crocodile Dundee' was playing to large audiences, and Mr Weringa conceived an idea to establish a crocodile farm in

Fremantle—although the port was many kilometres south of the usual habitat of the reptiles. He needed to do a lot of persuading—because crocodiles are unloved and unlovely, and the authorities did not share Mr Weringa's enthusiasm. However, he persisted, and he had done his market feasibility well. The crocodile farm has been a success—with 100 000 visitors and revenue of nearly $2 million in 1991.

The crocodiles are kept placid with doses of 'Valium' (lest they kill each other), and their growth is assisted by hormones. Excess numbers of crocodiles become crocodile products, with the skins going to handbag manufacturers, and the meat to restaurants. Even the crocodile urine is used—as a base by perfume manufacturers!

But, at the beginning, Mr Weringa had to convince others that his idea was not only a good one, but feasible as well.

Based on *Economist*, London (10 October 1992)[4]

The Spark of the Idea

Adam Smith, one of the earliest economists, said that consumption is the sole end and purpose of production.[5] Therefore, the challenge facing all entrepreneurs is to come up with an idea for a new product or service that consumers will want.

It can be exciting to conceive of market opportunities, or to develop a concept that has been brewing—provided that the person involved does not get carried away with the idea, thus allowing the idea to become an obsession that defeats logic and better judgment (see 'Common Misjudgments' p. 26).

CASE STUDY
Developing a Dream

The Smorgon family emigrated to Australia from the Ukraine in 1927 and set up a butcher's shop in Carlton, Melbourne. They quickly learnt to pre-sell, and developed a chain of butchers' shops and abattoirs. The family branched out into paper, packaging and a range of industries until, by the 1990s, the fourth generation of the family ran businesses worth more than a billion dollars. Victor Smorgon, the chairman, says simply, 'You have to have a dream, and it's all possible if people want to do it'.[6]

Smorgon Steel was listed on the stock exchange in 1999.

It is an old truism that, in every crisis, there is both danger and opportunity. Problems might present new opportunities, and opportunities might contain problems. David B. Gleichner, a management consultant, defines a problem as something that impedes an organisation in reaching its objectives, and an opportunity as something that permits the organisation to exceed its objectives.[7]

It therefore follows that ideas and possible projects must fit into the objectives of the business. McCarthy et al. (1994)[8] consider that a business must define specific and explicit objectives, and should have three general objectives:

- to be socially and economically useful;
- to develop an organisation to carry on its activities; and
- to earn a profit in the long run.

As an example of failure to achieve the last of these objectives, Compass Airlines (set up in 1991 to compete against Australia's two established domestic carriers) was a good idea, but was not able to turn a profit from its operations in the face of price competition from Ansett and Australian Airlines.[8]

When setting objectives, it is also useful to specify to what extent the owners are prepared to balance risk against potential return. Ideas for new projects that offer high returns almost inevitably carry with them high risks.

After defining objectives, the business should compile a mission statement. This is a philosophical and qualitative statement that determines the role of the business, defines the benefits it provides, describes its distinctive skills or competencies, and indicates its future plans—what it will do, what it might do, and what it will never do.[9]

In the course of investigation and contemplation, many possible opportunities might arise. In order to concentrate on the more promising projects, it will be necessary to screen out those that are clearly not feasible. There might be an identifiable market opportunity that is beyond the firm's (or the individual's) resources.

The First Step

The first and most important step in creating a new project is to define the nature of the idea that has bubbled its way out of the creative places of the mind and now must be given shape and substance. The concept has to be described. It is also necessary to compile an initial review to see if the concept is possible or impossible.

McDonald lists ten steps in the strategic marketing planning process, and these ten steps in marketing planning are broadly similar to the parts of the project evaluation. See Figure 2.2 (p. 23).

In the context of a discussion of project evaluation and feasibility analysis, after the business has determined its mission statement and its objectives (as in phase one above), the next stage is the equivalent of the market audit in phase two—a brief review of the situation to give a guide as to whether the proposal is possible or not.

An alternative model describes the process of real estate development in eight steps, which places the role of the project evaluation at the third stage, after the conception of the idea and an informal review of the market. See Figure 2.3 (p. 24).

Phase One: Goal Setting
1. Mission
2. Corporate Objectives

Phase Two: Situation Review
3. Marketing Audit
4. SWOT (Strengths, Weaknesses, Opportunities, Threats) Analysis
5. Assumptions

Phase Three: Strategy Formulation
6. Objectives and Strategies
7. Expected Results
8. Alternative Plans and Mixes

Phase Four: Resource Allocation and Monitoring
9. Budget
10. First Year Detailed Implementation Program

Figure 2.2 The Strategic Marketing Process

Based on McDonald (1995)[10]

Environmental Scanning

There is a technique called environmental scanning (not to be confused with environmental impact studies) which is intended to be a brief overview of the competition. It involves seeking information on competitors—who they are, what they are doing, what their plans are, and how they will affect plans for the new project.[12] The concept includes that of competitor intelligence. An emphasis upon competitor analysis makes it possible to anticipate competitors' actions—rather than having to react to them.

Environmental scanning can usefully serve as an initial analysis (or summary) of the local market—with a view to deciding whether there might be an opening in the market and whether a new proposal might be possible. It cannot take the place of a full and detailed study.

If management can make a reasoned decision that the project is at least possible, the process can be advanced to the next stage—the project evaluation itself (including a formal analysis of the market, of supply and demand, of the financial feasibility of the project, and of implementation strategies).

> **1 Inception of an Idea (Feasible/Not Feasible?)**
> A developer looks for needs, sees possibilities, has a number of ideas, and does some mental calculations of legal, physical and financial possibilities.

> **2 Refinement of the Idea (Feasible/Not Feasible?)**
> The developer finds a site for the idea, and considers physical feasibility, talking to lenders, professionals, and weighing up a tentative design.

> **3 Feasibility Analysis (Feasible/Not Feasible?)**
> The developer conducts a formal market study, considering benefits and costs, and presents the plans to government agencies.

> **4 Contract Negotiation (Makes Binding Contracts/ Cannot Make Binding Contracts?)**

> **5 Formal Commitment**

> **6 Construction**

> **7 Completion and Opening**

> **8 Property Management**

Figure 2.3 *Real Estate Development*

Kevin Baker
Based on Mile, Haney & Berens (1996)[11]

Scanning the Market Environment

A Victorian cattle farmer was considering extra ways to make ends meet. He and his wife had 500 hectares of idyllic farmland two hours' drive from Melbourne. On the property they had an old but well-kept shearer's cottage. One afternoon, the farmer had the idea that the property might be suitable for a farm tourism venture.

Before spending any money, or even developing the idea on paper, the farmer spoke to the local council and some neighbours—to assess whether the scheme might be a possibility. He also went to the library and was referred to a report on farm tourism published by the Research and Regional

Development Division of the Queensland Tourist and Travel Corporation. The report recorded that the market for farm tourism in Australia consisted of two segments—retired people and families with young children.

The farmer had limited financial means, but this initial review of the market, involving informal discussions and reference to published information, cost him nothing—and at least established that the concept might be feasible.

Based on a case study by Kidd
Cited in Stanton, Miller & Layton (1994)[13]

The Dialectical Inquiry Method

One way of reviewing a proposal before advancing to a formal project evaluation is to undertake a process known as the 'dialectical method'. The dialectical method can also be called the 'Devil's Advocate Method' (Stoner 1995).[14] An analyst considers possible opportunities in a new project, and then looks for problems and difficulties. When assumptions are made (for example, that economic growth will continue) the dialectical method suggests that the opposite assumptions should be made (that is, declining economic growth)—and the implications for the project are then determined.

This method looks for problems. Much time is spent on *problem-solving* in modern organisations, but very little time on the *problem-finding* that would enable the organisation to prepare solutions in advance and be more flexible and fast-moving in the market place.

The Basis of Consideration

In order to make an initial review, the developer or the entrepreneur must have basic information on the market and the product under consideration. There is an old saying that 'the cobbler should stick to his last'. The practical wisdom behind the saying is that business people should work in the fields they know well.

To be able to identify new opportunities, and then to seize them and develop them, an entrepreneur/analyst must be knowledgeable in five areas. He or she must have:

- marketing information—knowledge and expertise of the target market;
- product awareness—knowledge of the detailed operation and specifications of what is being offered in the market place;
- price sensitivity—ability to be flexible and adaptable to local conditions;
- knowledge of place—ability to locate operations efficiently and effectively; and
- expertise in promotion—ability to select the best channels.

Based on McDonald (1995)[15]

Tom Peters, author of *In Search of Excellence*, also compiled *The Shape of the Winner*.[16] Peters theorised that the successful corporations in today's global economy had certain traits—the first of which was to seek niche markets to develop in order to gain an advantage over competitors.

In the hospitality industry, developing a product for a niche market requires excellent knowledge of the market place, and a flair for selecting a product that no one has thought of before, and then developing that product for a market segment in a particular place.

Common Misjudgments

Entrepreneurs who seek to develop a new tourism or hospitality venture might make errors of judgment in a number of different ways.[17] Some common ones are described below.

Purchasing the land first and then looking for an appropriate development
A development such as a motel or a hotel is not like other real estate developments—because the market demand cannot be created easily, and factors such as the location of the property are absolutely critical.

Making unrealistic judgments about interstate and foreign demand
Some tourism and hospitality developments overstate the projected demand for their services by other than local sources.

Not allowing for site limitations
Any development must the meet physical limitations of the land and area, as well as limitations imposed by local community views, official approvals and environmental factors.

Acting on poor advice concerning marketing and financial factors
The quality of advice is dependent upon the expertise of the people giving the advice, as well as the validity of the process and the accuracy of the assumptions.

Pursuing a personal vision without sufficient regard for reality
Many of the best developments have come about when entrepreneurs sought to convert a dream into a reality. However, when developers are blind to the practical aspects of making their dream come true, the project might result in personal disaster.

Copying another development elsewhere
There is no guarantee that a project that is successful in one environment can be transferred to another. Local regional considerations must always be carefully considered before importing an existing concept.

Trying to satisfy all the market
Some developments can fail if they try to meet the demands of *all* segments of the market, and fail to properly satisfy any.

Mismatching the service and the demand
The market can be analysed properly and gaps in market demand can be correctly identified, but the service that is provided might not fill those gaps adequately.

Presenting the project in stages
Developers with limited financial resources sometimes try to construct a project one stage at a time—relying on ongoing revenue to finance the next stage. Unfortunately, this manner of proceeding sometimes fails to generate the revenue to meet existing commitments, let alone expanded commitments—because consumers are seldom attracted to properties that do not provide the full range of experiences that they promise.

CASE STUDY
Good and Bad Judgment

McDonalds stands as an example of a successful line of family restaurants. In 1954, an American named Ray Kroc, then aged 51, and a distributor of milk-shake mixers, received one of his largest orders. A restaurant owned by two brothers, Maurice and Dick McDonald, wanted no less than eight mixers. Their restaurant was clean, efficient, and had high-volume sales. Kroc visited the restaurant and negotiated with the McDonalds to franchise their restaurant concept. The new concept grew in leaps and bounds.

By 1966, McDonalds sales totalled $266 million, with growth rates of more than 25% a year. Other corporations saw McDonalds' success in the restaurant business and tried to emulate them. One such company was General Foods which, in 1967, acquired Burger Chef Systems—a chain of 700 fast-food hamburger restaurants similar to McDonalds.[18] The following year gave every promise of being a boom year. There seemed no reason for assuming that Burger Chef could not enjoy the same burgeoning growth as McDonalds.

Burger Chef embarked on an extensive expansion program. Within a year, there were 200 more stores, and the chain had gone international with stores opening in Canada. By 1970, there were more than 1200 outlets in the United States and Canada, and there was no apparent reason for believing that the growth should not continue.

However, in January 1972, the chain announced that, instead of expanding, it would be closing stores in an effort to recover its financial footing. Instead of a profit, the chain had made a loss of $83 million. In 1971, it had had a market share of 3.9% but, by 1972, this had fallen to 2.9%. The market share continued to decline marginally in the next two years—to 2.6% in 1973, and to 2.8% in 1974. Over the same period, McDonalds had no such problems, having 13.4% market share in 1971, climbing to 15.2% in 1972, to 17.7% in 1973, and to 19.8% in 1974.[19]

The management of General Foods, parent company of Burger Chef, was asking itself how its investment had gone wrong, and why its new restaurants had not built up sales to the same extent as its competitor, McDonalds. There were several answers, but they can be summarised in one statement—Burger Chef had not conducted adequate feasibility studies, including analyses of competitors, before it opened its new outlets.

General Food's management found that Burger Chef had suffered, in many cases, from poor site selection—influenced by the haste with which it had expanded. Large investors had contracted with Burger Chef to take area franchises—which had depended on setting up a number of outlets as quickly as possible. In contrast, McDonalds had conducted more-thorough feasibility analyses of sites for new stores, and had experienced few failures due to poor locations.

The quality of the buildings that Burger Chef occupied did not compare well with those of McDonalds (or with Kentucky Chicken or others)—which were identifiable, and of reasonable quality. Few Burger Chef outlets had comfortable amenities, and many had a 'temporary' atmosphere—rather than the 'family restaurant' image of McDonalds.

Burger Chef had also not conducted sufficient competitor analysis to keep pace with its competitors in the products it had been offering. While other fast-food restaurants had, after market evaluation, been adding options—such as fish burgers and double-decker hamburgers—Burger Chef had stayed with its limited range of hamburgers.

There had been other problems—such as the dispersion of operations, rather than the concentrating of sites to make supervision more efficient. A consideration of geographic factors in the feasibility studies (if such factors had been considered) might have indicated that this dispersion of operations would become a problem for management.

There are two lessons to be drawn from the case of the Burger Chef restaurant expansion:

1 Any new project requires a full project evaluation—including assessment of market supply and demand, and an analysis of competitors.

2 An emphasis on expansion into new projects at any price will bring disaster—no matter how large is the company behind the expansion, and no matter how large is the capital backing.

An Intangible Product

In the hospitality industry, because the industry is based on an intangible product—a service—entrepreneurs sometimes need an enhanced ability to visualise their proposed new service. Although these services can be provided out of tangible premises (requiring high capital input!), the product itself remains intangible. In the services industry, the product is *consumed* rather than *possessed*.[20]

Not only is the product intangible, but it also has high perishability—if the service is not used, it cannot be kept for another day. The capacity to provide entertainment or accommodation on a given night cannot be transferred to another night.

This sometimes makes it more difficult to express the idea (of a possible project) in a form that others can readily comprehend and appreciate. Thus, in the hospitality industry, the project evaluation is even more crucial.

A Last Word

The evaluation study has to be objective. A study conducted by a party with a vested interest in the outcome would be open to the possibility of subjectivity—leading to the delivery of a conclusion that coincided with that party's own interests, rather than those of the investor.

STUDY CHECKLIST #2
THE CONCEPT

- Corporate objectives: What are the purposes of the project?

- Financial objectives: What returns are sought?

- Operational objectives: Will the project be sold, or leased or managed?

- Is there a sufficient market?

- Is the project capable of obtaining necessary approvals?

Chapter 2 ■ Review and Questions

1 Indicate whether the following statements are true or false and give a reason for your answer:

a A trend of international business today is that large multinational companies are closely identified with the national characteristics of their founders. (True/False? Why?)

b One of the major trends that influences individuals today is the seeking of emotional escape in theme parks or fantasy routines. (True/False? Why?)

c Economist Adam Smith believed there were many purposes for the production of goods and services. (True/False? Why?)

d A project evaluation must always be the first step in the entrepreneurial process. (True/False? Why?)

e We should try to anticipate competitors' actions, rather than react to them. (True/False? Why?)

f If a hospitality service is not used, it cannot simply be kept for the next day. (True/False? Why?)

2 Insert the word(s) that best completes each of the following, selecting your answers from the following possibilities:
ideas; style; initial; financial plans; qualitative; momentum; earn a profit in the long run; quantitative; provide jobs; unimportant; weekend.

a A trend can be described as a sequence of events with . . . and durability.

b We might expect consumers who are 'stressed out' to give themselves rewards such as . . . skiing trips or holidays.

c Entrepreneurs have . . . and want to do something about them.

d In the view of McCarthy et al., a business should be socially and economically useful, should develop an organisation, and should . . .

e The mission statement of the business is both philosophical and . . .

f 'Environmental scanning' is an . . . assessment of the market.

3 Discuss the following in one or two sentences (for each statement):

a No one can make an accurate assessment of a market until a project is up and running and, until that time, all the research in the world is just conjecture.

b Market research must be uncertain because people are fickle, and can change their minds about a product overnight.

c Mission statements are all very well, but there is only one objective in business—to make money.

4 Analyse and discuss the following:
A project evaluation should be commissioned only after initial market reviews have indicated that the project should proceed. However, if that is the case, surely the project evaluation will duplicate work already done, and answer questions which have already been answered?

A Sample Project

BUILDING A BETTER BARBECUE

Some pitfalls to avoid when constructing a new hospitality venture!

Figure 2.5 *Who Will Be Attracted To Your Facility?*

Kevin Baker (after the style of Giles)

Chapter 2 Notes

[1] Kotler, P. 1994, *Marketing Management—Analysis, Planning, Implementation and Control*, 8th edn, p. 151, Prentice-Hall International, Inc.: New Jersey.

[2] Ibid., p. 152.

[3] Robbins, S. & Mukerji, D. 1994, *Managing Organisations—New Challenges and Perspectives*, 2nd edn, p. 457, Prentice-Hall of Australia: Sydney.

[4] From the *Economist*, London, 10 October 1992, p. 80, as quoted in Robbins & Mukerji 1994, op. cit., p. 153.

[5] Noted in McDonald, M. 1995, *Marketing Plans—How to Prepare Them and How to Use Them*, 3rd edn, p. 1, Butterworth-Heinemann Ltd: Oxford.

[6] Robbins & Mukerji 1994, op. cit., p. 457.

[7] Gleichner is referred to in Stoner, J. 1995, *Management*, 6th edn, p. 242, Prentice Hall, Inc.: New Jersey.

[8] McCarthy, E., Perreault, W., Quester, P., Wilkinson, J. & Lee, K. 1994, *Basis Marketing—A Managerial Approach*, p. 73, Richard D. Irwin Inc.: Sydney.

[9] McDonald, M. 1995, op. cit. (Note 5 above), pp 41–2.

[10] Ibid., p. 26.

[11] Mile, M., Haney, R. (Jnr) & Berens, G. 1996, *Real Estate Development Principles and Process*, p. 3, The Urban Land Institute: New York.

[12] Robbins & Mukerji 1994, op. cit., p. 167.

[13] Based on a case study by Jeffrey Kidd, Victorian University of Technology, Footscray, Victoria, In Stanton, W., Miller, K. & Layton, R. 1994, *Fundamentals of Marketing*, 3rd edn, p. 615, McGraw-Hill Book Co.: Sydney.

[14] Stoner, J. 1995, *Management*, 6th edn, p. 242, Prentice Hall, Inc.: New Jersey.

[15] Based on McDonald, M. 1995, op. cit., pp 403ff.

[16] Peters, T. 1989, *The Shape of the Winner*, Excel/California Limited: New York.

[17] Tourism South Australia 1993, *Development Guide for the Preparation of Feasibility Studies for Tourism Projects*, p. 1, South Australian Government: Adelaide.

[18] Hartley, R. F. 1992, *Marketing Mistakes*, pp 264ff, John Wiley & Sons Inc.: New York.

[19] *Advertising Age*, 14 May 1973, p. 93; 3 June 1974, p. 52; 30 June 1975, p. 49. Quoted in Hartley 1992, op. cit., p. 266.

[20] Czinkota, M. & Ronkainen, I. 1990, *International Marketing*, 4th edn, p. 525, The Dryden Press (Harcourt Brace College Publishers): Fort Worth, Texas.

CHAPTER 3

General Market Characteristics

Synopsis of Chapter

An evaluation report covers two main areas—market factors and financial factors.

This chapter describes market factors—what should be covered, how it should be covered, and where to find the information to support the analysis.

The quantitative and qualitative factors are described. Sources of information are listed, along with contact details. The chapter lists important trends and profiles of domestic and international visitors.

The Operating Environment

There are three parts to the process of matching a new product with the demands of consumers in the market place. These are:[1]

- the capabilities of the business or individual supplying the product;
- the wants of the customers/consumers; and
- the marketing environment.

The first factor, the capabilities of the business, will be considered later—in the context of the study of financial feasibility (Chapters 9, 10, 11), and the second factor, the wants of customers, will be considered in the detailed analysis of supply and demand (Chapter 4). The last factor, the operating (or marketing) environment, and its general characteristics, will be the first topic considered by the project evaluation, and the topic to be considered in this chapter.

What is the operating environment? No hospitality operation conducts its business in a vacuum. It operates in an environment, and that environment consists of its existing and potential customers, its competitors, and also other factors outside its control. There might be changes in the environment because of changes to various factors, including:[2]

- consumer wants;
- fashions;

■ technology;
■ environmental concerns;
■ legislation;
■ the economic climate; and
■ competition.

In fact, the operating environment is always changing in some respects, and its characteristics will be different from place to place, and from time to time. The operating environment can be monitored by a close examination of its general characteristics.

The success of a project is largely dependent upon planning. Good planning requires *market research* (to establish the likely demand for the services offered by the new project) and *financial research* (to establish whether the sales generated by the project will meet all the costs and allow a reasonable return on the capital invested).

The characteristics of the market within which the business operates, or plans to operate, can be assessed through *quantitative* and *qualitative* analysis.

Quantitative analysis deals essentially with numbers—that is, the total population of a region, or the total number of guests staying at hotels, or the numbers of guests in particular categories (such as business, conference or holiday visitors).

Qualitative analysis assesses factors which cannot be expressed numerically—such as the reasons people have visited a region and their satisfaction with their visit.

Quantitative and qualitative analysis can also be applied to the goals and objectives of the proposal, and an evaluation can be made of whether these goals are achievable in the operating environment.

Examples of *quantitative* criteria could include:

■ achieve sales of $750 000 within five years;
■ earn a long-term return on investment of 15% before tax on the new project; and
■ break even within one year on the new project.

Examples of *qualitative* criteria could include:

■ developing a quality product;
■ building on existing expertise;
■ developing the product within a preferred geographic area; and
■ expanding within identified trends.

The exercise of clearly defining criteria for the project forces decision-makers to understand exactly what they are trying to achieve. Solomon (1994) has considered this issue, especially in relation to restaurants, and he declares that it is fundamental to question the motivation for any development.[3] A desire to grow at any cost can lead to disaster.

If the operating environment is entirely new, the study of general characteristics could be in two stages. The *first* stage could be a situation analysis—which is an informal study of the opportunities and problems, and the available data relating to the issues. The *second* stage is the formal study of the market and how the project will relate to them.

What Should be Studied?

The analyst must choose the middle path between studying too wide an environment or too narrow a range of information. According to Kotler (1994): 'A problem well-defined is half-solved'.[4]

The type of project being considered will determine what factors are relevant, and how large an area should be studied. For example:

- a resort might draw its guests from a national (perhaps even an international) region;
- a neighbourhood restaurant will have a clientele that lives or works locally;
- a theme resort will draw its customers from a particular age group.

The information obtained over, say, a previous five-year period can be used for projections for growth over the next five years. A forecast that attempts to estimate trends more than five years in the future is chancing the ill winds of fate, and any analysis that draws conclusions for more than five years ahead must be treated with extreme caution. Analyses are like canned food—good for the next year or two, but decidedly 'dicey' after that time. After five years, the contents could be rotten.

If the market is a fast-moving one—such as with some types of restaurants—even five years might be too long a time period, and three years should be used. In contrast, with markets in which there are long time-spans of development, a longer period might be considered.[5]

With all market information, there must always be a proviso that projections drawn from historical data might not always be accurate indicators of the future. Circumstances change, and unforeseen catastrophic events can render a whole range of information unreliable. Even minor factors might have major effects—theorists have suggested that even the flutter of a butterfly's wings might cause a cyclone! Projections are always subject to probability analysis. A probability of one means certainty. Projections of growth in the tourism and hospitality industries might be close to a probability of one, but are seldom absolutely certain. When identifying trends and assessing the likelihood of their continuing into the future, it is best to project on a best-case/middle-case/worst-case scenario. For that reason, later analysis will generally identify a range of possibilities. The most successful punters hedge their bets. In evaluating a proposal, take both the optimistic and the pessimistic line, and balance the two—rather than taking just one or the other.

Another proviso is that the information be timely. Tourism trends can change relatively quickly, and what was an attraction in a region in one year, might not be so in the next year. The popularity of particular beachside areas with graduating students can change from one year to the next. Tourism data for such an area could show a high demand, but that demand can evaporate as quickly as a puddle of beer in the sun. If the data are not timely, an evaluation might be based on fads that have become out of date.

One other proviso should be kept in mind. Information from some areas of the media, or from those with political agenda, should be treated with caution. It is a little like buying a used car. That 1985 sedan might really be a dream car, little used, and at the peak of quality. It could also be a rust bucket with banana peel masking the noises in the gearbox! The trouble for the potential buyer is deciding which description best fits the car in question. Optimistic projections from a local politician could be accurate. However, they might be overstated. The agenda of a politician might be valid for the politician, but might not coincide with the agenda of a project analyst. Some published data are better than others. All should be reviewed critically before being accepted.

CASE STUDY

Forecasting the Asian Economic Collapse of 1997

It is difficult to plan for future demand. Even the year ahead can hold surprises. Project evaluations in Asia before 1997 would have routinely included optimistic forecasts for growth in the region. There were few commentators who sounded notes of warning. Some who did were not economists—such as the outgoing British governor of Hong Kong, Christopher Patten, who commented just six weeks before the handover to China in 1997:

> What has happened in Asia has been spectacular, but it does not amount to a miracle . . . and I don't think it's necessarily going to roll on exponentially.[6]

One area of Australia's hospitality industry that has been affected by the economic downturn in Asia is the Western Australian hotel sector. However, the changing economic conditions have produced a challenge for efficient management of capacity—rather than representing a threat to the sector's very existence. There is an excellent case study of the reaction of Western Australian hoteliers to the Asian crisis compiled by Ali-Knight, Williams and O'Neill (1998).[7]

In any investment there is a degree of risk. A project evaluation/feasibility study will make certain assumptions on the basis of the best expert opinion of the time, and it is better to make qualified assumptions on the basis of expert advice then not to do so—but it must always be borne in mind that historical trends cannot always be extended into the future.

Sources of Information

In designing the type of research to be undertaken into general market characteristics, the first question to ask is: What type of project? The second question is: What factors will affect its operation? After answering these questions, information can be sought on general characteristics through a number of sources—which can be termed *primary*, *secondary* or *tertiary* sources.

Primary Information

Primary information is that which relates specifically to the project, and is gathered at first-hand by the evaluation team. In marketing terms, primary information is that which is gathered by survey researchers—who seek out original data on attitudes and opportunities for a product or service. The term 'primary data' has been defined by McCarthy et al. (1994) as ' . . . information specifically collected to solve a current problem'.[8]

Such data can be collected in four ways:[9]

- by direct observation;
- by surveys;
- by focus groups (small groups who discuss a proposal in depth); and
- by experiment (studying responses to proposals by matched groups).

Within these categories, the information can be recorded by questionnaires, by sampling plans, or by direct contact methods (such as mail, telephone or personal interviewing).

Secondary Information

Other sources of information are government, local government and industry sources. Accessing these sources is referred to as 'desk research'.[10] These sources are termed *secondary* sources—because the information has already been gathered, summarised and categorised by industry or government organisations. The term 'secondary data' has been defined, again by McCarthy et al., as data that have ' . . . already been collected or published for purposes unrelated to those of the current project'.[11]

Tertiary Information

The present book also uses the term *tertiary* sources to refer to published analysis and comment—conducted upon previously collected data. Tertiary sources are those in which information (that has been previously gathered and collated) is now analysed and commented upon by third parties. The commentator adds another layer of information upon the collected data. Typically (although not always) industry journals and sector consultants who produce informed opinion are tertiary sources. An example of an academic analysis is the paper referred to above (Ali-Knight, Williams & O'Neill) on the Western Australian hotel situation.[7]

Taking into account primary, secondary and tertiary sources, there is thus a wide range of information available—and most of it is relatively easy and inexpensive to access. Some secondary and tertiary sources will be considered in this chapter—because such sources form a background and basis for research. Later in this book, when specific details of a project site and its environment are studied, primary information sources will be considered.

Information from all these sources should include both qualitative (descriptive) data and quantitative (statistical) data. *Qualitative* research will seek indepth opinion on services and products—using structured questions in surveys to focus on the needs and wants of consumers. Examples include mail or telephone surveys. *Quantitative* research records the absolute numbers of people using a service, or statistically records the characteristics shared by the group being surveyed.

In the project evaluation, only relevant data should be included, and these should be presented as concisely as possible.

General Factors

A project in the hospitality and tourism industry will be affected by a number of general factors. These include:

- external factors—national economic trends and other factors;
- population trends;
- local economic trends;
- attractions and special features of a region;
- the visitor profile; and
- cultural factors.

Each of these will be considered, in turn, below.

1. External Factors—National Economic Trends and Other Factors

Tourism and hospitality spending is largely discretionary for the non-business traveller—which means that if people have less money to spend, or if concern about future conditions causes them to save rather than spend, they will choose to do without a product or service that they see as unnecessary. Hence, any evaluation of a large-scale project should take into account national, and even international economic trends.

Even a smaller project, such as a restaurant, should take into account the prevailing economic climate and the likely changes in the near future. If interest rates are high, unemployment high, and confidence low, these factors must be taken into account. Niche ventures can do very well in certain climates—for example, backpacker hostels tend to increase their occupancy and their income in difficult financial times. However, properties operating in the upper range of the market might not find the same to be true for them. They should at least consider the matter, and judge the impact on the proposed operation.

Some external factors (economic and otherwise) that might affect the feasibility of a project include:

- interest rates;
- inflation rate;
- energy prices;
- international exchange rates;
- taxation policies;
- trade union militancy;
- government trade and tourism policies;
- immigration policies;
- regulations;
- new technology; and
- religious practices.

2. Population Trends

Trends in population growth, and the demographics of the population (such as whether there is a high proportion of aged people, or a high proportion of families) can affect the level of demand. The Australian Bureau of Statistics (ABS) collates its information on a regional and district basis, and the ABS can provide details on the breakdown of a local population by age, family structure, ethnicity, and income levels.

Government and local government bodies can also provide general population information (see list of sources of tourism and hospitality data, Figure 3.1, pp 40–1). In the author's experience, such bodies are always courteous and helpful and, if some information is not within their purview, they are prepared to recommend alternative sources.

The demographics of the regional population (the 'drawing area' of the project) will have an impact upon demand for services. The age and the population and the family profile will influence spending patterns. For example, tourists who travel as a family will generally seek budget accommodation and certain types of entertainment—particularly theme parks. Major demographic studies—such as those of the ABS—include data that allow assessment of such population trends as changes in ethnic makeup, educational attainment, household patterns and geographical shifts.

Marketing professionals seek to focus in on subgroups within larger populations. As an example, consider the following subdivisions (with associated acronyms):[13]

- school kids with income and purchasing power ('SKIPPIES');
- mother older, baby younger ('MOBYS');
- double income, no kids ('DINKS');
- dual earners with kids ('DEWKS');
- poor urban professionals ('PUPPIES'); and
- well-off older folks ('WOOFS').

Sources of Tourism and Hospitality Data

Australian Government Sources

Australian Bureau of Statistics

Contact:
Cameron Offices, Chandler Street,
Belconnen ACT 2617
Branch offices in capital cities
http://www.abs.gov.au

Notes:
Particular statistical series of interest
include:
Overseas Visitor Arrivals and
Departures (Catalogue No. 3401.0);
Accommodation Statistics—record
occupancy rates and guest expenditure
on a range of accommodation
categories.

Tourism Council of Australia

Contact:
40 Blackall Street, Barton ACT 2600

Notes:
The Council was founded in 1967 as a
statutory corporation with the objectives
of increasing the number of overseas
visitors to Australia and maximising the
benefits of tourism.

Bureau of Tourism Research

Contact:
4/20 Allara Street (GPO Box 9839),
Canberra ACT 2601
http://www.btr.gov.au

Notes:
The Bureau is a part of the
Commonwealth Department of Tourism
and is the principal source of
information on tourism and hospitality
statistics. It has a wide range of
research publications.
The Bureau maintains two important

registers of information: *The International
Visitor Survey* which collates information
drawn from entry cards filled in by all
international travellers to Australia; *The
National Visitor Survey* (which replaced
the Domestic Tourism Monitor in January
1998); surveys tourism information on a
geographical basis—from a national
level down to a division of states into
tourism regions; regions have their own
regional tourism authorities, many of
which produce Tourism Development
Plans on a three- or five-year basis, and
present information on local tourism
statistics and projections for growth (but
due to varying resources, the quality of
such plans is not uniform).
International and domestic tourism
forecasts are available on the Internet at
http://www.tourism.gov.au

The Australian Tourist Commission

Contact:
4/80 William Street, Woolloomooloo
NSW 2011

Notes:
The Commission's role is to represent
and promote Australian tourism
internationally. For example, the Tourism
Commission and Qantas have run
extensive advertising in Asia concerning
Australia as a tourist destination.[12]

Office of National Tourism

Contact:
PO Box 1545, Canberra ACT 2601

Notes:
The Office is part of the Commonwealth
Department of Tourism and its main role
is to support the development of
sustainable tourism throughout Australia.
The Office administers research and
grant programs.

Commonwealth Treasury

Contact:
Parkes Place, Barton ACT 2600
http://www.treasury.gov.au/Economic
Data

Notes:
The Treasury can supply information on
the consumer price index (CPI).

**Commonwealth Department of Foreign Affairs
and Trade**

Contact:
RG Casey Building, Barton ACT 2600
http://www.dfat.gov.au/geo/eeag/ind
ex.html

Notes:
The department provides economic
overviews of various international
economies.

Other Sources of Data

International Monetary Fund (IMF)

Contact:
http://www.imf.org

Notes:
For international financial statistics on
CPI, gross domestic product (GDP),
daily exchange rates, direct foreign
investment.

**Organisation for Economic Cooperation and
Development (OECD)**

Contact:
http://www.oecd.org

Notes:
For CPI and GDP data.

Figure 3.1 *Sources of Tourism and Hospitality Data*

Kevin Baker

A demographic assessment should address the question: Is the targeted population segment, or the population as a whole, sufficiently large to provide a local level of demand, and to provide projected staff requirements?

A trend analysis of population growth should be prepared, together with projections for future growth. A region of declining population might not be promising for expanding tourism and hospitality services—unless the region is within convenient travelling distance of a much larger population centre enjoying high growth.

CASE STUDY
Trend Anticipation — Club Med

Gilbert Trigano opened the first Club Med (from the French *Club Méditerranée*) in Greece in 1955 to provide a resort in an attractive region where guests could 'get away from it all' and enjoy themselves in a casual environment. The staff were informal, and all services and entertainment were provided within the property. The concept now embraces 104 Club Med 'villages' in 30 countries—mainly venues with sunny skies and warm weather.

However, in the 1990s, even Club Med found it necessary to modify its standardised mode of service. Although Club Med had clearly been successful, the market place had changed and, instead of catering mainly for single people, new Clubs began to cater for families with children. The geographical focus of new Club Med operations began moving towards the United States. The 'villages' became internationalised by the appointment of more non-French managers. Despite the emphasis on 'getting away from it all', some properties now featured computer workshops to allow business people to 'keep in touch'.

Clearly, feasibility studies for new Clubs have taken global and regional factors into account—and have planned accordingly.

Based on a report in *Asian Business* (January 1991)[14]

3. Local Economic Trends

Trends of economic development—the vigour and vitality of the region—can be assessed through evidence such as building approvals (listings available through local councils), and employment levels. The trend in building approvals over the previous five years will be an indicator of future economic growth or decline. Of course, a review of building approvals (undertaken with a view to assessing a new hospitality project) would highlight the construction of new tourism and hospitality facilities. These might indicate growing demand or, alternatively, a satiation of demand (indicating an oversupply in the market).

Approvals for new infrastructure projects are another indicator of the strength of local economic growth. Large local projects will normally reflect business confidence and the likelihood of further growth.

An evaluation of general regional characteristics should also consider transport projects and infrastructure—such as airport upgrades or highway development.

On a regional basis, there might be specific federal and state government financial initiatives to support local tourism/hospitality—to boost growth and employment. The local government authority might be a source of information on financial grants and other support available to new projects in the region. Alternatively, investigation might reveal that the local government authority has a negative attitude towards tourism development.

The general community support for tourism development can usually be assessed by a review of local newspapers and other media. Articles supporting tourism, a lively debate in the letters columns on the advantages and disadvantages of a development, and the level of advertising, can all be indicators of the attitudes of the local population. A careful reading of local newspapers might also indicate potential constraints on the local tourism industry. Council might be embroiled in debate over the need to upgrade water and sewerage, to rebuild an important highway, or to resolve chaotic traffic congestion in the main thoroughfares. Each of these points might not be important in itself but, taken together, they could be symptoms of a community that has reached its limits of development. Such an impression should flag concern, and the need to ask questions about what is being done to remedy the constraints on development.

In relation to local economic development, income statistics for a region will be relevant as an indicator of the propensity of the population to spend on travel and accommodation.

4. Attractions and Special Features of a Region

Attractions and special features of a region can be listed and assessed with the help of various sources. Some of the best sources are the directories of the state motorists' associations. Various associations exist to serve the needs of different classes of members.

Among other sources of information, the Restaurant and Caterers' Association can advise on the community's eating-out habits, and the Property Council of Australia can advise on issues affecting new developments. (See list of useful industry organisations, Figure 3.2.)

Tourism in the region under evaluation might be seasonal. Clearly a beach resort or a ski facility will have clearly defined periods of peak demand—based upon climatic and holiday factors. In some regions, however, there might be seasonal peaks and troughs that are not immediately obvious—such as the

Industry Organisations

Australian Automobile Association
Australian Amusement, Leisure & Recreation Association
Australian Federation of Travel Agents
Australian Hotels Association
Australian Youth Hostels Association
Bus and Coach Association
Caravan Parks' Association
Caravan Trade and Industry associations
Fast Food Industry Association
Meetings Industry Association of Australia
Motorists' associations (various states)
Property Council of Australia
Registered Clubs Association
Restaurant and Caterers' Association
Retailers' Association
Tourism Training Australia
World Tourism Organisation

Figure 3.2 *Industry Organisations*

Kevin Baker

grape-harvesting period in a wine-growing district, or a period of high demand at the time of a local festival. Some industry associations can assist in an evaluation of whether regional demand is likely to be seasonal. Travel journals or feature articles in the general press can indicate whether the proposed resort will have to cope with excess seasonal demand at certain times and, conversely, low occupancy at other times.

If there are specific attractions in a region, the evaluation will need information on the likely numbers of visitors, and the nature of those visitors. This will include information on whether they are usually day visitors or (because of distance or night attractions) whether they will require accommodation. The type of attraction might mean that the visitors are likely to repeat their experience. Whale-sighting is an example of an attraction that draws visitors back time and time again.

The regional attractions might be such that they draw a particular group. Senior citizens are more likely to visit a region for a festival of gardens and flowers than are young families. Senior citizens are more likely to purchase meals in the area, and souvenirs, but are less likely to attend side-shows or carnival rides.

A region might not have attractions of its own, and might not be a destination in its own right, but could still be important as a transit area. Districts halfway between the capitals of the eastern mainland states have high numbers of transit visitors and, typically, such visitors seek budget accommodation.

Aspects of regional tourism and relative attractions can often be studied in tertiary sources. Tertiary sources of information include trade publications (see list of subscription trade journals, Figure 3.3, p. 45). Major business periodicals are usually indexed, and the index should assist the researcher to find references to topics that are under their microscope.

A researcher can also find information in academic journals—although the topics covered in such publications are usually more specialised. One such academic journal is the *Australian Journal of Hospitality Management*, published by the University of Queensland. Another source of both secondary and tertiary data, and one that is often overlooked, is the local library. The local library might also have links to other libraries and be able to obtain detailed information and statistics from local, regional and national groups.

The first step in making reference to tertiary sources should be the use of a computerised search. An Internet search can provide sometimes interesting and varied responses to a word search but, for more specialised searching, there are online indexing services available. One such is *ABI Inform*, which covers approximately 800 major business journals.[15]

Another tertiary source is the use of private subscription consultancy services. These are commonly conducted through stockbroking advisory services, merchant banks and specialist consultancies. An example of the last is Horwath and Horwath, which conducts indepth analysis of the hospitality industry on a national and international level. Another example is the National Institute of Economic and Industry Research, which examines macroeconomic variables—

Subscription Trade Publications

Australian Hotelier (National Publishing Group, NSW)

Convention and Incentive Marketing (Rank Publishing Company, NSW)

Hospitality: Foodservice, Beverage, Accommodation (APN Business Publishing, Vic.)

Hotel Watch (quarterly report on hotel performance; Blake, Dawson & Waldron, NSW)

National Liquor News (National Publishing Group, NSW)

Restaurant and Catering Australia (Association of Restaurant and Catering, NSW)

Tourism and Hospitality Review (Genesis Multimedia, NSW)

Traveltrade (Reed Business Publishing P/L, NSW)

Travelweek (APN Business Publishing, Vic.)

Figure 3.3 *Subscription Trade Publications*

Kevin Baker

such as the CPI, GDP and exchange rates. Consultancy services usually charge for providing information for a commercial project—reflecting their costs in gathering, monitoring and analysing data on trends. It is a case of, 'you pays your money and you takes your choice'.[16]

To contact consultancy services, or to refer generally to what might be available, the *Yellow Pages* (the telephone directory of business numbers) can be a useful source—albeit an often overlooked one.

5. The Visitor Profile

In assessing the general characteristics of hospitality and tourism in a specific region, it is also useful to compile a profile of domestic and international visitors. This involves a comparison of the numbers of domestic and international visitors, and a comparison of the level of spending of each group. The growth patterns for the past five years should be assessed, as well as the growth projections for the next five years for each group within the region. Their preferred transport needs and preferred standard of accommodation should be listed. Consideration should also be given to the duration and the times of year of their travel.

For the international visitors, the home country of visitors should be noted, and numbers from each of the major countries of origin should be compared. External factors might contribute to a growth or decline in overseas visitors— including exchange rates, and economic conditions in countries of origin. (See Figure 3.4, p. 46.)

Care must be taken when analysing international markets and marketing variables in those markets, because it is more difficult for those outside a culture to identify the risks involved in considering particular factors.

The farther from familiar territory, the greater the risk of making major mistakes.

McCarthy et al. (1994)[17]

Much of the above information might be difficult to obtain, but regional tourism bureaux often prepare profiles of domestic and international visitors.

Exchange Rate Facts

The Important Currencies to Consider

International tourism is very sensitive to exchange rate fluctuations because overseas travellers wish to go where their local currency will buy the most for them. It is important in making projections of future economic conditions to consider likely movements in various exchange rates. The most frequently traded currencies, and their percentage of average daily foreign exchange transactions worldwide (before the introduction of the 'Euro'), were:

United States Dollar (82%)

German Mark (40%)

Japanese Yen (23%)

British Pound (sterling) (14%)

Swiss Franc (9%)

Other currencies (32%)

The reader will note that the total of these percentages exceeds 100%. In fact, they total 200%—because each transaction must involve two currencies and, therefore, the total volume must be 100% × 2.

The introduction of the 'Euro' in 1999 impacted upon foreign exchange trading, and it has become the second-most-commonly traded currency.

Figure 3.4 Exchange Rate Facts

Based on Daniels & Radebaugh (1995)[18]

6. Cultural Factors

The visitor profile, and the general characteristics of a region, should be assessed in terms of cultural factors. For example, a proposal for a fixed venue for rock concerts hoping to attract school leavers might not sit well in a conservative rural area. Alternatively, it might be welcomed. At least the project evaluation should consider this cultural aspect of the general environment.

Culture includes far more than ethnicity. Culture includes intangible features (such as attitudes, beliefs and languages) and tangible features (such as products and works of art). Cultural values are in a continual state of flux. Recent cultural changes that might affect the planning of hospitality projects include:

- *moving from* a savings ethic *to* spending freely on credit;
- *moving from* a work ethic *to* self-indulgence and having fun;
- *moving from* male domination *to* equal male/female roles; and
- *moving from* postponed gratification *to* immediate gratification.

Stanton, Miller & Layton (1994)[19]

A project that has a strong theme—such as an hotel embodying 'outback' values and offering ranch-type entertainments—should take cultural aspects into account in the course of its design and development. These factors could prove to be a source of market differentiation and advantage, but they could also be a disadvantage.

CASE STUDY
Tasmania as a Tourism Destination

The small state of Tasmania relies heavily on the tourism industry. More than $220 million was spent in the industry by 350 000 visitors in 1980. The Tasmanian Department of Tourism researched the profile of visitors and discovered that almost all (95%) of the visitors were Australians. The department therefore emphasised cultural features of the state in its marketing—the penal settlements and early historical buildings. The department also emphasised another 'cultural' feature—the Wrest Point Casino and Hobart's night life. In addition, the natural environment was an attraction which appealed to the increased appreciation of nature and heightened environmental values in Australian society.

Based on Stanton, Miller & Layton (1994)[20]

Interpreting the Information

What does it all mean? The information collected through an analysis of general market characteristics must always be subject to a review process to ensure that it is interpreted correctly—especially if statistics have been used, or sample surveys completed.

Statistics should be cross-tabulated, or subject to referral to a second source of information—to ensure that the data are consistent with other studies. Samples used in surveys must be representative of the population from which the sample was taken. Questionnaires must also be checked, and any inconsistent responses reviewed. It might be that responses reflect the personal biases of the respondents, or reflect a deliberate attempt to mislead the questioner. Perhaps some people try to be helpful, and are therefore too optimistic in their predictions of future trends.

The validity of conclusions is dependent upon the validity and accuracy of the information collected. If the information is in doubt, the research should be repeated—if possible with different sources.

Conclusion to the Assessment

Having compiled information on general market characteristics from secondary and tertiary sources, the analyst should summarise the background to the project evaluation, supporting the information with supporting tables and schedules where appropriate, and highlighting any problem-specific data brought to light by the analysis.

A Last Word

The analyst should not form conclusions too early in the appraisal process. As open a mind as possible should be maintained until all the information has been gathered and analysed. The analyst should then take a short break before returning to the material, and formulating conclusions.

STUDY CHECKLIST #3
GENERAL MARKET FACTORS

- What is the national economic situation?

- What is the regional economic situation?

- What is the economic situation at the point of origin of our likely clients?

- What is the current national/state government policy towards this type of project?

- What social or economic factors will influence this project?

- What are the global/local trends in hospitality that will influence the project?

- What are the growth patterns and projections in the global and local market?

- What is the international/domestic visitor profile?

Chapter 3 ■ Review and Questions

1 Indicate whether the following statements are true or false and give a reason for your answer:
   a Qualitative research seeks indepth opinion. (True/False? Why?)
   b Smaller projects, like restaurants, can safely ignore the prevailing economic climate. (True/False? Why?)
   c Religious practice is an example of an internal factor that might affect a project. (True/False? Why?)
   d The trend in building approvals in a region is not a good indicator of the economic growth in that region. (True/False? Why?)
   e Local newspapers have nothing to offer an analysis of development in a region. (True/False? Why?)
   f Visitor profiles include such things as comparative numbers and patterns of spending. (True/False? Why?)

2 Insert the word(s) that best completes each of the following, selecting your answers from the following possibilities:
   special; attitudes, beliefs and languages; register; profile; well-defined; first-hand; quantitative; sports; quickly; watching; rejected; external.
   a The characteristics of a market can be assessed through . . . and qualitative analysis.
   b 'A problem . . . is half-solved.'
   c Primary information is that gathered . . . by the evaluation team.
   d Interest rates and energy prices are examples of . . . factors that might affect the feasibility of a project.
   e In order to assess the general hospitality and tourism characteristics of a specific region, it is useful to compile a visitor . . .
   f Culture includes tangible and intangible factors, and examples of intangible factors are . . .

3 Discuss the following in one or two sentences (for each statement):
   a Visitor profiles are useless, because profiles produce only a theoretical average—and no one is average.
   b Demand for a new product does not exist but has to be generated by good marketing.
   c The development of tourism and consequent increased visitor numbers must change the characteristics of a region and might affect the very features that attracted visitors to the region.

4 Analyse and discuss the following:
   Many sources of information have their own reasons for collecting data, and their own reasons for summarising and presenting that data in formats that suit themselves. This means that source information could be skewed and unreliable—so why use it?

A Sample Project

BUILDING A BETTER BARBECUE

Some pitfalls to avoid when constructing a new hospitality venture!

Figure 3.6 *Is There a Demand for Your Proposed Service?*

Kevin Baker (after the style of Giles)

Chapter 3 Notes

[1] McDonald, M. 1995, *Marketing Plans—How to Prepare Them and How to Use Them*, 3rd edn, p. 4, Butterworth-Heinemann Ltd: Oxford.

[2] Ibid. p. 13.

[3] Solomon, J. 1994, 'To Grow or Not to Grow: Contemplating Expansion in Uncertain Times', *Restaurant USA*, January 1994, pp 18–21.

[4] Kotler, P. 1994, *Marketing Management—Analysis, Planning, Implementation and Control*, 8th edn, p. 131, Prentice-Hall International, Inc.: New Jersey.

[5] Lewis, G., Morkel, A. & Hubbard, G. 1993, *Australian Strategic Management—Concepts, Context and Cases*, pp 82ff, Prentice Hall of Australia: Sydney.

[6] Quoted in *Business Week*, 12 May 1997, p. 31.

[7] Ali-Knight, J., Williams, P. & O'Neill, M. 1999, 'The Impact of the Asian Economic Downturn Upon the Management of Capacity in the Western Australian Hotel Sector', *Australian Journal of Hospitality Management*, 1999:6(1).

[8] McCarthy, E., Perreault, W., Quester, P., Wilkinson, J. & Lee, K. 1994, *Basis Marketing—A Managerial Approach*, p. 113, Richard D. Irwin Inc.: Sydney.

[9] Kotler, P. 1994, op. cit., p. 135.

[10] McDonald, M. 1995, op. cit., p. 351.

[11] McCarthy, E. et al. 1994, op. cit., p. 113.

[12] Ibid., p 445.

[13] Kotler, P. 1994, op. cit., p. 156.

[14] Author not noted, 'A New Course for Club Med', *Asian Business*, January 1991, pp 96–8.

[15] McCarthy, E. et al. 1994, op. cit., p 113.

[16] Anonymous: from a peepshow rhyme. See Lean, V. S., *Collectanea* (1902–04).

[17] McCarthy, E. et al. 1994, op. cit., p. 98.

[18] Daniels, J. & Radebaugh, L. 1995, *International Business—Environments and Operations*, 7th edn, p. 332, Addison-Wesley Publishing Company: Massachusetts.

[19] Stanton, W., Miller, K. & Layton, R. 1994, *Fundamentals of Marketing*, 3rd edn, p. 124, McGraw-Hill Book Co.: Sydney.

[20] Ibid., pp 523–9.

CHAPTER 4

Analysis of Supply and Demand

Synopsis of Chapter

This chapter continues the examination of the market place, presenting a detailed analysis of supply/demand factors by segment.

Three crucial questions of market demand are posed and discussed:
1 Is demand for the service greater than supply?
2 Is there a demand for a new product?
3 Is there a demand for a different quality of product?

The benefit-matching model is described.

Market supply factors are considered—including the use of market analysis tools such as competitors' inventory, 'fair-share' and 'normal occupancy' methods.

Market place reactions are also discussed.

Market Factors

The supply-and-demand section of the project evaluation is intended as a detailed analysis of market factors—including the competition in the target market. This analysis provides crucial information about whether the proposed project has an acceptable chance of success in the market place or not.

In an earlier age, in the 1960s, it was hardly necessary to ask, let alone answer, questions about supply and demand. This was because, in the typical Australian city/tourism destination, there was a shortage of good hotels and restaurants. The only question to ask was whether the site chosen for the project was a suitable one for a hotel/restaurant—if not, there were generally many other sites to choose from. The 'tyranny of distance' that helped to shape Australia's economic growth meant that travellers had to go long distances from one accommodation place to another. A hotel was insulated, as it were, from competition—simply because prospective guests could not easily travel on to an alternative.

In the 1980s, there was another boom period for hoteliers, when worldwide economic activity reached a peak, and financial deregulation in Australia resulted in a ready supply of financing. Hotels raised room rates, and there was an unprecedented number of new hotels built.

At the start of the 1990s, economic activity dived—resulting in the 'R-word'. This expression referred to the strange spectacle of government and industry spokespersons being reluctant to use the word 'recession'. After all the years when they had 'talked up' the economy, popular media commentators jokingly used the term 'R-word' instead of the word 'recession'! Due to this recession and room oversupply, there was a drop in sales and profitability for many hospitality operations. There was also an extensive strike of Australian airline pilots in 1989, and this delivered a sharp blow to demand for hotel accommodation. Overall, during the first years of the 1990s, the hotel industry experienced losses, staff cuts and declining service. Many tourists sought lower room rates, with the result that four-star and five-star hotels, in particular, suffered badly.[1]

Any project developer has to be careful to ensure that the proposed venture will suit market conditions of supply and demand. If it does not, the project evaluation should provide a clear conclusion—the project should not go ahead.

Market Demand

There are three questions to ask when considering demand factors relating to a new project:

1 Is the existing or potential demand for the service greater than the existing supply?
2 Is there a demand for a new market product that is not being met by the existing service providers?
3 Is the quality of the existing product being offered appropriate to the demand?

Each of these questions will be discussed in detail below.

Is Demand for the Service Greater Than Supply?

There are three steps involved in answering this question:

■ first, define what group or groups constitute the demand for the services of the proposed project;
■ secondly, determine from where the market groups of travellers will originate—whether they will be from local, regional, national or international origins; and
■ thirdly, assess the implications of the conclusions about supply and demand.

1. Define the Market Group

The group that constitutes the demand for the services of the proposed project needs to be defined. What is the target market, or market segment? For a hotel, resort and associated restaurant facilities, the demand for services comes from three main groups—business travellers, conference travellers and recreation/holiday travellers.

These groups can be subdivided further. For example, business travellers can be divided into private-sector and public-sector travellers; holiday travellers can be subdivided into travellers on a tourism package and backpackers; and so on. Each subgroup has different spending habits. However, too much subdivision might overload the analysis with too much information—some of which might not be relevant.

There are also other groups that might or might not be significant to the project—such as sporting groups and other special-interest groups.

For each group that is considered, the level of existing demand and the likely growth in demand for a five-year period must be determined—with estimates divided into low-range growth projections (conservative), mid-range growth projections, and high-range growth projections (optimistic).

Examples of relevant information include the following:

- for *business* travellers: information on market demand could include growth in local airport traffic and growth in office-space occupancy; high demand in these areas often being reflected in the demand for hotel/restaurant services;
- for *conference* travellers: relevant information to seek out would include the number of conferences held in the area, the number of participants, the length of stay and the level of spending of participants;
- for *recreational or holiday* travellers, the analyst should seek statistics on the number of tourists, their geographical origin, average length of stay, level of spending, the length of the tourist season, and any potential changes to the season.

Growth in demand can be assessed only with 'legwork' (that is, physically going out and assessing the situation). Regional tourism authorities and other secondary sources (see pp 43–5) can often assist with broad figures for growth in demand, and possibly with details concerning length of stay and typical expenditure. However, for much of this information, the analyst has to assess this information personally, or 'do the rounds' (as it is often termed).

Local sources of information on the growth of demand and the character of that demand include: (i) comparable hotels in the area; (ii) travel agents and tour operators; (iii) other local businesses; (iv) real estate agents; and (v) personal observation. Each of these is discussed below.

Comparable Hotels in the Area

Management or other staff at comparable hotels in the area might be prepared to discuss such statistics as occupancy and average room rate, and the mix of their guests. If they are reluctant to discuss these matters—and such reluctance would be understandable—information on the number of guest rooms and their tariff will be available through advertising material.

A schedule of hotels should be compiled. This should include the number of rooms and advertised rates. The advertised rates are known as 'rack rates', and are typically 10–20% above the actual rates charged—due to discounting for various reasons.

Although hotel management might not be prepared to disclose information to an appraiser, or might give false information in the hopes of discouraging further development, there are advantages to cooperation. By cooperating with the appraiser, current hotel operators can discover the status of planned hotel projects, and have the opportunity to adjust their own planning. The benefits of cooperating with market appraisers have been discussed by Cahill (1988).[2] In general, hotels within a region are usually prepared to share information such as occupancy and average room rate. For example, fourteen hotels in Canberra fax each other monthly with details of occupancy and average room rate for the month before. The information is useful to all the participants—not just to compare their own performance, but to understand regional trends in the industry.

Local Travel Agents and Tour Operators

Usually, people employed in the local travel industry will be more than prepared to talk about accommodation and other services—especially if they are aware that investors are looking at setting up new tourism operations in their area, and might put business their way. It is these people who are more likely to give estimates about occupancy rates in local properties.

Projected occupancy figures used in feasibility studies will always contain a degree of error. Tarras (1990) examined discrepancies between projected figures and actual operating results in hotel feasibility studies—including the question as to whether studies understate or overstate occupancy.[3]

Local travel agents and tour operators can also give advice on the seasonality of demand—a factor to take into account when forecasting occupancy rates for the project. It might be that travel agents 'talk up' an area, and an analyst must be aware of this possibility. However, if the person compiling the study interviews several agents, any agent who sounds unduly optimistic or pessimistic can be factored out.

Other Local Businesses

Other local businesses—whose trade is dependent upon the number of visitors—can be interviewed. These might include managers of bus lines, or car-hire firms.

They can offer advice on the number of business travellers in the area (who usually rent cars), and recreational travellers (who are more likely to use bus travel than are business or conference travellers).

Real Estate Agents

Real estate agents can be a source of information of the level of development in an area, and likely growth in demand for properties and tenancies—which might reflect a demand for accommodation and restaurant facilities.

Personal Observation

Another valid technique of research—provided it is conducted as an adjunct to more formal study and interview, and provided it is not used as the sole source of information—is personal observation. This is sometimes known as 'RBWA'—research by wandering around!

The appraiser could sit outside the proposed site of the project, or walk around the area, and assess the following sorts of questions:

- How many pedestrians and vehicles go past?
- How busy are the local shops?
- Are there plenty of parking spaces? Or is the area so busy that parking spaces are few?
- Does the district look prosperous?
- Are there shops shuttered up?
- Are there other developments in the area?
- Is it far to the business centre of town, or far from transport, or far from recreational centres?

An Ethical Issue

Researching information on competitors without their specific knowledge, especially information that could be considered confidential, can lead a researcher into ethical issues.

For example, is it ethical to discuss, with a disgruntled ex-employee of a potential competitor, such matters as confidential inside information about the competitor's development or marketing plans? What about discussing such matters with a junior employee who does not understand the sensitivity of the information being divulged?

It is clearly unethical and inappropriate to use information that has been gained in a secretive fashion from unauthorised sources. It is appropriate to make estimates, and to gather information from oblique sources (such as getting information on taxi movements, for example)—but such activity involves imagination, not outright theft of private data.

2. Determine the Origin of the Target Group

The first step in working out whether demand for a proposed new service is greater than supply was to define the market group. Having done that, the second step is to determine the origin of this target group. The proposer of the project needs to determine where the market groups of travellers (business, conference and recreational) will come from—that is, whether they will be from local, regional, national or international origins.

The discussions and interviews conducted in defining the target group (see pp 55–7) should have included queries about the origin of travellers and visitors. The appraiser should have ascertained the size of the 'feeder area' of the project— that is, from how far it will draw its guests, customers or clients. With information on these feeder regions, the analyst should then take the steps described below.

1 The analyst should re-assess the information on general market characteristics assembled in the first step of the study, and collate data on the particular feeder areas of travellers.

2 The analyst should, if possible, interview conference organisers and corporate travel officers in the areas from where the visitors will travel. These people might have less-detailed information, but they might be able to indicate characteristics of the wider area, and relay what they have heard in feedback from their clients. They can also indicate future travel plans. Large universities employ travel officers, and they can indicate popular conference and business destinations (which, of course, are often other university cities).

3. Assessment of Conclusions About Supply and Demand

The third step in the supply/demand question is carefully to assess the implications of the conclusions reached.

If the Study Concludes that Demand DOES Exceed Supply

If the study concludes that the supply of a service has *not* met the demand, there should exist some corroborating evidence as to how the market has adjusted to this situation. Has overall growth in the area been stunted by the short supply of hotel beds? Have room rates increased, or been higher than the average elsewhere, as a result of the undersupply of the service?

Evidence of a market with an undersupply of a service could be:

- high levels of development in a competing centre;
- the emergence of alternatives such as home-accommodation;
- instability in the local economy as a result of tourist-orientated activities operating at less than optimum;
- a distortion in the market whereby visitors are commuting long distances; and/or
- a cutback in demand to match the difficulties of undersupply.

In seeking this sort of corroborating market evidence (to back up a conclusion that there is, indeed, an undersupply), the analyst obviously needs to have some conception of the size of the market area in which to seek the corroborating evidence. How big is the market area? Many years ago, the local market area was restricted to one or two hours walk. That is, a town might have two or three hotels/inns which constituted the local market area—because prospective guests would not be prepared to walk to the next town. Today, however, if services are not satisfactory in one venue, a discerning traveller can take advantage of readily accessible transport to travel on to another destination. In these circumstances, a hotel or restaurant several kilometres away (or perhaps even a hundred kilometres or more away) can be a competitor.

In coming to its conclusions about a perceived undersupply, the project evaluation should have three dimensions. As well as a review of the *present* situation, and a five-year projection of operations into the *future*, there should be a five-year analysis of *past* activity. That analysis should show evidence of local facilities having taken action to cope with the undersupply—such as expanding accommodation.

Finally, in making a judgment that there is, indeed, an undersupply, there is always a proviso. Are competitors moving to fill the gap? The analysis of the competition (see pp 62ff) should consider this.

If the Study Concludes that Demand DOES NOT Exceed Supply

If the existing demand for the proposed service is assessed as being less than the available supply, the other two questions remain:

- whether there is a market need for a new product; and/or
- whether there is a market need for a different quality of product.

Is There a Demand for a New Product?

Is there a demand for a new market product that is not being met by the existing service providers?

To answer this question, it is necessary to assess the information gathered as for question 1, and to make a judgment about who are the likely consumers of the new product.

An analysis of a new product has its special difficulties, because an analyst obviously cannot examine existing operations in the area to be served by the proposed new product. There are three options:

- survey;
- small-scale test; and/or
- study of similar product.

Survey

The analyst can conduct a survey of potential consumers of the product. This option requires a clear definition of the target market, and also requires having access to a statistically significant sample of consumers.

Small-Scale Test

The proposer of the new project can set up a small–scale operation of the proposed product within the new area. This option is feasible for, say, franchised operations that are conducted on retail sites, but is less feasible for a large operation (and large investment) such as a hotel.

Study of Similar Product

The assessor can examine a similar product (if there is one) in another area. This third option is the cheapest one, and can be an accurate gauge—provided that the characteristics of the area in which the similar facility operates is comparable to the area where the proposed facility is to be established. For example, false conclusions could be drawn if the results of establishing a water amusement park in a beachside area were used to assess the likely success of operating a similar operation in a colder, inland area. The two areas and the market demand might be comparable, but they should not be assumed to be so.

Name Central Tourist Hotel	
Occupancy	72%
Tariff	
Single	$45
Double	$55
Location	
Central Business District	
Inner Suburban	
Outer Suburban	✗
Harbourfront	
Airport	
Quality	
Luxury	
Mid-Range	✗
Budget	
Backpacker	
Facilities/Services	
Restaurant	✗
Bistro	
Coffee Shop	
Night Club	
Swimming Pool	✗
Conference Centre	
Business Centre	
Efficiency of Operation	Good
Impression of Property	Good
Other Comment	In need of renovation

Figure 4.1 Worksheet for Market Inventory

Kevin Baker

Is There a Demand for a Different Quality of Product?

Is the quality of the existing product being offered appropriate to the demand? This is the third question to answer in an overall assessment of the market environment.

Various studies suggest that matching consumer demand with level of services should be one of the main objectives of management in developing a new hotel.[4] In assessing the quality of a product, an appraiser should, if possible, make a decision based upon objective factors. There are many sources of objective information.

Objective information can be obtained from formal or informal surveys of visitors and industry sources. Operatives in one part of the tourism industry that is dependent upon another can be quick to comment upon the comparative quality of services. For example, rental-car agency employees are partly dependent upon the level of hotel occupancy in the area, and will say whether they perceive that there is a market segment that is not catered for.

Statistics on repeat visits to a region can indicate whether quality meets demand. If visitors come once, but do not return, it is possible that the standard of service that they received was less than expected.

Evidence of a 'gap' in the range of services offered can be obtained by comparing accommodation statistics in one area with another. Assuming a similar visitor profile, the demand for each category of accommodation (five-star, four-star etc.) should be broadly comparable in one region with the demand in another.

With all statements concerning supply and demand in the tourism/ hospitality industry, it must be remembered that there might be reasons for a gap in the range of services. For example, there could be an absence of budget accommodation in an isolated resort area because the area is expensive to access and, consequently, budget travellers do not come in sufficient numbers to warrant expansion in that segment of the market spectrum. There might be a variation in visitor profiles that is not readily obvious.

The Benefit-Matching Model

The 'benefit-matching' model was developed to assist in the analysis of market supply and demand in the tourism industry.[5] The model is primarily used for considering market destinations. It identifies the benefits that travellers and visitors are seeking, and then identifies the benefits that the area or resort can offer.

The model permits a tight focus on market needs and, consequently, an emphasis upon marketing to particular segments of the market. For example, the market segment of outdoor vacationers would seek clean air, quiet surroundings and beautiful scenery—a nature resort would therefore provide the sort of benefits this segment is seeking.

Markets	Benefits Sought	Benefits Match	Benefits Provided	Destinations
		s = supermatch		
		m = match		
		n = mismatch		
U	A, B	s	A, B	X
V	B, C	m	B, D	Y
W	C, D	n	E, F	Z

Figure 4.2 *The Benefit-Matching Model Illustrated*

Based on Woodside (1982)[5]

Market U seeks benefits A and B, and Destination X provides these benefits. Therefore Destination X can assess market U with a view to determining, with accuracy, factors of supply and demand.

Market V seeks benefits B and C. Destination Y has some of the benefits (B) sought by Market V, but not other benefits being sought (C). Destination Y could therefore assess Market V with some accuracy in determining supply and demand.

Market W seeks benefits C and D. Destination Z has none of the benefits sought by market W and will not consider that market segment at all—because it clearly cannot meet the demand.

In a project evaluation of supply and demand, the use of the benefit-matching model can lead to a high degree of accuracy in predicting occupancy and room rates that match the demand of the target market. For example, young backpackers might be seeking low-cost accommodation—the average expenditure by backpackers in Australia in 1998 was $59 per day.[6] They might be seeking this accommodation in a region where there are plenty of outdoor attractions, and where the climate is conducive to outdoor activity. A selected northern coastal region of New South Wales offers cheap accommodation in caravan parks, and beach recreation—such as swimming, boating and fishing. There is a super-match between the market and the destination. An entrepreneur might consider expanding park/camping type accommodation venues.

Market Supply

Analysis of Competitors

What competitors should be considered? In other words, has the proposer of the new project determined the market geography (how far afield in listing competitors?), the product (should the backpackers' hostel be considered a competitor to a new motel?) and the segment (is the new proposal mainly offering accommodation services or entertainment services?).

In 1980, Marriott Hotels believed that there was an opportunity in the market place for a new style of suburban hotel. The company conducted a competitor analysis by examining all the sectors of the lodging market (budget, mid-price and luxury) in a number of geographical areas. The company discovered increases in travel by older people and families. Based on this information, Marriott Hotels judged that there was a 'gap' in the market place—an opportunity for mid-price products below what was typically being provided. The company followed up this analysis with a customer analysis conducted through focus-group interviews and a study of segments in the market. This reinforced the conclusions of the competitor study, and found a need for simple services in a secure and functional environment.[7]

In entering a new market, or extending services in that market, management must be confident that it can obtain a market share. If the market is restricted in some way—for example, by tied arrangements between hotels/motels and travel agents/transport operators—the following discussion and calculation based on obtaining a share of the market becomes superfluous. Therefore, the first aspect of competition that should be considered is whether the market is fairly open to new entrants. In most cases in the hospitality industry, the market is an open one and the existing operators are subject to competition—although some have advantages through the size of the operation or through other factors (such as brand recognition).

The proposer of a new project should consider not only actual competition (as listed from research of the area, and other sources such as the *Yellow Pages*), but must also consider the potential competitors. Local council authorities can supply some information on other development projects that have reached application stage. But to obtain information about rival projects that are only at a concept stage, or information about those that are still at a stage of project evaluation, the proposer of a new project might have to rely on interviews with local agents and people in the industry.

How does one get detailed information about competitors? One author has suggested that 95% of the strategic information required about competitors is available and accessible to the public.[8]

Compiling an Inventory of Competitors and Their Services
General
By referring to the sources described above (such as directories, listings, *Yellow Pages* etc.), or by using old-fashioned 'legwork', the analyst can compile an inventory of the competition. In the case of a hotel development, that inventory will list existing (and proposed) accommodation establishments in the market area, and will include those establishments that will be competitive by reason of:

- the type of services;
- rating (two-star, five-star);
- size;
- location; and
- rates.

The study could include information on whether the competitive properties are independent or affiliated to a chain. Information on the range of services offered (such as restaurants, bistros, entertainment etc.) could also be included. These factors could be appended to the analysis in notes, or as a listing by services. Some factors are difficult to assess—for example, the benefits of location, or heritage value. Such factors are clearly qualitative, and require a qualitative judgment by the appraiser.

The inventory of competitors can be expressed in quantitative terms—for example, by listing number of beds and other statistical factors. For purposes of calculating projected revenues at a later stage, the inventory should include details of tariffs—for both single guests and doubles. More subcategories of tariffs could overload the inventory with detail, and extended tariff subcategories should always be described by way of note. Tariff details will usually be found in hotel brochures and advertising material. Special advertised rates for 'low periods', or as part of a package, should not be taken into account here—because it can be assumed that such special rates will not apply often (unless the property is in a highly seasonal operating environment).

Average Room Rate

The average room rate will be an important figure in calculating likely revenues—because most hotels use such a figure in revenue projections, rather than using published rates (since most hotel guests receive some sort of discount). This average room rate statistic might be difficult to obtain in some cases, so an estimate is used. The estimate is usually based on a presumed discount of 15% less than the double rate.

Occupancy

Best available figures should be used for this assessment—either a statistic from local tourism sources, or an estimate if there is no figure available from a source within the local accommodation sector. There is a pitfall with forecasting occupancy rates—as there is in most forecasting! The pitfall is that occupancy is usually based on performance in a previous year, with the assumption that economic and market factors will continue into future periods. Some people say that this is market analysis based on a 'wishbone'.[9]

Average Nightly Demand

This figure will be used in assessing whether the demand for accommodation is such that the market can support a new development. It is obtained by multiplying the total beds in each hotel by the estimated occupancy. *Beds* are used rather than *rooms* in order to get consistency of calculation with the projected demand for beds. If *rooms* were used as a basis, the complication of having to assess double and single occupancy would arise.

Average Spread

The difference between the double rate and the single rate can be a broad indicator of demand—the greater the demand for hotel rooms, the smaller the 'spread' (that is, the smaller the difference between double and single rates). Because the hotel operator has a high demand for rooms, the operator is reluctant to sell a room for a single rate if a double rate can possibly be obtained.

In practice, tour operators rarely distinguish between double and single rates—especially at the four-star and five-star levels. This is because the costs associated with selling the room are virtually identical. The rate is based upon the room, rather than the bed.

For example, where services such as conference facilities are important in the proposed venture, the project evaluation should compile an inventory of the competitive facilities—which might include more than just other hotel properties.

As in the larger study, the study of conference venues assesses the existing facilities by size, quality and range of services offered. The participants are examined by origin, preference and spending patterns. The type of conferences, in terms of size and special requirements (such as technical facilities) should be listed. The mode of transport of participants—whether they are likely to travel by air through local airports, or by road or by sea transport—might influence plans for developing the conference venue. Changing trends in the sector should be noted. All this information should be obtainable through the sources listed above, particularly regional tourism offices.

Another useful division into subcategories is the division by individual/ group travellers. Group travellers can include some business travellers, some conference travellers, and some recreational travellers. The division might be useful at the feasibility stage—because the costing for group travellers is different, and the margins might be tighter.

Sub-Categories Within the Analysis of Competitors

The competitor analysis inventory can be expressed in spreadsheet format. Note that the maximum hotel beds in each property are totalled, as well as the total 'average nightly demand'. The latter remains an estimate. In a later section dealing with occupancy projections in further detail (p. 69), variations such as seasonality will be considered. For the purposes of assessing the supply/demand situation, one average and estimated figure will be used.

A fictional example of competitors for a proposed 100-room hotel development in a non-CBD metropolitan area is illustrated in Figure 4.3 (p. 66).

Property*	Beds in hotel	Sgle Rm Rte	Dble Rm Rte	Ave Rm Rte**	Occupancy (average)	Average Nightly Demand
Hotel # 1	180	$65	$75	$64 75	0%	135
Hotel # 2	68	$45	$53	$45 72	0%	49
Hotel # 3	89	$54	$58	$49 82	0%	73
Hotel # 4	165	$62	$70	$60 80	0%	132
Hotel # 5	122	$43	$50	$43 70	0%	85
Hotel # 6	100	$48	$55	$47 75	0%	75
Hotel # 7	90	$55	$65	$55 85	0%	77
Hotel # 8	224	$59	$67	$57 70	0%	157
Totals	1038					783
Averages		$54	$62	$52	76.1%	

* First column is a list of properties (similar to proposed) considered in the Competitor Analysis
** Fifth column: Average Room Rate—assume 15% less than double

1 Average Nightly Demand = 783 divided by 1038 = 75.4%
2 Average Room Rate (estimated) = $52
3 Average Spread (Double less Single rate) = $8

Figure 4.3 Competitor Analysis: Average Nightly Demand/Rate Comparison

Kevin Baker

Calculations of Supply/Demand

Determining Growth in Demand by Market Segment

Having prepared a list, or inventory, of the competitors, the next logical step is to compile calculations of how demand will match supply.

Guests are divided into categories (or segments) of the market for hotel beds. The common categories are:

- business travellers;
- conference or convention travellers;
- recreational or vacationing travellers; and
- permanent residents.

Using primary, secondary and tertiary sources, the analyst should estimate the likely growth (or decline) in demand for each of the categories.

Continuing with the example of Figure 4.1 (p. 60), let us suppose that the proposed 100-room property is in an area where there is a number of technical institutes, and that local sources have informed the analyst that several international conferences are scheduled for the next two years. This could imply an increase in business travellers, and an increase in conference travellers, and it could be anticipated that this high rate of growth will continue. It could also be assumed that there would be a small increase in recreational travellers in line with population and economic growth generally, and that there will be almost no increase in the number of permanent residents

The increase in each category is assessed, and then a composite percentage is obtained by multiplying the percentage of each category by the percentage increase of that category. Then simple addition of the composite growth of each segment gives a total composite growth figure.

Category of Guest	Existing Percentage of Demand	Annual Rate of Growth	Composite Growth
Business Travellers	55.0%	6.0%	3.3%
Conference Travellers	20.0%	10.0%	2.0%
Recreational Travellers	15.0%	4.0%	0.6%
Permanent Guests	10.0%	0.0%	0.0%
Totals	**100.0%**		**5.9%**

Figure 4.4 Estimate of Composite Growth in Demand

Kevin Baker

The composite growth figure of 5.9% can then be applied to the existing statistic of the demand for hotel rooms—the average nightly demand (783 rooms per night).

Extending growth projections over five years means that the present average nightly demand number is increased by 105.9% each year (compounded). Figure 4.5 (p. 68) provides data for the estimated increase in demand for hotel rooms based on a 5.9% increase each year. For comparison purposes, compound growth of 4% a year and 2% a year are also calculated for later analysis.

Note that the segments of higher growth might be termed 'high-priority segments'—because both the new projects and competitors will be striving to pick up an increased proportion of this segment. By contrast, there are 'maintenance-priority segments' (in which operations would strive to retain their market shares), and 'low-priority segments' (where there will be little marketing effort and expenditure because the segment is declining).

Figure 4.3 (p. 66) suggests that the average nightly demand is 783 rooms. Figure 4.5 (p. 68) suggests that, with a growth in demand of 5.9%, the average nightly demand one year from base date will be 829 rooms; after two years it will be 878 rooms; and so on.

The crucial question to be asked in the analysis of supply-and-demand factors for a new 100-room hotel is this: Is there a sufficient demand for hotel rooms to enable the operator of the new hotel to achieve the required occupancy target? There are two methods that can be used for assessing whether the market demand can support the new project in addition to existing competitors. One is the 'fair–share method' and the other is the 'normal occupancy method'.

Growth of 5.9%

Year	Demand	Annual Rate of Composite Growth	Future Demand for Rooms
# 1	783	105.9%	829
# 2	829	105.9%	878
# 3	878	105.9%	930
# 4	930	105.9%	985
# 5	985	105.9%	1043

Growth of 4%

Year	Demand	Annual Rate of Composite Growth	Future Demand for Rooms
# 1	783	104.0%	814
# 2	814	104.0%	847
# 3	847	104.0%	881
# 4	881	104.0%	916
# 5	916	104.0%	953

Growth of 2%

Year	Demand	Annual Rate of Composite Growth	Future Demand for Rooms
# 1	783	102.0%	799
# 2	799	102.0%	815
# 3	815	102.0%	831
# 4	831	102.0%	848
# 5	848	102.0%	865

Figure 4.5 Estimate of Growth in Demand for Rooms—Different Demand

Kevin Baker

Assessing Market Demand—the 'Fair-Share Method'

The 'fair–share method' totals the number of rooms in the target market place, and calculates the new project's contribution to that total.

For example, the analysis of competitors reveals that there are 900 available rooms in the regional lodging property market. The new property is for 100 rooms. This will make a total of 1000 rooms. The 'fair share' is calculated as 100 divided by 1000. The fair share of the market that the new development could expect is 10%.

The market could be further divided into business, conference and recreational travellers, if those statistics are readily available.

The fair share could be amended by what is called a 'penetration factor'—by which market analysts assess whether the project could achieve more than its proportionate share of the available market (due to advantages of branding and chain support).

The fair-share method has the advantage of being simple and quick to use. However, it has a disadvantage in that it takes no account of existing occupancies. If the occupancies of existing properties are *low*, a new competitor will achieve a fair share of a declining market. If the existing occupancies are *high*, the new property has a good likelihood of achieving high occupancies.

The fair-share method also cannot tell the analyst how many rooms under-supply there might be in the market place. Also, in extreme cases, the fair-share method might lead to a false analysis. For example, if the new property is disproportionately large, the method might suggest that the new hotel could pick up, say, 40% of the market. This assumes that the market is able to sustain a large increase.

Assessing Market Demand—the 'Normal-Occupancy Method'

For the purposes of analysing supply and demand, assume that the required occupancy target for achieving a reasonable profit is 70%. It can also be assumed that this occupancy figure, if achieved on average by all hotels in the target market, would allow a reasonable profit for all. Regional and national statistics support the judgment that a 70% occupancy is a 'normal' statistic—it is the 'normal occupancy'.

The 'normal-occupancy method' requires information on existing competitor occupancy rates. It is a better tool to use than the fair-share method because it is more precise in measuring market undersupply. The method requires an assumption of what is a normal occupancy in a particular area at a particular time.

For the purposes of analysing supply and demand, assume that the required occupancy target for achieving a reasonable profit is 70%. It can also be assumed that this occupancy figure, if achieved on average by all hotels in the target market, would allow a reasonable profit for all. Regional and national statistics support the judgment that a 70% occupancy is a 'normal' statistic—it is the 'normal occupancy'.[10]

The Disadvantage of the 'Normal-Occupancy Method'

The disadvantage of the 'normal-occupancy method' as opposed to the 'fair-share method' has been touched upon. The occupancy method requires a calculation of occupancy rates at competitors' properties. To the extent that those occupancy calculations are accurate, the occupancy method will also be accurate. However, if estimates have to be made (as often they do), the accuracy of the method declines.

The best course, in calculating likely demand, is to use both calculations. The 'fair-share method' is straightforward, requires little time to calculate, and is based on a verifiable statistic (available rooms) which is easily available from brochures of other hotels. Both methods will usually produce consistent forecasts, and the 'normal-occupancy method' simply adds additional detail and information about the degree of oversupply or undersupply.

Calculating Supply/Demand and Future Supply/Demand of Services

The next step in the process of establishing the feasibility of building an additional 100-room property is to assess whether there is (and will be) an undersupply or oversupply of rooms in the market. This is done by calculating a notional figure for the required total of daily hotel rooms to achieve a balance between supply and demand.

Let us say that the average nightly demand is 783. A reasonable occupancy statistic is 70%. Dividing 783 by 70% equals 1119 rooms. Let us also say that existing rooms available in the market (as determined by the rooms total in the inventory of competitors) is 1038. The notional demand for rooms is thus 1119 and the supply is 1038, so there is a notional undersupply, or shortfall, of 81 rooms per night in the target market area. At the present time, an additional 100 rooms will thus create an oversupply.

After one year, when the anticipated composite growth of 5.9% has occurred, the average nightly demand will be 829. Dividing 829 by 70% equals 1184 rooms. Existing hotel rooms (if there is no other construction) remain 1038. Subtracting 1038 from 1184 reveals a shortfall of 146 rooms after one year. Therefore, one year from now, an additional 100 rooms will meet part of the shortfall of supply over demand of 146 rooms and a new hotel will be feasible.

Figure 4.6 (p. 71) extends these calculations for five years. Figure 4.6 also includes calculations based on other scenarios—that instead of all hotels averaging 70%, all average 73% (a slight decline from the existing situation), or all average 76% (the existing average occupancy). In these last two scenarios, the shortfall of supply over demand is much less, and makes construction of a 100 rooms more risky.

It then becomes a management decision as to whether a new hotel can effectively take away some of the guests from the existing properties, or whether those properties will be successful in maintaining their regular guests and their share of new guests. The management decision then has to consider qualitative factors about the nature of the current demand for rooms. The segment of conference travellers is quite large, and such travellers have less brand loyalty than business travellers—so there might be a possibility of winning some of this segment of the market.

The statistic for the shortfall of rooms can also be an indicator of the space in the market place—that is, whether there is room for the entry of other competitors, and whether existing competitors can also achieve gains. The larger the shortfall, the greater the likelihood of success for new entrants. The third scenario in Figure 4.6 assumes that all hotels retain their current occupancy rate of 76% (probably an unlikely one). This indicates that there is limited space for new entrants, especially a new entrant planning an addition of 100 rooms to the supply, until year 3, when there will be a shortfall of 186 rooms in supply over demand.

Assuming 70% Occupancy All Hotels

Year	Present and Future Demand	Assume 70% Occupancy All Hotels	New Total for Available Rooms	Existing Rooms Available	Shortfall in Supply of Rooms
Current	783	70.0%	1119	1038	81
# 1	829	70.0%	1184	1038	146
# 2	878	70.0%	1254	1038	216
# 3	930	70.0%	1329	1038	291
# 4	985	70.0%	1407	1038	369
# 5	1043	70.0%	1490	1038	452

Assuming 73% Occupancy All Hotels

Year	Present and Future Demand	Assume 70% Occupancy All Hotels	New Total for Available Rooms	Existing Rooms Available	Shortfall in Supply of Rooms
Current	783	73.0%	1073	1038	35
# 1	829	73.0%	1136	1038	98
# 2	878	73.0%	1203	1038	165
# 3	930	73.0%	1274	1038	236
# 4	985	73.0%	1349	1038	311
# 5	1043	73.0%	1429	1038	391

Assuming 76% Occupancy All Hotels

Year	Present and Future Demand	Assume 70% Occupancy All Hotels	New Total for Available Rooms	Existing Rooms Available	Shortfall in Supply of Rooms
Current	783	76.0%	1030	1038	-8
# 1	829	76.0%	1091	1038	53
# 2	878	76.0%	1155	1038	117
# 3	930	76.0%	1224	1038	186
# 4	985	76.0%	1296	1038	258
# 5	1043	76.0%	1372	1038	334

Figure 4.6 Estimate of Growth in Demand for Rooms—Different Occupancy

Kevin Baker

Calculating Worst-Case and Best-Case Scenarios

With all of the above calculations, a proviso must be noted. The calculations are projections based on *assumptions*, and the quality of the conclusions depends upon the quality (accuracy) of the assumptions. The projections are for five years, and projections of longer than that period are subject to a greater margin of error. The further into the future one attempts to project, the greater the potential error.

It is possible to use supply/demand assumptions with estimates of composite growth to develop worst–case/best–case scenarios. Because the estimates of growth and future projections are so dependent upon assumptions, it is best to provide a range of projections, rather than just one. It is a proven military tactic that it is easier to strike a target if a salvo (a simultaneous firing of several guns) is fired, rather than if a single round is fired. Overstreet (1989) found that over-optimistic feasibility studies are often blamed for the lack of success of new hotels.[11]

A *worst-case scenario* could take the least optimistic occupancy estimate—that is, 76% (which assumes that all other hotels maintain all their existing guest profiles and that a new hotel must attract its guests from market-growth factors). This could then be combined with the worst-case growth factor—in this case 2%. The worst-case scenario revealed in Figure 4.7 suggests that a new hotel will not be able to operate within a shortfall of supply until at least year five.

The *best-case scenario* suggests that, with 70% occupancy and 6% composite growth, there will be, within a year, a shortfall of supply that will be able to accommodate an additional 100 rooms. This will probably be within the construction time of the new property.

Supply/Demand Analysis—Other Factors

Other Quantitative Factors

There are other factors of supply and demand that are not included in the above model. These include such factors as spending patterns, length of stay of guests, and use of in-house facilities. Length of stay and use of facilities are difficult to predict for a new property, and it is often necessary to rely on industry 'rule-of-thumb' estimates.

These statistics, although useful, are not as crucial as occupancy rates and growth estimates, and are best treated separately in order to keep the supply/demand projections as simple as possible.

Forecasting the Reaction of Competitors

The proposer of a new venture must be wary of other competitors, and be conscious that they will probably react to new competition by reducing prices or by offering special package deals for upgraded services. The new venture might determine its room rates, and then discover that the competitors have reduced their rates, even below full cost-recovery in the short term, in order to squeeze out the new competitor.

If the new enterprise sets its rates at an existing level, and then fails to modify them to take account of competitors' strategy, the new enterprise provides what is referred to as a 'price umbrella'. This protects the competitors and means that

Worst Case:
76% occupancy in existing hotels and 2% composite growth (existing hotels retain their market share and the new project snares only the overflow

Year	Present and Future Demand (2%)	Assume 76% Occupancy Existing Hotels	New Total for Available Beds	Existing Beds Available	Shortfall in Supply of Beds
Current	783	76.0%	1030	1038	–8
# 1	799	76.0%	1051	1038	13
# 2	815	76.0%	1072	1038	34
# 3	831	76.0%	1093	1038	55
# 4	848	76.0%	1116	1038	78
# 5	865	76.0%	1138	1038	100

Best Case:
70% Occupancy in all hotels and 6% composite growth

Year	Present and Future Demand (2%)	Assume 76% Occupancy Existing Hotels	New Total for Available Beds	Existing Beds Available	Shortfall in Supply of Beds
Current	783	70.0%	1119	1038	81
# 1	830	70.0%	1186	1038	148
# 2	879	70.0%	1256	1038	218
# 3	931	70.0%	1330	1038	292
# 4	986	70.0%	1409	1038	371
# 5	1044	70.0%	1491	1038	453

Figure 4.7 Worst-Case/Best-Case Scenario

Kevin Baker

the new enterprise endures the economic 'storms' of falling guest demand.[12] The new venture might therefore need contingency plans for room rates—including the possibility of price–cutting strategies.

CASE STUDY

Competition Analysis in an Inner Melbourne Suburb

In 1993, a development company purchased a small two-star hotel in Melbourne called 'The Lady of Shallot'. It was situated approximately three kilometres from the centre of Melbourne and consisted of public and saloon bars, an 80-seat dining room, a bistro seating 40 people, and 16 double rooms with private facilities.

The competition consisted of similar properties within a radius of approx-imately a kilometre. A brief analysis of competitors involved listing those properties and noting their strengths and weaknesses.

The competition faced by the new owners of 'The Lady of Shallot' at that time included:

- 'The Sword and Stone Hotel':
  65 years old; last modernised in 1988; smaller than 'The Lady of Shallot' ('Sword & Stone' has 11 rooms); good, well-patronised bistro seating 70; catering to local business and professional people; profitable and well managed;
- 'The Merchant Prince Hotel':
  95 years old; needing modernisation; more rooms than 'The Lady of Shallot' ('Merchant Prince' has 22; limited use); larger bistro than 'Lady of Shallot' (seating 120), but offering limited services to the lower end of the market;
- 'The Five Feathers Hotel':
  60 years old; minor work 30 years ago; only 13 rooms; occupancy rate of 77%; well-reputed 20-seat dining room; '1960s' atmosphere;
- 'McLaren's Hotel':
  limited bar trade; 10 rooms (almost unused); renovations required; site for sale for an extended period; and
- 'The House of Cards Hotel':
  60 years old; renovated two years before; catering for young profes-sionals; providing extensive entertainment; late liquor licence; very busy and apparently profitable.

Summary

There were four real competitors (although a purchaser of 'McLaren's' might have provided new and different competition). The four real competitors catered for the range of demand—including low-priced bar trade, business people, younger clientele, and older nostalgia-seeking clientele.

A redevelopment of 'The Lady of Shallot' would have to compete directly for one of these market segments or, alternatively, seek a niche market (and the success of 'The Five Feathers' indicated that there could well be a demand for a 'theme' hotel).

In this case, comparative or average occupancy figures are not extracted because, in one hotel ('The Five Feathers'), the occupancy was very high at 77%, whereas, in the other hotels, the occupancy of rooms was very low (down to 15% at 'The Lady of Shallot' and probably less at 'McLaren's'). Hence, an average figure in the 40s (calculated on one high figure and several very low figures), would be meaningless.

Based on Ellis, cited in Stanton, Miller & Layton (1994)[13]

If there are many competitors, and if the new project will therefore be just one of many players in the market place, the reaction of competitors might be muted. However, if the competition consists of, say, only four hotels/motels, and the new project is a large motel, the proposed venture is attempting to take approximately 20% of the available market, and competitors would certainly react to that situation. In the latter case, the project evaluation must include an analysis of competitors' likely strategies—and moves to counter them.

In considering the possible strategies of competitors in countering new developments, the analyst must take proper account of the size of the project. A comparatively small project might not be able to successfully compete with a number of larger competitors who have the advantage of economies of scale. The concept of 'economy of scale' simply proposes that a larger property (of 500 rooms) can achieve economies of operation that a smaller property (of 50 rooms) cannot. Such economies would be achievable, for example, in purchasing goods in large quantities, or in arranging specialist services—the cost of which could be spread over 500 rooms rather than 50 rooms.

Hotels from a higher market segment might also compete directly by lowering their rates to match those of a new entrant in the local market. That is, if the new project is a three-star hotel, four-star and five-star hotels might become direct competitors. Liatsos has discussed this issue with an academic case study of hotels on Cyprus.[14]

In assessing the supply/demand factors of a target market, an appraiser might also discover that there are external factors that impinge upon the operation of the market. For example, other properties might have been developed to take advantage of tax laws and benefits—such as relief from land taxes or subsidies for development. Overstreet (1989) has discussed how some regions in the United States have an oversupply of hotel rooms due to external factors.[15] Overstreet has also discussed a case study of the hotel market in Charlottesville, where nearly half the hotel rooms of the city were developed over six years (1983–89), resulting in an oversupply.[16] What had been a profitable market became soft.

When external non-market factors are involved, supply/demand assessments can be distorted.

CASE STUDY
The Pudong Shangri-la Hotel

Sometimes investors/owners must make their investment decisions on limited market information. An example of a large hotel constructed in a new area is the 'Pudong Shangri-La Hotel', which opened in August 1998 in a new region in Shanghai, China, called the Pudong district.

The Pudong is an extensive development which commenced in 1991 and which is intended to be a major international financial and commercial centre, opposite the existing business districts of Shanghai. There are other regions of Asia planned as 'new cities' and free-trade areas, but the Pudong development is the largest single project of its kind.

With no existing operations, and little infrastructure in an area, it was not possible to conduct a detailed analysis of local competitors, or even a market review—although a citywide review was possible. This indicated that there were 4376 five-star hotel rooms available in Shanghai in 1996, and 6765 four-star rooms.[17] In the larger urban area of Shanghai, there are excellent tourism analyses and projections, but it was uncertain how much competition would be provided by the existing hotels in the older area of the city— separated from the newer area by a major river.

The basis for investment in a major hotel in Pudong would have to be considered in the context of the regional development.

The Pudong Shangri-La was conceived as a five-star 612-room property and the decision to proceed with construction in 1994 was made in conformity with a long-term strategy of developing in fast-growing regions or Asia, rather than to meet short-term investment targets. Shanghai can be termed a 'gateway' market, and the strategic aim is to obtain a foothold in the gateway with a view to being able to dominate the market.[18]

The Pudong Shangri-La project cost US$140 million, and opened in September 1998 in a difficult market environment—due largely to a decline in visitor arrivals (down by 8.83% for the twelve months to August 1998). A local magazine commented: ' . . . glut of hotel rooms in Shanghai, aggravated by a widespread slump . . . and a . . . plummeting in the numbers of tourists, has triggered cut-throat competition among local hoteliers'.[19]

Occupancy rates for four-star and five-star hotels in all of Shanghai had declined from 67% in 1997 to 59% in 1998, and average room rates had seen a decline of similar magnitude—down from US$106.82 in 1997 to US$92.50 in 1998.[17] In the Pudong area there were, by that time, three hotels and, whereas occupancy rates had been (and remained) higher than the rest of Shanghai (76% in 1997 declining to 66% in 1998), average rates were lower (US$91.51 in 1997 to US$82.08 in 1998). The rates have been subject to heavy discounting, driven down by the market.

Despite the difficult market, the decision to proceed (based on an analysis of regional statistics of demand) appears to have paid off, and the hotel has achieved its occupancy targets in its first months of full operation. To date, it has benefited from limited competition in the area—only three hotels of four-star or five-star standard have been completed in Pudong, and there are few local food and beverage outlets to lure guests.

Supply/Demand Factors for Other Tourism Ventures

The above example of market analysis for a proposed 100–bed hotel can be used for other types of tourism ventures involving short–term and long–term accommodation—such as motels or caravan parks.

Caravan parks, in particular, have a high ratio of permanent and semi-permanent residents which, for a new operator, indicates that a lengthy period of time must be allowed to establish the business and build up the number of permanent residents. Motels and caravan parks might also be more seasonal in operation than the city hotel described in the example above. For motels and caravan parks, the calculation of average nightly demand should be amended to an annual basis. Calculating guest-nights spread out over a year makes the numbers larger, but the principles remain the same.

Holiday units, like caravan parks, normally return occupancy figures on an annual basis—although occupancy could be broken down into peak periods and non-peak periods, with differential rates, and two calculations could be made for projected returns.

Some of the principles outlined above—such as assessing supply/demand factors and making an inventory of competitors—are also applicable to a project evaluation for a new restaurant. However, restaurants are more difficult to compare because of the wider range of services/products that they offer consumers. In addition, the restaurant market is more fast-moving—and this makes five-year projections less accurate. Nevertheless it is essential to compare trends and occupancies and prices of competitors before investing in a new restaurant.

Other, more specialised, tourism ventures—such as tours, cruises and theme parks—are not as easy to assess in terms of market supply and demand. This is because there might be few regional competitors, or the competition might come from different industries. For example, a theme park might have to compete with sporting events in a region—such as motor racing or football. Feasibility analyses for ventures such as these must involve more sophisticated marketing assessment techniques—such as sample surveys.

In his book on conducting feasibility studies for tourism projects, Tonge has produced a number of checklists that can be used in assessing the feasibility of a number of different projects, and they are recommended as further reading for specific projects—such as, for example, caravan parks.[20]

Having analysed supply-and-demand factors, and having assessed the competitors, the next step is to consider the site and its possibilities, and likely occupancy and rates. Then, after considering the likely number of guests and what they should be prepared to pay, the study can discuss the size and quality of a project developed to meet market needs.

A Last Word

It should be remembered that, at the very time when the developer thinks that all options have been covered, there always seems to be one more that has been overlooked!

STUDY CHECKLIST #4
SUPPLY/DEMAND ANALYSIS

- How many hotels, motels, units, caravan parks, and camping grounds are there in the region?
- What services do they offer?
- What markets are they aimed at?
- What is the range of prices?
- How many properties have been constructed in the past five years?
- How many tourism/hospitality projects are under construction?
- What are the constraints on growth in the region?
- Are there local and regional tourism organisations?
- What is the rate of population growth?
- Are there plans for improved transport links?
- Are there seasonal patterns to demand?
- Are there unique features or events in the region?

Chapter 4 ■ Review and Questions

1 Indicate whether the following statements are true or false and give a reason for your answer:

   a Low-range growth projections are usually preferred to 'optimistic' ones. (True/False? Why?)

   b 'Research by wandering around' is a useful tool of analysis. (True/False? Why?)

   c High levels of development in a competing centre could be an indicator of undersupply in the market under study. (True/False? Why?)

   d Matching consumer demand with level of services is not one of the main objectives in developing a new hotel. (True/False? Why?)

   e 'Benefit-matching' concerns the benefits a developer hopes to receive from their project. (True/False? Why?)

   f It is misleading to use average room rates as a guide to likely financial returns. (True/False? Why?)

2 Insert the word(s) that best completes each of the following, selecting your answers from the following possibilities:
high-priority segments; fair-share; three; quality; external non-market; inventory; analysis of past operations; review; heuristic; projection of future operations; costing of present operations; fall-back plan.

   a A project evaluation should have three dimensions—a review of the present situation and an . . . as well as a . . .

   b There are . . . options for analysing the market for a new product.

   c Information on probable competitors is presented in an . . . of those competitors and their services.

   d Guest categories/segments of higher growth might be termed ' . . . ' for new projects.

   e The . . . method of assessing market demand totals the number of rooms in the target market place, and calculates what proportion to that total the new project will contribute.

   f Supply/demand assessments can be distorted by . . . factors.

3 Discuss the following in one or two sentences (for each statement):

   a If a new hotel is built in an area, overall visitor numbers will increase, because new properties generate extra demand through their marketing and advertising.

   b The discrepancy between advertised rates and average room rates means that guests are being deceived by being offered so-called 'discounts' which have already been costed into the system.

   c Either all guests should be offered discounts or none should.

4 Analyse and discuss the following:
A project evaluation must always be inaccurate, because it is using historical information to try to make assessments about future occurrences, and the past is not a good guide for the future because circumstances are always changing.

A Sample Project

BUILDING A BETTER BARBECUE

Some pitfalls to avoid when constructing a new hospitality venture!

Figure 4.9 *What Will the Competition be Doing?*

Kevin Baker (after the style of Giles)

Chapter 4 Notes

[1] Carter, R. School of Marketing, University of New South Wales, quoted in Stanton, W., Miller, K. & Layton, R. 1994, *Fundamentals of Marketing*, 3rd edn, p. 717, McGraw-Hill Book Co.: Sydney.

[2] Cahill, M. 1988, 'Hoteliers Can Reap Rewards by Welcoming Appraisers', *Hotel and Motel Management*, vol. 203, no. 12, pp 18ff.

[3] Tarras, J. 1990, 'Accuracy of Hotel Project Evaluation Projections', *FIU Hospitality Review*, vol. 8, part 1, pp 53ff.

[4] Pyo, Sung-Soo, Chang, Hye-Sook, Chon, Kye-Sung 1995, 'Considerations of Management Objectives by Target Markets in Hotel Feasibility Studies', *International Journal of Hospitality Management*, vol. 14, no. 2, pp 151–6.

[5] Woodside, A. 1982, 'Positioning a Province Using Travel Research', *Journal of Travel Research*, 20 (Winter 1982), pp 2–6; described in Czinkota, M. & Ronkainen, I. 1995, *International Marketing*, 4th edn, pp 764ff, The Dryden Press (Harcourt Brace & Company): Fort Worth.

[6] Lound, M. & Battye, R., Report of the *International Visitor Survey September Quarter 1998*, Bureau of Tourism Research: Canberra.

[7] Hart, C. 1986, 'Product Development: How Marriott Created Courtyard', *The Cornell Hotel and Restaurant Quarterly*, November 1986, p. 68.

[8] Robichaux, M., 'Competitor Intelligence—A Grapevine to Rivals' Secrets', *Wall Street Journal*, 12 April 1989, p. B2; quoted in Robbins, S. & Mukerji, D. 1994, *Managing Organisations*, 2nd edn, p. 167, Prentice Hall of Australia P/L: Sydney.

[9] Yesawich, P. 1988, 'Planning: the Second Step in Market Development', *The Cornell Hotel and Restaurant Administration Quarterly*, February, 1988, p. 72.

[10] Horwath & Horwath 1998, *Survey of Operations, Australia and New Zealand Hotel Industry*, Horwath International, Worldwide Hotel Industry: New York.

[11] Overstreet, G. 1989, 'Profiles in Hotel Feasibility', *Cornell Hotel and Restaurant Administration Quarterly*, February 1989, pp 8–19.

[12] McDonald, M. 1995, *Marketing Plans—How to Prepare Them and How to Use Them*, 3rd edn, p. 300, Butterworth-Heinemann Ltd: Oxford.

[13] Drawn from a case described by Ellis, R. B., of Victoria University of Technology, In Stanton, Miller & Layton 1994, op. cit. (Note 1), p. 171.

[14] Liatsos, G. 1996, 'A Project Evaluation for the Renovation of a Four-Star Hotel in Nicosia, Cyprus', MSc thesis (unpublished), University of Surrey, Guildford, UK.

[15] Overstreet 1989, op. cit., pp 8–19.

[16] Ibid., pp 10–18.

[17] Statistics courtesy of the Pudong Shangri-La Hotel.

[18] In smaller Chinese cities, such a strategy has led to problems for many operators who sought to develop properties at the top end of the market where supply had exceeded demand by the late 1990s. See Brooks, S. & Killory, F. 1997, 'Examining China's Hotel Boom', *Asian Hotelier*, December, pp 12–13.

[19] Yu, T. 1998, 'Making Money in a Depressed Market', *Shanghai Today*, September, pp 28–9.

[20] Tonge, R. 1997, *How to Conduct Feasibility Studies for Tourism Projects*, 6th edn, R. Tonge & Associates, Gull Publishing: Queensland (available from Australian Bankers' Association, Melbourne).

The Project—Physical Characteristics and Issues

Synopsis of Chapter

The selection and utilisation of the site for the proposed project is obviously crucial.

There should be an initial evaluation of the physical aspects of the site and its surroundings, followed by an evaluation of the proposed construction on the site, and possible risk factors. This will take into account the size and quality of the facility.

The characteristics of the site should also be taken into account when planning associated development—such as landscaping and access.

Review of Objectives

No evaluation or study should proceed until the investors or initiators of the project have formulated the objectives of their project. In addition, the major opportunities and risks of the project should be described—at least in outline. For example, there is no point conducting a study for a five-star hotel in a rural area where such developments are not permitted, and the authorities are unlikely to be persuaded to change the rules.

Once the objectives have been formulated, and the general characteristics of the region and market have been examined, the evaluation study can proceed to detailed consideration of the *physical characteristics* of the project—starting with an assessment of the physical characteristics of the site chosen for the development. First the site itself is assessed, then the design concept of the proposed construction, and then the site surroundings—which can serve as an introduction to the environmental impact study as necessary.

The Initial Site Evaluation

The location of a proposed development is among the most important of all factors to evaluate. Academic research indicates that 'effective utilisation of location characteristics' is one of the two most important management objectives to be considered when proposing a new hotel development (the other being maintaining customer satisfaction).[1]

The evaluation of the site is carried out through a variety of sources. The visual inspection of the site itself and its environs is an example of research at a primary level. The condition of the site must be assessed, including its aesthetic aspects. Is it a pleasant area, and would it be attractive to tourists?

An assessment must be made as to whether the site will require extensive preparation—for example whether it has slope or drainage problems. Are there existing constructions or old buildings which must be cleared? The site must be accessible to transport arteries and hubs. The area must be large enough for the proposed purpose and, if future expansion is being considered, an assessment of the site's suitability in this respect must also be made. Major services such as water, sewerage, electricity and gas should be provided to the land.

The area around the site should be compatible with the proposed project. The project might have a positive or a negative impact on its surrounds. Are there competitive properties adjacent? Are there noisy industries close by, and does heavy traffic pass the property? Would building work produce special problems—for example, would it affect the frail condition of heritage properties close by? There might be issues relating to historic preservation. Is there likely to be opposition from the surrounding building owners—with resulting public relations issues? Are there other developments in the surrounding district that might affect the project?

If the project is dependent upon a unique and distinctive visual impact, will that fit into the surrounding development? Although a personal visit to the site is a 'must' for all prospective developers, most research into the site will probably be carried out by reference to various authorities, and by obtaining professional opinion on the possibilities and constraints of development.

There will be legal constraints on development on the site, and these will largely be determined by reference to state and local government authorities. Special submissions and approvals might be required from state government departments—such as main roads authorities. Tourism projects are often influenced by the policy of the current government because of the potential of such projects to create jobs and boost local spending. It might be that there are incentives and financial encouragements for particular types of tourism and hospitality development.

Local government authorities (such as town/shire/regional councils) provide information on zoning requirements—although the individual parcel of land might have particular caveats (legal restraints). Local authorities can also advise on building and development regulations, and can advise regarding requirements for formal submissions for council approval. They might also advise on other developments that are before council awaiting public comment and approval. Local councils might also have information on possible major works by themselves or by state authorities.

CASE STUDY
Councils and Resorts

Excelsior Waves Resort Company has applied to Starbuck Bay Council to purchase land and to seek approval to construct a 200-unit luxury resort on a headland owned by the council. The land was previously used as a council-owned caravan park. Local council has, among its roles, the promotion of economic development in the council's area. The headland is zoned for use as a caravan park, but Excelsior makes a submission to council to change the zoning to permit construction of the resort—which will bring employment and consumer spending to the region.

Clearly, the council has a conflict of interest—in meeting its role of promoting development, it bestows a benefit upon a private company. Stanton and Aislabie (1992) have written a long case study on the process and limitations of local council involvement with coastal resort development on the east coast of Australia.[2]

Initial approaches to a council might be best done through council's professional officers on a confidential basis. Once the council is approached in a formal manner, the matter might be discussed openly at a council meeting—and details of a proposal can rapidly find their way into public discussion. Media discussion can be useful to gauge local feeling on a project, but it is crucial to handle media releases appropriately. In some cases, if details of the project (either correct or incorrect) leak out prematurely, the proposal might be hijacked by an ill-informed public debate. Alternatively, aspects of the proposal could be 'leaked' to the media to gauge public reaction to sensitive elements of the project.

A well-prepared media package should be a part of the final documentation on a project. This should be ready for release if the project evaluation recommends that the project go ahead.

Council officers can also advise as to whether public hearings might be necessary for the development, and whether the objections of surrounding landowners might influence the approvals. They might give their opinion on public feeling about development in the council area, and whether there will be a positive or negative reaction to the proposal. If the proposal is likely to be environmentally sensitive, it is wise to confront this early. It is important not to discount the political influence of the environmental lobby—especially at local government level. (See Chapter 8.)

Construction Aspects of the Site

A project evaluation for a large project should include a boundary survey and details of the legal titles. There should be a survey of topography and soil analysis, and drawings of where services (gas, power, water) are located.

In preparing outline plans for the site, a number of alternative site-use plans should be included—as well as concepts for the construction. It is important to compile a concept of 'optimum site-use', although this might have to be scaled back because of financial constraints. The aim of a developer should be to put the site to optimum use, even if that involves developing the site in stages. Outlining the stages of development—even while a project evaluation is being compiled, and before a single sod is turned—means that subsequent development of the site (if proceeded with) can be done according to a consistent and coherent plan.

The site should be 'organised'. This involves such matters as determining where the entrances for hotel guests will be, where the function spaces should be situated, and where receiving and services areas should be located. Which is the best aspect, or view, from the site, and what is its context with the surrounding buildings? Where will the lobby of the hotel be, and which direction will it face? Will the public access be prominent and reflect the status of the project?

Some Site 'Rules'

'Oh Mum, Please Dash'

Orientate the new building to utilise the sunshine and views, and minimise or maximise the prevailing wind.
Make the new building clearly visible from the road.
Provide a view for as many rooms as possible.
Develop an attractive presentation for the building so it makes a favourable impression when seen for the first time.
Allow room for subsequent expansion.
Separate the entrances for guests, functions, staff and goods.
Hide areas such as parking from the immediate view of guests.

Site Risks

The initial assessment of the site might have identified problems. In Macomber's words:

> Hazardous waste and the remains of old foundations are just two . . . invisible surprises.

> Macomber (1989)[3]

A developer could find many invisible, unpleasant surprises—especially on a rehabilitated site with unknown risks. Usually a builder will add on the costs of dealing with any unforeseen site problems, and these could cause a substantial 'blow out' in the price of a new hotel.

Examples of potential site risks include:

■ a lack of manoeuvring room due to the siting of entrances or the size of the site;

- traffic problems associated with construction on the site, and with congested streets;
- inadequate analysis of the soils or the presence of boulders; and
- previous uses—particularly those involving hazardous substances (such as the petrol tanks of an old petrol station).

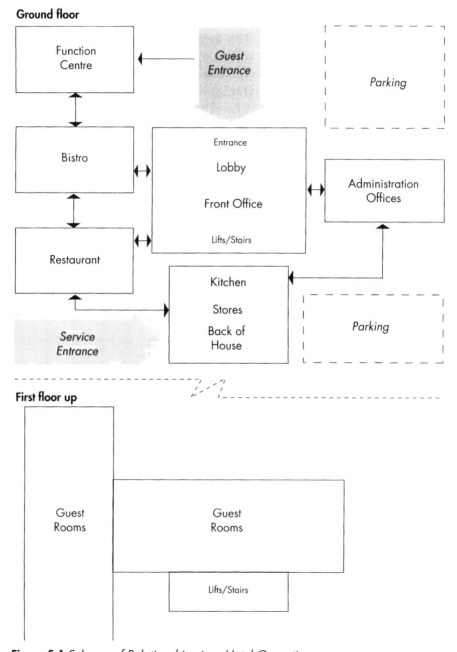

Figure 5.1 *Schema of Relationships in a Hotel Operation*

Kevin Baker

The Size and Quality of the Facility

Often such questions as the size of a proposed hotel or resort, the standard of the services it will provide, and its inclusions, will have been discussed when the proposal was at concept stage. In the case of a restaurant, an investor might have in mind the size and theme of the operation which is proposed. The starting point of the project evaluation was a description of the objectives and purpose of the project, and these should be referred to again at this stage. A project evaluation, provided it is conducted properly, should identify the constraints that the proposal will face, and the market and financial imperatives for its operation. Within those constraints, the study can list an outline of design studies—also referred to as concept-design studies.[4]

It is important that the development be of the appropriate size, and that the size allows for increased future capacity to meet expanded market demand.

Some questions to be asked at this stage of the study/evaluation are:

- How many rooms will there be, and how many suites? Indeed, should the new property provide only suites?
- How many guest floors will there be?
- What should be the capacities of the principal meeting rooms and function rooms? What should be the area of these?
- How many food and beverage outlets should there be?
- Should there be retail outlets, and where and how should they operate?
- What sort of recreational facilities (such as a gym, swimming pool and the like) should be provided?

These questions are asked so that a general outline of the project on the site can be assessed. Obviously, the analyst will use the answers to these questions at the stage of preparing design outlines. However, for now, the questions are considered in order to determine the size and quality of the property, and whether it will be appropriate on the selected site.

The determination of the size and quality of the hotel will also act as a guide for the preliminary design study—because such attributes as the area of *public* space compared with the area of *support* space will be influenced by the number of rooms and the class of the hotel.

Public space within a hotel includes spaces such as the lobbies, lifts and corridors, and facilities that the public might use—such as food and beverage outlets, conference and meeting rooms, ballroom and the like. These public spaces should be clustered around the lobby as far as possible.

Support space within a hotel comprises those spaces which are used by services—such as housekeeping, kitchens, receiving and stores, office and administrative space and so on. The kitchens, receiving area and stores area should be on the same floor. Food and beverage outlets should be clustered around the kitchen.

Accommodation properties of different classes will utilise different ratios of public/support space to guest-room space within their total area. For example:

- a 100-room hotel would have 10% of its space dedicated to public/support areas and 90% to guest rooms;
- a 250-room hotel would have 25% of its space utilised by public/support areas and 75% by guest rooms—because a larger hotel requires proportionately more service areas and access ways;
  To take another example:
- a budget hotel of 200 rooms would dedicate only 10% of its total space to the public/support function;
- a mid-range hotel of the same size would utilise 20% of total space in public/support purposes; and
- a top-of-the-range facility of this size would dedicate 30% of total space to public/support purposes—because it would provide a greater range of services, and therefore greater space would be required for these.

The target market and location of the property might also affect the allocation of space within the plan. Convention and resort hotels (which typically have longer average stays) will require more public space than, say, airport hotels (which generally cater for overnight stayers).

The number and location of recreation and conference facilities should also be considered. These facilities should be separated from the central functions of the hotel.

External Site Factors

In considering the site for a new development, after assessing aspects of the building itself, there are three other factors to evaluate:

- the property identification;
- landscaping; and
- parking.

Property Identification

The property must be easy to access by visitors and the public. To facilitate that access, the property should be identifiable and the place of access should be easy to find. The identification of the property will involve signage, and perhaps an identifying feature. If the property is part of a chain or a franchise, the brand identification will already be determined, but the questions of placement and size of signage are still important.

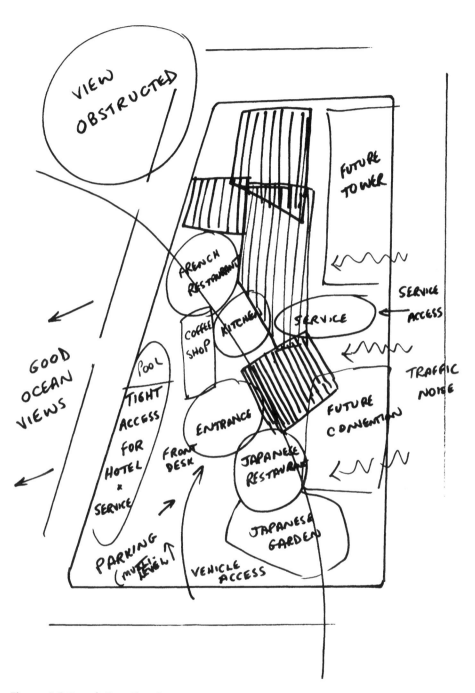

Figure 5.2 Rough Site Sketch

Kevin Baker

There will probably be local government requirements relating to the size and location of signage and brands, and there might even be other requirements (for example, if the building is heritage-listed). It is important to consider the issue in the project evaluation because, if the project will be hidden—perhaps by surrounding development or limitations on the signage—its marketing will be impeded, and the value of the location thus discounted.

Landscaping

Landscaping, including sculptural artworks, can be important as a feature in development—because it often moulds the first impressions that visitors have of a property. Distinctive landscaping can also assist in marketing and public perceptions of the property.

Parking

Parking is important to consider. The provision of parking might be mandated by local government development and building approvals, and the requirement might severely limit the possibilities of the site—as well as being the cause of considerable expense.

The number of parking spaces to be provided might be determined by:

- the number of guests resident;
- the volume of the food and beverage outlets, and function spaces; and
- the preferred mode of travel by target markets—that is whether prospective guests will probably arrive by car or coach.

Reviewing the Development on the Site in Advance

Clearly, the size and quality of the project will influence the cost of construction, and this, in turn, will affect financial considerations. A new hotel or tourism development involves considerable investment, and it therefore makes sense to utilise all available technology in order to review the impact of the development upon the site and its environment. The expense of producing three-dimensional (3-D) computer modelling can be a sensible precautionary investment. As well as 3-D modelling and imagery, computers can also produce 'fly-through' animation— giving an interested party the experience of what it will be like to walk through the property.

CASE STUDY
South Stradbroke Island, Queensland

South Stradbroke Island, off the coast of Queensland, is in a sensitive environmental area. The Couran Cove Resort development was planned to include a hotel, marina, holiday homes, and a number of facilities for aquatic recreation. The development was to be extensively marketed because the market place for holiday properties on the Queensland coast is already a very competitive one.

To meet the needs for a careful review of the environmental impact of the development, and its various constructions, as well as to provide a sophisticated marketing tool that would be particularly useful to prospective investors and agents, a photomontage was produced which incorporated 3-D imagery. This allowed for a high-quality presentation to clients in a way that stood out from comparable resort projects. This presentation was especially useful for interested parties in other regions and countries who would gain a feel for the resort—without having to undertake expensive and time-consuming travel.

Figure 5.3 *Couran Cove—3-D image*
Published with permission of Mark Windsor of Burchill Partners Pty Ltd

The analysis of the market place should have provided information on market segments. Will the proposed development meet the high range, the middle range, or the low range of the market? Users of mid–priced hotel rooms represent the largest segment of *demand* for hotel accommodation, but the largest category of room *supply* is also from mid–price hotels. The analysis of competitors should indicate likely segments of undersupply.

Projections of Occupancy and Room Rates

Prospective room rates and likely occupancy rates must be considered again—this time in the context of the size and quality of the facility. For example, would a 200-room development be too large in terms of achieving a desirable occupancy rate? If a smaller development is proceeded with, should the developers seek higher room rates to achieve a desired return on investment. If so, should they provide a higher standard of service? The issues of occupancy and rates will arise at several points in the project evaluation—because they are crucial issues that determine revenue levels and net income.

The analyst returns to the market analysis to consider what quality of property is likely to achieve a higher occupancy, and whether the provision of that class of property fits in with the objectives and purposes of the developer.

With information on market competition, and an analysis of likely occupancy and rates, the study can proceed to the stage of preparing an outline design.

A Last Word

It must be emphasised that there is no better way to assess the possibilities of a site for development than to visit the site and its surroundings, and to stay there a while to absorb the atmosphere—the *sensus loci*, or 'sense of place'.

STUDY CHECKLIST #5
THE SITE CHARACTERISTICS

- What is the physical appearance of the site?

- Has it had prior use?

- Are necessary approvals likely?

- Will there be environmental implications in the development?

- Are there appropriate and adequate services to the site?

- Are the surroundings attractive?

- Do the surroundings match the nature of the project?

- Are the approaches and access adequate?

- What is the traffic flow around the site?

Chapter ■ 5 Review and Questions

1 Indicate whether the following statements are true or false and give a reason for your answer:

a Customer satisfaction and site utilisation are the two most important management objectives when proposing a new hotel development. (True/False? Why?)

b Visual inspection of a site is relatively unimportant. (True/False? Why?)

c Details of boundary surveys and legal titles are best left to the planning stage after the project evaluation is completed. (True/False? Why?)

d Signage and site identification are not generally covered by council regulation. (True/False? Why?)

e The volume of the food and beverage outlets will influence the number of car-parking spaces required. (True/False? Why?)

    f A top-of-the-range facility has a lower proportion of total space devoted to public space, because the suites are bigger and more private. (True/False? Why?)

2 Insert the word(s) that best completes each of the following, selecting your answers from the following possibilities:

future expansion; landscaping; expensive operations; optimum site-use; manoeuvring room; property identification; parking; risks; physical; costing.

    a A project evaluation should have three dimensions—a review of the present situation and an . . . as well as a . . .

    a The aim of a developer should be to compile an ' . . . ' concept.

    b Although wishing to utilise the site properly, a developer should nevertheless allow for the possibility of . . .

    c A rehabilitated site might have site . . .

    d After assessing aspects of the building, a study will consider other factors such as . . . , . . . and . . .

    e Size and quality of the development are . . . characteristics.

    f Poor siting of entrances can lead to a lack of . . .

3 Discuss the following in one or two sentences (for each statement):

    a A good designer could build an attractive hotel on any site.

    b The best properties have been built on the least-promising sites because challenges bring out the best in creative designers.

    c There are only three factors to consider in a prospective hotel site—position, position and position.

4 Analyse and discuss the following:

Ensuring the compatibility of the development with the site and its physical characteristics is the single most important factor to be considered by the project evaluation.

Chapter 5 Notes

[1] Pyo, Sung-Soo, Chang, Hye-Sook & Chon, Kye-Sung 1995, 'Considerations of Management Objectives by Target Markets in Hotel Feasibility Studies', *International Journal of Hospitality Management*, vol. 14, no. 2, p. 151.

[2] Stanton, J. & Aislabie, C. 1992, 'Local Government Regulation and the Economics of Tourist Resort Development: An Australian Case Study', *Journal of Tourism Studies*, December 1992, pp 20–31.

[3] Macomber, J. 1989, 'You Can Manage Construction Risks', *Harvard Business Review*, March–April 1989, p. 158.

[4] Two good texts on hotel design are: Baucom, A. 1996, *Hospitality Design for the Graying Generation*, John Wiley & Sons: New York; and Knapp, F. 1995, *Hotel Renovation, Planning and Design*, McGraw-Hill: New York.

Design and Construction Issues

Synopsis of Chapter

Having examined the site, the study then considers the design of the facility.

The analysis of design issues will take into account current market trends when the theme and building outline of the new project is developed. The design of a hospitality project concerns marketing and operational aspects as much as it does aesthetic factors.

The facility must service the needs of primary and secondary markets. The floor space and layout must meet the needs of public, guests and staff.

The construction budget should be considered in the context of preparing the design outline, as well as the timing of the project.

Design Aspects

A project evaluation must include an outline of the design and outlines specifications in order to assess whether it is possible to finance and construct the design. It might include conceptual renderings and models. In general, hotel designers will endeavour to make the building stand out by incorporating new and different aspects into the design.

The outline design section of the project evaluation follows the earlier steps outlined in this book—analysis of general and market characteristics, and an evaluation of the site.

The building design must respond to market needs, and must function adequately. The building must also fit the image and objectives of the developer, and it must meet any limitations imposed by outside bodies such as local government. There might also be time constraints in the construction of the property—time constraints imposed by marketing requirements (perhaps to preclude competition). The construction must also stay within the capital budget of the developer, and the design of the building is generally conducted in conjunction with capital budgeting. Finally, the design formulation should be comprehensive and have a degree of flexibility—such that the possibility of change during the construction process is limited.

The design concept for a proposed development will usually be prepared by an architect—another of the outside sources of expertise required in a well-conducted project evaluation.

There is a number of current trends in hotel design that must be considered in any new lodging property development. These include:

- new fashions in hotel design;
- a focus on business travellers;
- new technologies in hotel operations;
- increased facilities in hotels;
- changes in food and beverage outlets;
- increased need for 'no-frills' accommodation;
- need for flexibility of design;
- new design and building techniques;
- redesign of former non-hotel properties; and
- renovation

Each of these will be considered below.

New Fashions in Hotel Design

There are always new fashions in hotel design and development. One of the trends of the mid-1990s was a 'boom in small, offbeat hotels where the interior design is cutting-edge or richly opulent . . .'.[1] These were also termed 'boutique' hotels. They catered for a particular market segment—usually people who had the wealth and inclination to seek something different and exclusive.

Another fashion is the trend towards privacy. In earlier times, there was a certain imperative to 'see and be seen', but this is less important now (although it still exists in parts of Asia and the Middle East).[2]

In creating the design concept for the new building, the developer or the architect should be aware of current fashions and how to interpret them.

A Focus on Business Travellers

One of the largest segments of the market consists of the business travellers, and they have particular needs. These include telecommunications (for example video-conferencing), small meeting rooms (for client appointments), and secretarial support.

Studies have indicated that tele-conferencing and tele-beaming facilities are becoming increasingly attractive to business travellers.[3] The guest room itself might become a 'business room' with in-room fax, on-call printer, access to the Internet, and two or more phone lines. This concept of the 'business room' has been developed by a number of large chains (such as Marriott's 'Room that Works', Westin's 'Guest Office' and Hyatt's 'Business Plan').[4]

CASE STUDY
Business Services — the Concorde Hotel, Singapore

The Concorde Hotel in Singapore has 515 rooms and a marketing focus on business travellers—a focus that reflects its location on Orchard Road in the commercial district of the city. To cater for its selected market, the hotel has a range of suites of business quality, and also includes some suites designed specifically to appeal to business guests from Japan and South-East Asian countries. The range of services offered in suites includes:
- a fully equipped business centre;
- NHK and CNN news channels; and
- telephones with IDD service.

As well as en-suite services, the hotel's business centre also caters especially for this segment of the market. In addition to the usual facsimile/telex and cable facilities that business travellers would expect, the business centre includes:
- secretarial and dictation services;
- photocopying;
- Internet connections;
- binding and printing services;
- library facilities; and
- presentation rooms with overhead and slide projectors.

The hotel also runs a shuttle service to the larger business and convention centres.

New Technologies in Hotel Operations

Recent technological advances have changed the way that hotels can operate. Rapid changes in telecommunications technology mean that connections for television, computers and business telecommunications might be desirable in guest rooms. Smart-card access systems can enhance and monitor guest security, and can also monitor the movement of staff. Computerised reservations and check-in/check-out functions can change the way in which front-office facilities are designed and operated.

Increased Facilities in Hotels

Guests expect to be able to access a wide range of entertainment in the course of their stay. These include theatres, IMAX (giant screen) facilities, interactive recreational facilities for families, cabaret, and restaurants on a variety of themes. Some hotels (such as resorts or casinos) are specifically developed in the context of entertainment packages.

Changes in Food and Beverage Outlets

Food and beverage outlets might be contracted out in 'innovative, symbiotic relationships in hotel dining that help build incremental revenue and foster brand identity'.[5] Brand restaurants, in particular, are creating new demands for hotel services—often from the general public, as well as from guests who are actually staying in the hotel.

Hotel dining rooms have had a reputation for being 'stuffy, expensive, slow, behind the curve [and] these are not exactly enticements'.[6] About 80% of hotel guests prefer to eat outside their accommodation venue—for reasons of convenience, and also so they can sample the area and its restaurants.[7] It is up to hotels to attract their guests to use the facilities.

Westin Hotels is changing the concepts of their restaurants to reflect various themes. These include 'carnival', 'horse-racing', and 'Mediterranean-bistro' styles.

> People want to go to an interesting place and they want interesting, eclectic food.
>
> Fischer (1997)[8]

The quality of hotel restaurants has improved in recent years, and the trend continues.

Increased Need for 'No-Frills' Accommodation

Along with the trend for increased services (as described above), there is also a trend for the provision of 'no-frills' accommodation. The aim is to create a simple (although not Spartan) design with good, durable furniture and finishes.

Flexibility of Design

Flexibility of design is important for at least two reasons.

Owners of lodging properties understand that they might have to change the theme of the property, and redecorate frequently, to keep up with changes in the market place.[9]

Another issue related to flexibility of design is the requirement to be able to meet a number of markets. Henry Vergnaud, general manager of the 93-room 'Le Mirador' in Mont Pelerin, Switzerland, states, 'Hotels in Europe cannot survive on a single market'.[10] What is true of Europe is generally true of other regions.

New Design and Building Techniques

Developers are becoming more closely involved with the design and building of projects, and are including in-house expertise on estimating, design and construction—in order to achieve a greater control over costs and efficiency in the construction phase. This also permits 'fast-track construction.'[11]

Redesign of Former Non-Hotel Properties

Some older properties that were not built as hotels originally are being redeveloped into accommodation properties—mainly to cater for niche markets (such as the heritage tourist). For example, some former convents and religious houses are being redeveloped in this way.

The 'Hotel Costes' in Paris is a former eighteenth-century convent, and the 'Casa de Carmona' in Seville was a seventeenth-century mansion.[12] In Sydney, New South Wales, a new Intercontinental Hotel is being developed within a large building that was formerly a department store operated by Grace Brothers.

Renovation

Existing accommodation properties, provided they have good location and are structurally sound, are being renovated to achieve a higher return on investment, and to enhance the value of the property. Typically, the enhanced value should be 10–30% more than the cost of the refurbishment.[13]

CASE STUDY
'Entertainment Architecture'

The Walt Disney Company has constructed a number of lodging properties along themes. These developments provide a new dimension to accommodation—for the guest is immersed in a 'milieu', as it were. One of these new developments is the 'Dolphin and Swan' in Orlando, Florida—a hotel designed to be 'entertainment architecture'.[14] Each hotel provides an environment intended to replicate that of another place or time. There is the full range of services and comforts, but they are concealed where necessary (for example, television sets are enclosed in cabinets) to ensure that the overall theme is not disturbed, and to ensure that guests can avail themselves of an experience by immersing themselves in a totally different atmosphere.

The Design Theme

The developer might already have in mind a theme for the development. Determining a theme is an important aspect of the project, because it goes beyond the 'artistic'. It has marketing implications.

> Hotel design is as much about marketing and sales as aesthetics. Strong style creates a unique identity for hotels and makes them stand out in their markets.
>
> Scoviak-Lerner (1995)[15]

Resort accommodation in an area that attracts environmental tourists, for example, might incorporate a strong theme into its design. An instance is the Gagudju Crocodile Hotel at Jabiru in the Kakadu National Park in northern Australia. This hotel is shaped in the form of a crocodile.

In the course of the project evaluation, the conducting of market research to refine new concepts and themes for the development can sometimes be worthwhile. Market research on a new concept for Marriott Hotels revealed that guests of mid-price hotels did not stay in a hotel because they liked the hotel, but because it was functional.[16] This market research conclusion led to the new design's emphasis on functional and security elements—rather than on a different theme. It was decided that the hotel should reassure guests that staying there was like staying in their own homes. The result of this research and creativity was the 'courtyard concept'—conceived as a new hotel model for suburban sites.

Whatever the chosen theme, it should be 'right for the guest and right for the setting'.[16]

The Primary/Secondary Market Concept

> Before we design a guest room, we will have to look at what the property's primary market is and what is the secondary market.
>
> McCarty, quoted by Scoviak (1996)[17]

In conceptualising the new hospitality operation, the developers and those drafting the design outline should be aware of the idea of the *primary* and *secondary* markets of a lodging property. For example, a hotel's primary market might be business travellers, and the hotel would therefore cater for their particular needs (as noted above). But there might also be an important secondary market of family recreational travellers. The implications for the design will be that the guest rooms should be as large as possible (to meet the needs of business travellers, and those of families). However, not every guest room will need facilities such as in-room fax lines. The design of the guest room should be flexible, but should be done with an eye to both the primary and secondary markets.

Hyatt Hotels' senior vice-president, architecture and design, states:

We have to start giving customers what they really want instead of what we think they want.

Quoted by Scoviak (1996)[18]

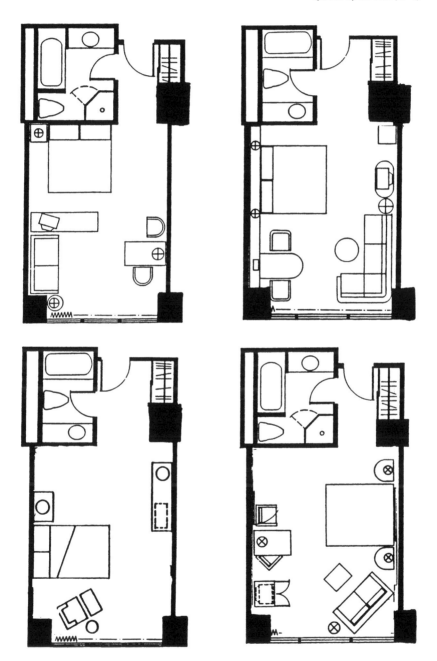

Figure 6.1 *Room Layout—Considering Alternatives*

Kevin Baker

Other Design Issues/Considerations

There are other considerations that could be taken into account at the design-concept stage—provided that they could have a significant effect on the construction of the building. These include such matters as people with disabilities, issues to do with automation, and 'special' design features.

People with Disabilities

Requirements to accommodate people with disabilities should be included at this stage. If the property has been especially conceived to meet the needs of aged people, making the building not only accessible to people with disabilities, but also user-friendly to them, might require consideration even at the design-concept stage.

Developers need not 'go overboard with complex modifications that might be quite expensive to implement' (Wagner 1995).[19] However, they should be aware of requirements (some slightly larger rooms, ramps, heights of services, Braille visual signals for warnings etc.), and design a solution that balances requirements, expense and aesthetics.

It is useful to take account of these aspects, even at the design-concept stage, so that the building or detailed designs do not need retrospective amendments.

CASE STUDY
Special Features

The 280-suite 'Embassy Suites' property in Lake Buena Vista, Florida, opened in 1991.[20] It was designed so that a proportion of suites (six out of the 280) would be user-friendly to people with disabilities. The alterations to the basic suite design (to make the facilities more appropriate) were not obtrusive.

Other measures for accessibility were incorporated at design stage. For example, the atrium lobby was designed with an inclined access, and corners and intersections provide space for wheelchairs to turn around. Telecommunications systems to assist those with visual and hearing impairments were also included from the beginning.

Automation

Another issue for design of lodging properties design is increased automation. For example, the preparation and supply of meals is becoming more automated, and this will affect the design of back-of-house areas. (The term 'back-of-house' generally describes service functions such as kitchens, laundry etc.—all those areas of a hotel not observed by guests and the public.) A large property might have only one kitchen—due to the savings on staff and efficiencies.

Special Features

A third issue is whether to have a feature incorporated in the design to make the new project unique—to create a talking point among consumers.

In the 1980s, it became popular to the point of being fashionable among designers to put a large water feature in the lobby of the new hotel. However, this was not always appreciated. In the words of Meg Greenfield:

> I have stayed in hotels with waterfalls in the lobby, with rivers, with canals and with what looked to be . . . an attempt at re-creation of the elaborate irrigation system of early Sumeria. I have been in hotels where you needed a kayak to get to the news-stand . . . How many weary late-arriving . . . travellers have actually drowned in hotel lobbies?
>
> Greenfield (1986)[21]

Construction Aspects

The design concept within the project evaluation should also take account of construction aspects—for these might impact heavily upon construction costs. The timing of the construction will also be crucial for the costing and financing plans.

The construction of a large building is divided into components. Separate component headings might include:

- site work;
- excavation;
- foundations;
- structural work;
- external walls and windows;
- internal walls and divisions;
- plumbing and drainage;
- electrical systems;
- plastering;
- painting;
- furniture and fixtures;
- landscaping;
- paving and parking; and
- signage.

Floor Space and Layout

Even at the project-evaluation stage, the design outline should consider such aspects as the dimensions and layout of a typical room and suite. If the project is a franchised one, minimum dimensions for rooms and public areas might be specified in the franchise-approval documentation.

After the dimensions of the guest rooms have been defined, other dimensions will be decided—such as corridor width, room-attendants' areas, and core area (stairs and lifts). In the example of the 100-room hotel used in an earlier chapter, a decision might be made at design-concept stage (after evaluation of the site and local government requirements) that the hotel will be six floors.

Guest Rooms

Guest rooms might take up 60% of the total floor area of the development (excluding parking and external access areas). Another 7–8% will be taken up with floor circulation space (for example corridors) and room-attendants' room. A further 8% might be taken up by the core area (stairs and lifts). Guests' rooms and access will thus take up three-quarters of the floor space of the development. The dimensions of the typical room therefore become a crucial issue in determining the overall size of the building.

In recent years, hotel rooms and suites have been getting bigger, and bathroom facilities are also larger and more luxurious than they used to be.[22] More space obviously means higher construction costs—costs which have to be recovered in the course of operations.

Public Areas

How much space for public areas should be allowed in the construction? That depends on how many food and beverage outlets there are to be, and how large the coffee shop (or the entertainment lounge, or the speciality restaurant) is to be. There might also be function and meeting rooms. Again, there is a trend towards providing larger meeting rooms that can also function as boardrooms and dining rooms.[23] The use of movable partition walls allows for flexibility of meeting spaces.

The lobby space is important. Lobbies are as much meeting places and business areas as they are check-in venues.

In all, approximately 12–14% of the available floor space might be taken up by public areas. The design outline should also indicate the quality of finish of the construction to allow for a cost estimate.

Service Areas

For service areas, approximately 2% of floor space should be allowed for administrative areas, and the balance of floor area (9–11%) would be taken up by food preparation, inventory receipt and storage, laundry and housekeeping, engineering and maintenance, and employee areas (such as locker rooms and amenities).

Construction Contracts

Within these constraints of floor space and external matters (such as parking and access to the property), methods of construction should be considered. In considering functional priorities, whether the site and the design provide any special problems should be taken into account. An estimate of the cost of the development can be made on a square-metre basis—with an allowance for difficulties of construction.

Then comes the critical issue of estimating the time required for construction. The total capital budget must take into account the timing of progress payments to the builder as various stages are completed, because those payments will usually attract finance costs (that is, interest on the amounts advanced due to a lender).

Projecting the total cost of the development might depend on the type of construction contract that has been negotiated. Some common types of building contracts and risks include:[24]

- a lump–sum contract;
- a guaranteed maximum price; and
- a time–and–materials contract.

A lump-sum contract

This means that the builder takes the risk of cost overruns (and takes the benefit of cost savings).

A guaranteed maximum price

This means that the owner receives the benefit of savings on construction costs.

A time-and-materials contract

This means that the owner gets any cost savings, but also takes the risk if there are cost overruns.

If there is an estimated lump sum for construction, this figure can be used for the analysis of financial feasibility. If the developer chooses a form of contract that entails the risk of higher costs than those estimated, there should be a provision for cost overruns. The project evaluation should factor (into the cost calculations) a best-case and worst-case outcome for building costs.

Value Engineering

Obviously, the costing of the design is a complex process—as well as being crucial in assessing the feasibility of the project. 'Value engineering' is a technique that has become more important in recent years. It compares alternative products and costs at each stage of the building process. As design decisions and owners' needs have become more complex, value engineering has been developed as a 'systematic method of analysing needs versus costs versus resources'.[25]

The process can take place at the design stage—when site considerations, market conditions and the proposed time schedule can mean big differences in the end-cost of the project. It is a process that involves all the parties involved in construction—including the developer, the architect, and the likely building contractor.

For large projects, value engineering is probably essential. However, even for smaller projects, developers can benefit from going through a systematic analysis of the cost/value of various components and finishes with their architectural adviser.

Value engineering is very similar to cost-cutting. It involves taking each component of the construction and analysing whether there are cheaper options available that are just as adequate for the purpose. It can involve big questions that will have a substantial effect on the construction budget—such as considering the amount of space allocated to room-attendants' rooms—or it can involve lesser matters. For example, where a finish of high-quality marble is envisaged, will another finish provide the same aesthetic and practical effect? Where customised bathroom fittings are planned, can 'off-the-shelf' fittings be used just as easily?

Even something such as the specified headroom (height of the ceiling) might be subject to value engineering—because an extra ten centimetres of headroom can add substantially to the cost of a component. If there is a height restriction on the building, shaving ten centimetres from the headroom of each floor in a 24-storey building (still allowing for minimum headroom requirements) could allow one extra floor to be built.

Cost of Construction

The construction budget is normally determined in conjunction with an architect, and possibly with a quantity surveyor. At the project-evaluation stage, detailed costings are not prepared (and nor are they required), but good estimates of costs are compiled for the purpose of assessing financial feasibility, and also for accessing finance if there is a decision to proceed with the project.

The budget will be heavily influenced by the quality of finishes and also the cost of any features—but some typical percentage figures can be used as a basis for cost estimates. Cost estimates must include such items as pre-opening expenses—because they will have to be financed from the capital investment (because there will not be operating revenue to cover them).

Items on the project budget and guides for percentage costs are as shown in Figure 6.2.

Figure 6.3 (p. 108) is an estimate of the cost of building a 100-room hotel, including an estimate of the cost of fitting it out with furniture and equipment.

Time of Construction and Its Implications

Along with the estimate of the cost of construction, there should be an estimate of the time it will take. This will assist planning and staffing, and arranging finance for particular dates. This time estimate can be compiled and presented in graphic form—normally as a bar graph. At the project evaluation, these estimates are not as refined as they will be when a decision is made to proceed with the project—and formal contracts for construction and financing are then drawn up. Consequently, it might be best to include provisions for extra time, just as there were provisions for extra costs.

Type of Cost	Estimate (allow approx.)
Development Costs	12%
project evaluation; architect's and engineer's fees; project manager/ consultant; legal costs; building and development approvals; building insurance; surveys and site testing; franchise fees (if applicable); contingency amount	
Construction Costs	60%
site work; building costs; utilities; contingency amount	
Fitout (including furniture, fixtures and equipment)	12%
interior design; kitchen equipment; laundry/housekeeping equipment; telecommunications systems; security systems; linen etc.; tableware etc.; contingency amount	
Construction Finance	7%
Pre-Opening Expenses	4%
salaries and training; marketing and advertising; office expenses	
Initial Working Capital	3%
Balance	2%
(to be retained for initial operating deficit)	
Total Budget	100%

Figure 6.2 *Percentage Costs of Budget Items*

Kevin Baker

Required Project Investment

Land	$630 000
Development Costs	$600 000
Siteworks	$290 000
Building (incl. architects etc.)	$3 260 000
Equipment & Fittings	$800 000
Bridging Finance	$200 000
Pre-opening Expenses	$120 000
Start-up Working Capital	$70 000
Contingency	$50 000
Total	**$6 020 000**

	Borrowings	Equity	Total
Land	$0	$630 000	$630 000
Development Costs	$0	$600 000	$600 000
Siteworks	$0	$290 000	$290 000
Building (70% mortgage)	$2 282 000	$978 000	$3 260 000
Equipment & Fittings (75% fin.)	$600 000	$200 000	$800 000
Bridging Finance (interest only)	$0	$200 000	$200 000
Pre-opening Expenses	$0	$120 000	$120 000
Start-up Working Capital	$0	$70 000	$70 000
Contingency	$0	$50 000	$50 000
Totals	**$2 882 000**	**$3 138 000**	**$6 020 000**

1 There are three partners in the project—an individual and two companies—each of whom contribute $1 046 000 in equity to the project.

2 The partners' equity is slightly more than half the total cost of the project.

Figure 6.3 Capital Investment Estimates

Kevin Baker

One aspect of construction strategy (the trend to use designer/builder combinations) has been mentioned above. It remains more common for a developer to use the services of an architect for the design and contract the construction to a builder. There will be time involved in drawing up contracts, and in gaining building approvals before construction commences.

Advice on the timing of construction should come from the architect who provided the design concept. The pace of construction can sometimes be increased—but at a cost. An architect and builder can accelerate the building schedule—by employing more people, by having them work overtime, or by deciding to spend less time on some areas of construction and finish. This last option—compressing the schedule—increases direct costs, but it can produce savings in lower overhead costs. However, there is often a penalty in reduced quality of building as compressing the schedule makes supervision more difficult.[26]

Again, there should be a provision—by allowing contingency factors in the timing—for any overruns of the estimated time of construction.

Another option to increase the pace of building is called 'fast-track' scheduling. This involves dividing the project and its design up into many separate contracts, and starting them as soon as possible—even as the major structural elements are being completed.[26] With this option, work on the building might be well advanced even as the architectural team is still finishing the drawings for the interior design. There are economic advantages to fast-tracking a project, but there is also a risk if the design team falls behind its schedule.

First Six Months

Months from Decision to Proceed	1	2	3	4	5	6
Preliminaries	X	X	X	X	X	X
Construction						
Plans & Approvals	X	X	X			
Tenders				X	X	
Building						X
Plumbing & Electrical						X
Finishing						
Plant & Equipment						
Specifications				X	X	
Supply & Installation						X
Interior Design						
Design		X	X	X	X	
Fitout						
Pre-opening Activities						
Marketing & Advertising				X		
Management Team Recruitment						
Staff Recruitment						
Purchase of Inventories						

Second Six Months

Months from Decision to Proceed	7	8	9	10	11	12
Preliminaries						
Construction						
Plans & Approvals						
Tenders						
Building	X	X	X	X	X	X
Plumbing & Electrical						X
Finishing						

Months from Decision to Proceed	7	8	9	10	11	12
Plant & Equipment						
Specifications						
Supply & Installation	X	X	X			
Interior Design						
Design						
Fitout						X
Pre-opening Activities						
Marketing & Advertising				X		X
Management Team Recruitment						
Staff Recruitment						
Purchase of Inventories						

Third Six Months

Months from Decision to Proceed	13	14	15	16	17	18
Preliminaries						
Construction						
Plans & Approvals						
Tenders						
Building	X					
Plumbing & Electrical	X	X	X			
Finishing				X	X	X
Plant & Equipment						
Specifications						
Supply & Installation						
Interior Design						
Design						
Fitout		X	X	X	X	
Pre-opening Activities						
Marketing & Advertising					X	X
Management Team Recruitment			X	X	X	X
Staff Recruitment						X
Purchase of Inventories						X

Figure 6.4 Construction Timeline—Le Hu Hotel

Kevin Baker

The timeline for construction is often presented as a 'critical-path' diagram in which critical building activities (such as concrete pours) are highlighted. The timespan of these activities is noted by a straight line on the timespan, and the completion of each critical activity is represented by a circle, or a node. Delays to these critical activities will lengthen the time required to complete the project, whereas non-critical activities might not delay the construction overall as time can be made up later.

This is also referred to as the 'critical path method'. It also records the order in which activities should be undertaken, and indicates what will be delayed if a prior activity is delayed.

Once the timelines for construction have been determined, the time period in days can be transferred to a calendar—with possible starting dates high-lighted. This will enable the developer to judge how construction of the project might be affected by public holidays or other external events. The allowances for extra time—the contingency factors—might have to be increased because of public holidays, unless the developer wishes to speed construction and meet the cost of penalty rates for the building workers.

Other Construction Issues

As with any estimate, there might be problems. In fact, the mythical 'Murphy' is said to have composed a law—'Whatever can go wrong, will go wrong'. Designs might prove to be complex in construction. Building might strike problems in the course of construction—with difficulties in the supply of labour or materi-als. The timing of the project might have to include contingencies for these aspects of the design, especially if the work involved is to be new and complex. A typical contingency for extra costs will be 5–10%.

One other construction issue that should be considered is protection for the developer if things go awry. In determining the contract for development, the developer should always have adequate legal advice. Contracts should include appropriate penalty and bonus clauses to reduce any losses due to deficiencies of the builder. Proper insurance should also be negotiated. These provisions might add to the costs of the project but, without them, a developer would be very vulnerable to heavy loss. Included in the protection clauses should be a disputes-settlement procedure, and a named arbitrator (in case an arbitrator should become necessary).

The project evaluation might also note the way in which tenders (for design and construction work) will be let. Although this might not seem to be central to a project evaluation (which is essentially about whether the project will go ahead), this information is important to a financing authority. Because the pro-ject evaluation will be a crucial tool in arranging finance, it is useful to include information on the proposed tendering process—at least by way of note.

The design and construction stage of the project evaluation is crucial—since it expresses an idea in bricks and mortar, and can assist in catching the imagina-tion of finance or venture partners. However, it can also be crucial to success in that the design must be a practical one and match not only the developer's idea and needs and financial means, but also the requirements of the market place.

A Last Word

It must be noted that it is not easy to retain the inspiration of a creative idea while considering mundane issues of time and cost. However, the effort must be made to do so—in order to be true to the human need to strive after an ideal.

STUDY CHECKLIST #6
DESIGN/CONSTRUCTION
ISSUES

- Is the theme of the design consistent and attractive?

- Does the design suit its surroundings?

- Does the design have appropriate internal work flows?

- Does the design have appropriate external work flows?

- Are there problems in the type of construction?

- Is the construction timeline reasonable?

- Is the quality of construction appropriate to the project budget?

Chapter 6 ■ Review and Questions

1 Indicate whether the following statements are true or false and give a reason for your answer:
   a Most hotel guests will prefer to eat in a food and beverage outlet on the premises rather than eating outside their accommodation venue. (True/False? Why?)
   b Today's guests are not in the least attracted by 'no-frills' accommodation. (True/False? Why?)
   c A hotel designer should have in mind marketing aspects of the property when preparing the concept. (True/False? Why?)
   d It is a satisfactory outcome if renovation and refurbishment increase the value of the property by at least the cost of the refurbishment. (True/False? Why?)
   e Because hospitality is a people-orientated industry, there is little opportunity to automate any part of the services. (True/False? Why?)
   f Construction time can be cut if the owner is prepared to accept a cost penalty. (True/False? Why?)

2 Insert the word(s) that best completes each of the following, selecting your answers from the following possibilities:
   tourists; business travellers; function; disputes-settling; angry; time-and-materials; critical-path; all hostels; systematic; variation; complaints; unimportant.
   a A hotel must respond to market needs, but must also . . . adequately.
   b . . . would value telecommunications and secretarial services.
   c A . . . contract means the owner incurs the risk of cost overruns.
   d 'Value engineering' is a . . . method of analysing needs versus costs versus resources.
   e A construction timeline can be presented as a ' . . .' diagram.
   f Protection clauses should include a . . . procedure.

3 Discuss the following in one or two sentences (for each statement):
   a Hotels are essentially all the same because their function— accommodation—is the same for everyone.
   b Investors should not spend too much in building a hotel, because these days the building will have a lifespan of only 10–15 years.
   c The physical surroundings a guest experiences are less important than the quality of service he/she receives.

4 Analyse and discuss the following:
   Every design has a natural lifespan and it is vital to plan to recover an adequate return on an investment as soon as possible within that lifespan.

Chapter 6 Notes

[1] Dickey, C. 1996, 'Niche for the Night', *Newsweek*, 9 December 1996, p. 71.

[2] Scoviak-Lerner, M. 1996, 'Market-Driven Design Trends for the Millennium', *Hotels*, May 1996, p. 58. [Note that this author sometimes publishes as 'Scoviak' and sometimes publishes as 'Scoviak-Lerner'.]

[3] Plummer, A. 1992, 'Projected Growth in Technologies Required by a Teleresort', Pacific Asia Travel Association, *PATA Conference 1992*, San Francisco, pp 267–8.

[4] Scoviak M. 1996, 'The Full Service Business Room of the Future', *Interior Design*, June 1996, p. 154. [Note that this author sometimes publishes as 'Scoviak' and sometimes publishes as 'Scoviak-Lerner'.]

[5] Hensdill, C. 1996, 'Partnerships in Dining', *Hotels*, February 1996, p. 57.

[6] Rowe, M. 1997, 'The New F&B Rules', *Lodging Hospitality*, March 1997, p. 20.

[7] Taylor, S. 1997, 'Food for Thought', *Lodging Hospitality*, March 1997, p. 27.

[8] Kurt Fischer, vice-president of food and beverage, Westin Hotels, cited in Rowe, M. 1997, 'The New F&B Rules', *Lodging Hospitality*, March 1997, p. 20.

[9] Scoviak-Lerner, M. 1995, 'One-of-a-Kind Design', *Hotels*, May 1995, p. 30. [Note that this author sometimes publishes as 'Scoviak' and sometimes publishes as 'Scoviak-Lerner'.]

[10] Scoviak-Lerner, M. 1996, op. cit. (*Hotels*, May 1996), p. 60. [Note that this author sometimes publishes as 'Scoviak' and sometimes publishes as 'Scoviak-Lerner'.]

[11] Terpak, M. 1989, 'The Fast-Track Construction Alternative', *The Real Estate Finance Journal*, Winter 1989, p. 75.

[12] Dickey, C. 1996, op. cit., p. 71.

[13] Mankarious, R. & Nehmer, J. 1992, 'Structuring the Contractual Relationship in a Hotel Renovation Project', *The Real Estate Finance Journal*, Winter 1992, p. 91.

[14] Russell, J. 1991, 'Value Engineering the Disney Way', *Architectural Record*, December 1991, p. 24.

[15] Scoviak-Lerner, M. 1995, op. cit. (*Hotels*, May 1995), p. 29. [Note that this author sometimes publishes as 'Scoviak' and sometimes publishes as 'Scoviak-Lerner'.]

[16] Hart, C. 1986, 'Product Development: How Marriott Created Courtyard', *Cornell Hotel and Restaurant Administration Quarterly*, November, 1986, p. 68.

[17] Dennis McCarty, director of project management for Radisson Hotels International, quoted by Scoviak, M. 1996, 'Hotels: The Next Generation', *Interior Design*, June 1996, p. 150. [Note that this author sometimes publishes as 'Scoviak' and sometimes publishes as 'Scoviak-Lerner'.]

[18] Unnamed, quoted by Scoviak, M. 1996, 'Hotels: The Next Generation', *Interior Design*, June 1996, p. 150. [Note that this author sometimes publishes as 'Scoviak' and sometimes publishes as 'Scoviak-Lerner'.]

[19] Wagner, G. 1995, 'ADA: A Look Back', *Lodging Hospitality*, October 1995, p. 47.

[20] Ohlin, J. 1993, 'Creative Approaches to the *Americans with Disabilities Act*', *The Cornell Hotel and Restaurant Administration Quarterly*, October 1993, pp 19ff.

[21] Greenfield, M. 1986, 'Who Put the Lake in the Lobby?', *Newsweek*, 13 January 1986, p. 76.

[22] Scoviak-Lerner, M. 1994, 'The New Look of Hotels—12 Trends Influencing Today's Design', *Hotels*, May 1994, p. 52. [Note that this author sometimes publishes as 'Scoviak' and sometimes publishes as 'Scoviak-Lerner'.]

[23] Ibid., p. 54.

[24] Macomber, J. 1989, 'You Can Manage Construction Costs', *Harvard Business Review*, March–April 1989, p. 164.

[25] Russell, J. 1991, 'Worth Less', *Architectural Record*, December 1991, p. 21.

[26] Kemper, A. 1979, *Architectural Handbook*, p. 289, Wiley: New York.

CHAPTER 7

Management and Operation

Synopsis of Chapter

Having considered site and design issues, the study turns to issues of management and staffing.

The new facility might be a stand-alone operation or part of a chain or franchise—either the project will be operated under a management contract, or the investors will manage the facility directly. If the latter, decisions will have to be made on the management structure and staffing levels.

Labour costs can be estimated once the structure and staff are determined. The labour budget must also take into account when management and staff will be engaged. Once the labour budget has been compiled— both for the initial operating period and for normal operations—it can be carried forward into the overall budget for the project.

Property Management

One of the first matters to consider in relation to management and staffing is whether the property will be run by managers and executives employed directly by the organisation, or whether the developers will enter into a management agreement with a hotel management company. If the latter, the management company would contract to manage the property and to be recompensed by a proportion of gross revenue (say, 3%) and a percentage of gross operating profit (say, 10%). Such a contract is useful where a hotel investor does not wish to be involved in the day-to-day operation of the business.

In the 1960s and 1970s, such contracts generally favoured the hotel operator. However, Simons (1994) observes that, in the late 1980s to 1990s, the terms of management contracts swung around to favour the owner-investors.[1]

Whether the developer chooses to manage the property directly, or chooses a franchise arrangement, the following issues of staffing will still be relevant, and should be addressed in the project evaluation.

Staffing and Operational Issues

After the project evaluation has outlined the design concept, timing, and capital costs, there should be a section (in the final Report) on staffing and operational issues. How many staff will be required? Are skilled staff available?

Some of the recent trends in hotel design concepts and service will require more staff, some will require less. Food services in some properties have undergone radical changes—away from full-service restaurants towards food courts and kiosks. These dramatically reduce food and beverage costs and staffing, yet still provide what guests need. The trend towards business travellers using hotel rooms as their offices has meant an emphasis on room-service amenities.

It appears that the demand for increased room-service amenities is not limited to the business segment. Ted Mosley, senior vice-president of Quorum Resorts, believes that room-service business as a whole is increasing and that, in recent times, it has increased from 15% to 30% of food-service business.[2] This change in the proportion of room-service to food-service business will result in changes to the traditional staffing ratios in food and beverage outlets.

Other trends, such as the increased dependency on technology, will affect staffing in security areas. New features—including fine-tuned locking systems, cameras (in corridors and externally), and in-room safes—will all reduce the need for higher staffing in the security department.[3]

Technology might even change the nature of the check-in process. In the next generation of hotels . . .

> There is no registration desk. Just follow your escort to the guestroom, have your thumbprint scanned, and enter the hotel room of the future.
>
> Scoviak (1996)[4]

Depending on the level of service that the property will provide, the first step is to compile a staffing schedule that lists the number of employees by department and shift. Decisions made about the type of service to be offered will influence the number of staff required. For example, the food and beverage programs might be contracted out. If they are not, a schedule for each service should be compiled—depending on hours of operation, seating mixes, menus, capacity, and so on.

A number of food-service outlets will obviously add to costs. In some properties, there is a move away from restaurants on a specific theme to providing a variety of themes through measures such as extending menu choices, or creating a different atmosphere for breakfast, lunch and evening meal. The result is an economical variety of themes.[5] Determining staffing levels means going back a step in the project evaluation to consider again what sort of theme and service will be provided on the property.

The degree of supervision required will impact upon labour costing. To ensure high levels of services for guests around the clock, seven days a week, a large number of supervisors is needed. However, how many supervisors do the supervisors require? In other words, how many layers of management should there be?

At the Sheraton Sydney Airport Hotel, management revised a traditional structure of having seven or eight management 'layers' and redrew their organisational structure. The hotel was able to operate with a high quality of service with only *two* layers of supervision. The new management structure was a success because it encouraged employees to use their initiative in meeting guests' needs.[6]

Estimating Labour Costs

The project evaluation must include a section on staffing and operational issues because the question of an adequate supply of skilled labour has relevance at this stage. However, the question of an adequate supply is not the only issue. A project evaluation must estimate staff numbers because there are *financial implications*—the number of staff required and the timing of their recruitment has a cost dimension.

One way of assessing the costs is to undertake a detailed analysis of staffing for each department—breaking labour requirements down into hours, and cost per hour for each category where possible. Using hours as the basic unit of measurement allows for adjustments if there are changes in wage and salary levels. There is no alternative to this if the project embodies new concepts and there are no comparisons.

However, if comparisons can be made with other operations, there can be a shortcut to staffing estimates—provided that there is an in-built tolerance in those estimates (that is, provided that the project is not a high-volume, low-margin operation where close estimates are vital).

The breakdown of labour and other expenses by department can be done using the categories of the 'uniform system of accounts'. This is a common format for financial statements which was developed in New York in the 1920s, and which has since become widespread around the world. Under the system, labour and related expenses (that is, wages, salaries, payroll tax, superannuation, employee benefits and so on) are assembled under the following departmental headings:

- rooms;
- food and beverage;
- telephone;
- other operating departments;
- administrative and general;
- marketing; and
- engineering/maintenance.

Where the proposed development is an extension of an existing service, or where it is a franchised operation with similar properties carrying out their business in similar locations, comparable statistics can be taken from other operations to come up with a likely staffing schedule and likely staffing costs. For example, the analyst might examine a similar established property and discover that staff costs are divided as shown in Figure 7.1.

Division	Percentage (of Total Wages/Salaries Costs)
Rooms Division Labour	34%
Food and Beverage Labour	32%
Functions & Conferences Labour	8%
Administrative Staff	12%
Marketing Staff	7%
Engineering/Maintenance Labour	7%

Figure 7.1 *Staff Costs*

Kevin Baker

Moreover, total wages and salaries usually equals 35% of the revenue of this comparable property. It would be acceptable to use this statistic as a 'rule of thumb' to estimate what wage and salary costs might be in the new operation—provided that it is recognised that not all hotels are the same, and that labour costs can vary markedly depending upon various factors.

When budgeting for labour expenses in a new project, there will be significant labour costs even before the property is operational—because most staff will have to commence duties for orientation and training purposes, and for start-up tasks weeks or months before opening.

All the cost categories in the financial project evaluation will be *estimates* to some degree and, as long as the analyst provides *best estimates* (based upon real evidence drawn from a reputable and objective source), a limited tolerance of error is acceptable. Nevertheless, it is up to the analyst to demonstrate that the basis of this comparison of labour requirements and costs is well founded.

The First Operational Priority—the Marketing Campaign

The first operational issue to consider is the work that will take place even before the property is completed and ready to receive its first guests/customers. The pre-opening marketing campaign will be crucial to the success of the project in its early days, and it is certainly sufficiently important to consider in the context of the project evaluation.

The project evaluation should include an outline marketing plan so that the plan can be budgeted and provided for, and so that it can be synchronised with the construction phase. The cost of marketing and advertising will be only one aspect of the pre-opening expenses—but possibly one of the more important aspects.

Operating Within a Chain or Franchise

The number of owner-operated hotels is declining. This is due to increasing demands on management expertise, and to changes in economic conditions.

If the new project is part of a chain or a larger entity, one of the first operational issues that must be addressed is the design of policies and procedures in the new property to ensure that they meet the standards of the chain, and conform to the image that the brand presents in the market place. This issue, because of its importance and complexity, will be considered at greater length in Chapter 12.

CASE STUDY
Quality of Staff Service

The Ritz-Carlton Hotel Corporation operates 23 hotels in the United States and two in Australia. It aims at the luxury market. In 1989, the chain brought in 'Total Quality Management'—a formal process that aims at continual improvements in all aspects of operations. The president and chief executive officer of Ritz-Carlton, Horst Schulze, sought to increase the chain's existing high standards by emphasising customer service. Employees were given authority to make decisions to meet customer needs immediately—without seeking management approval. To achieve higher standards, Schulze chose a two-pronged strategy of (i) improving executive management and (ii) training a committed work force. In 1991, the chain was awarded 121 quality-related awards, and surveys of guests indicated that 95% considered their stay a 'memorable visit'.[7]

It might be that the management team of the new project will be drawn from existing operations. As the property gets close to opening, the new appointees should go through a process of team-building. How this is to be done might be noted in the project evaluation—for the quality of service in the new operation will largely depend upon the quality of management.

Other Operational Issues

The Recruitment of Employees

The project evaluation should consider whether local sources are sufficient to provide the number of staff members necessary to meet the demands of the shifts and the hours of operation, and whether local people are likely to have the skills required.

The service that a guest receives, and the impression that the guest takes away, might very well depend upon limited face-to-face contact between the guest and the hotel employee—who most often will be one of the base-level employees.

Jan Carlzon, president and chief executive officer of Scandinavian Airlines (SAS), revived the fortunes of that airline between 1981 and 1989. He did it by emphasising quality face-to-face service, even though the 'average person' who flew by SAS came into contact with only five of its employees face-to-face, and even though each contact lasted, on average, only 15 seconds—not much of a period to create a favourable impression of the friendliness and service of its staff![8]

The Appointment of Executive Staff

The timing and the source of appointment of executive staff should be considered as an issue in the project evaluation. There are practical and budgetary implications. For example, it would be usual to appoint the general manager even before the hotel nears completion, so that he or she can attend to matters associated with marketing and commissioning the new facility.

The appointment of senior marketing executives will also take place well before the project is close to being commissioned.

Training of Staff

Even if the new project seems likely to attract staff already skilled in hospitality work, there will still be a need for training because every property is different. A new property will inevitably have 'teething problems'—although good managers should be able to keep these to a minimum.

These staffing and operational schedules are carried forward to the financial feasibility stage of the study.

A Last Word

Labour costs are one of the largest expenses in operating a hospitality operation, but this is only to be expected—for it is a *service* industry. Plans can be made for staff numbers, but it is more important to plan for the intangible factor of *quality* service from that staff.

STUDY CHECKLIST #7
OPERATIONAL ISSUES

- Will the property be sold, leased or managed?

- Will the property be placed under management contract and, if so, how will the management be selected?

- What will the organisation structure be?

- What will the management structure be?

- When will the management team be engaged?

- What will be the timeline for opening and marketing the project?

Chapter 7 ■ Review and Questions

1 Indicate whether the following statements are true or false and give a reason for your answer:

   a Hotel management contracts refer to the employment contracts of managers. (True/False? Why?)

   b There is a trend towards providing only full-service food and beverage outlets in hotels. (True/False? Why?)

   c In the view of some people, room-service business as a whole is increasing. (True/False? Why?)

   d The number of employees by department and shift depends on available funds, not on services. (True/False? Why?)

   e Costing of labour will be influenced by the degree of supervision required. (True/False? Why?)

   f Hotels can provide good service with as few as two layers of supervision. (True/False? Why?)

2 Insert the word(s) that best completes each of the following, selecting your answers from the following possibilities:
design trends; franchises; airlines; technology; McDonalds; wages and salaries; hamburgers; capitalisation.
  a ... might change the nature of the check-in process.
  b ... comprise approximately 35% of the revenue of some properties.
  c Linked properties carrying out the same business in different locations can be referred to as ...

3 Discuss the following in one or two sentences (for each statement):
  a It is unwise to employ a general manager to commission and then operate a hotel, because the two tasks are very different and no one person is likely to have the range of skills needed to perform both tasks adequately.
  b A strong general manager is needed in a start-up operation, because they will have to weed out staff who perform poorly when tested for the first time.
  c It is better to employ a good team (that is, a financial controller, marketer, rooms manager, engineer) all at once, rather than employ one manager to organise all the others.

4 Analyse and discuss the following:
Guests have limited face-to-face contact with senior hotel staff, so it is essential that even base-level staff (such as room-attendants) have the authority to make decisions in response to the needs and complaints of guests.

A Sample Project

BUILDING A BETTER BARBECUE

Some pitfalls to avoid when constructing a new hospitality venture!

Figure 7.3 *Have You Built Your Facility in the Right Place?*

Kevin Baker (after the style of Giles)

Chapter 7 Notes

1 Simons, M. 1994, 'Hotel Management Contracts. Some Recent Trends in Relation to Dispute Resolution in Australia', *International Journal of Hospitality Management*, vol. 13, no. 2, p. 143.

2 Ted Mosley, senior vice-president of Quorum Resorts, reported in Taylor, P. 1997 'Food for Thought, *Lodging Hospitality*, March 1997, p. 27.

3 Scoviak, M. 1996, 'Hotels: the Next Generation', *Interior Design*, June 1996, p. 151. [Note that this author sometimes publishes as 'Scoviak' and sometimes publishes as 'Scoviak-Lerner'.]

4 Ibid., p. 150.

5 Rowe, M. 1997, 'The New F&B Rules', *Lodging Hospitality*, March 1997, p. 21.

6 Carter, R., School of Marketing, University of New South Wales, described in Stanton, W., Miller, K. & Layton, R. 1994, *Fundamentals of Marketing*, pp 716–18, 3rd edn, McGraw-Hill Inc.: Sydney.

7 Stoner, J., Freeman, R. & Gilbert, D. 1995, *Management*, 6th edn, pp 232–3, Prentice Hall Inc.: New Jersey.

8 Robbins, S. & Mukerji, D. 1994, *Managing Organisations: New Challenges and Perspectives*, 2nd edn, p. 445, Prentice Hall of Australia P/L: Sydney.

CHAPTER 8

The Environmental Impact Study

Synopsis of Chapter

This chapter examines the important aspect of the environmental impact assessment.

All new projects must consider how the development will affect the local environment—even if a formal study is not required by law.

The chapter describes the background to environmentalism, and outlines the circumstances where a formal study will be required. New projects can have varying degrees of support for environmental issues—ranging from a strict legal posture to a significant commitment to the issues involved.

General Aspects

Environmentalism has had an important impact upon marketing and development. It has been defined as:

> . . . an organised movement of concerned citizens and government to protect and enhance people's living environment.

> Kotler (1994)[1]

In the view of many environmentalists, the goal of business and marketing should be to enhance the quality of life—and quality of life means more than the quantity and quality of goods and services available to the consumer. It also means the quality of the environment that the consumer enjoys.[1]

Manufacturing industries have faced additional costs with the imposition of such measures as stricter pollution controls. The tourism and hospitality industry has not been exempt from the imposition of such environmental controls—especially at the project development stage. Some developers, who have endorsed environmental values, have found that they have enhanced the value of their investment.

One aspect of hospitality operations that has an impact upon the environment is energy usage. Although not as consumptive of resources as are some industrial processes, hotels *are* high users of energy in air-conditioning and other services, and they have a high profile in the community. Therefore hotel management has a role to play in amending energy practices—by saving energy in its own business, and by encouraging education on ways and means of conserving energy. Many hotels have been in the forefront of recent campaigns to use energy sensibly, and the lead they have taken is one which can inspire domestic users to conserve energy. After all, the difference between a kitchen in a hotel and a kitchen in a private household appears to be one of scale rather than function (with apologies to some fine hotel chefs!).

Environment Australia has recorded case studies of energy conservation and environmental education in large hotels in Sydney (the 'Hotel InterContinental' and the 'Regent') and in Melbourne (the 'Parkroyal'). Conservation measures that were used included:

- re-assessing peak and off-peak energy usage;
- improving the efficiency of air-conditioning (even down to the use of swing doors to retain warmth or cool air); and
- the dimming of lights when not needed.

The Australian Hotels Association conducted a study of thirteen hotels in 1994 and examined a large number of ways that hotels could conserve energy and contain costs.

Even smaller-scale projects—such as restaurants—should take into account environmental factors when feasibility analyses are conducted. A comprehensive survey of six Canadian food-service operations found that substantial benefits to the environment could be achieved by reducing polystyrene waste.[2]

Environmental Impact Studies

Larger projects, such as a resort development, might be required by regulation to conduct an environmental impact study (EIS).

Usually, an EIS will be required if:

1 crown land or reserves, or national parks and wildlife sanctuaries, are to be affected by the proposal;
2 rare species of animals or vegetation might be threatened, or if there will be extensive clearing of bushland;
3 the quality of water or water flow is to be affected (by clearing land, or by building work near marine areas and watercourses, or by diverting natural flow);
4 existing water or power supply services might be insufficient for the project, or be subject to heavy demand;

5 existing sewerage and waste-disposal services might be insufficient or subject to heavy demand;

6 existing road and parking facilities will be insufficient, or subject to heavy demand (by increased traffic to and from the site);

7 there will be a substantial effect on the local environment from noise or visual impact; or

8 sites of heritage value, or Aboriginal sites, are to be disturbed.

The EIS will usually start with a full description of the project—with outline plans of the building and construction works. The study must then take into account a number of factors, depending upon which of the above circumstances apply.

If large areas of land are to be cleared, or endangered native flora and fauna threatened, the study will have to detail how that clearing work would be done, and the likely physical changes to the land and natural flow of water.

Where water and sewerage services might need augmenting, the study will have to state the level of demand for services and how it would affect existing services.

Where traffic will increase, the study will have to provide estimates of the likely increase, and the provisions that will be made to cope with the demand—such as additional parking and access works.

If the operation will increase noise levels substantially (say from entertainment or functions), and if that noise will be heard in surrounding areas, the noise levels should be estimated and the geographical areas that will be affected should be described.

Possible changes to heritage properties must be noted. The term 'heritage property' includes more than mere buildings, and the expression 'changes' includes comparatively minor works. This is especially so with reference to Aboriginal heritage sites, and the EIS should refer to the details of even minor damage that might be done. This applies also if that damage is likely to be temporary—such as damage during construction work that is to be rectified after building is completed.

The EIS must also include such details as:

■ the exact site location;
■ the boundaries of the site;
■ the boundaries of the project itself;
■ zoning requirements (and any necessary zoning changes); and
■ the nature of the land ownership (that is, whether the developer owns the land, and the tenure of ownership).

Assessing the Importance of Environmental Concerns

In considering the environmental aspects of a proposed venture, the project evaluation should comment on how much time and attention should be paid to environmental concerns. Certainly, the project must comply with specific laws and regulations, but it might be necessary to go beyond what is strictly required by law.

A large development with increased loads on sewerage and waste-disposal facilities will be seen to be a polluter, and could invoke in the local community the 'NIMBY' ('not in my back yard') factor. If local public opinion is strongly in favour of environmental action (and this should have become evident in local research and interviews), and if the project might have a significant impact on the environment, the study should include options to reinforce a positive public perception of the project.

There are four levels of support for environmental issues that can apply to new projects. They can be characterised by different 'postures' as follows:[3]

- the 'legal' posture;
- the 'market' posture;
- the 'stakeholder' posture; and
- the 'dark-green' posture.

The Legal Posture

This describes an attitude in which organisations comply with all laws and regulations so that they are beyond legal challenge, but will use the law to their advantage where possible.

The Market Posture

This describes organisations that respond to the environmental preferences of their customers. In the tourism industry, this means that service organisations will provide environmentally friendly products to their guests/customers.

The Stakeholder Posture

In this posture, organisations actively seek out ways of encouraging their stake-holders (employees, managers, agents etc.) to develop more environmentally appropriate ways of operating—such as reducing waste and energy usage in a hotel.

The Dark-Green Posture

This describes organisations that choose to involve environmental values in all aspects of the project construction and operation (for example, by using recycled material wherever possible).

It is up to the backers of the project to determine what posture they will take. In the study, the analyst should report on environmental issues in accordance with that posture. In fact, the objectives of the project should include reference to environmental concerns. Even if the investors choose to accept a posture of legal compliance only, that should be spelled out, for prospective financiers or investment partners will look for it. If the environmental aspect is neglected, the project could be involved in unexpected costs or litigation or amendments—or even public opprobrium.

There can certainly be advantages in catering for the growing market for vacations that are environmentally friendly. The properties involved in environmental tourism can be at the top end of the market—not just aimed at the lower end of the market (such as the young backpacker clientele). As an example, a project evaluation for a new four-star resort hotel in Halkidiki, Greece, found evidence that environmental tourism was increasing in the region, and that top-of-the-range properties had the potential to tap a market that had both quantity and quality.[4]

CASE STUDY
Do Not Neglect Environmental Factors

Boise Cascade is a company that began as a timber mill in 1913. By 1970, it had developed into a diversified corporation marketing a range of building products. It was also a large landholder—its investment in land having begun when it purchased timber leases.

By 1970, the company held a large amount of recreational land, and had acquired another company called US Land Company, which had five lake resort properties in the course of development. The future of Boise Cascade was seen to be in developing and selling recreational communities which offered such attractions as water sports, golf, swimming and, in some cases, skiing.

The strategic move seemed a good one because market studies confirmed a strong growth in recreational spending, especially in California. On the basis of that growth potential, Boise Cascade invested in a lakeland resort development 75 minutes' drive from Los Angeles, and in a US$38-million recreational community at Palos Verdes, also in California.

Boise Cascade's resort development managers had considerable autonomy, and 'tended to be of the old school'.[5] Their attitude was described as 'cut it up, develop it, sell it and get out'.[6]

The marketing and feasibility surveys conducted by Boise Cascade did not take adequate account of changing attitudes towards environmental issues, particularly in California. Public opinion was moving against aggressive marketing and development of recreational land, and a number of Boise Cascade's resorts were on shorelines (such as Puget Sound). The damage caused by the initial development was highly visible. Conservation movements launched public debates about the values of development, and obtained front-page publicity in local media.

Local authorities demanded that the resorts provided more open space than originally planned, that utility services be placed underground, and that sewage treatment be upgraded.

The costs of the resorts escalated at the same time as sales fell. The company had heavy debt commitments, and the resultant squeeze on its cash flow rapidly brought on a crisis. Boise Cascade was forced to start selling off assets to meet its debt, and its top management was replaced. The new management team divested the company of its recreational developments, and returned to its core business to build up its assets.

Robert Hansberger, the president of Boise Cascade during its expansion years, put the failure of the resort developments down to 'social changes . . . Environmental issues . . . came suddenly upon the company . . . We could not change quickly enough'.[7]

Based on Hartley (1992)[8]

The marketing and feasibility studies that were done for the proposed resorts did not take adequate note of the changes in public opinion regarding environmental issues. In that, Boise Cascade was hardly alone during that period.

A Last Word

There should be no tendency to underestimate the influence of environmental issues on proposed developments. The quality of a project will be judged by intangible as well as tangible factors.

STUDY CHECKLIST #8
ENVIRONMENTAL ASPECTS

- Does the project have a defined lifespan?

- Will the environment be affected by the operation over that lifespan?

- What are the plans for waste and effluent disposal?

- Will the project be subject to laws or regulations relating to environmental considerations?

- Are there heritage aspects to consider?

- Are there aspects that will impact upon indigenous people?

- Are there special features of the project that make it environmentally friendly?

Chapter 8 ■ Review and Questions

1 Indicate whether the following statements are true or false and give a reason for your answer:

   a Environmentalism is an organised movement. (True/False? Why?)

   b Quality of life depends on a person's material wealth. (True/False? Why?)

   c Practices to conserve energy can result in substantial cost savings. (True/False? Why?)

   d Smaller-scale projects need not take into account environmental factors. (True/False? Why?)

   e The project evaluation should consider what environmental posture developers wish to take. (True/False? Why?)

2 Insert the word(s) that best completes each of the following, selecting your answers from the following possibilities:
national unimportance; three; ways of operating; heritage value; four; only private; all; two; dividends.

   a There are . . . levels of support for environmental issues.

   b Organisations should encourage their stakeholders to develop environmentally appropriate . . .

   c . . . developments must comply with environmental laws and regulations.

   d Generally an environmental impact study (EIS) will be required on sites of . . .

3 Discuss the following in one or two sentences (for each statement):

   a Environmental factors are overrated as far as hotels and resorts are concerned, because even the largest hotel does not threaten the environment as much as does a factory that is discharging pollutants into the atmosphere.

   b It is best to understate heritage values in a site, because otherwise owners might lose substantial control over the project to government heritage authorities.

   c The problem with conducting environmental studies is that it is difficult to quantify the costs and benefits.

4 Analyse and discuss the following:

   Most of the energy-reduction measures that can be carried out in hotels (for example, dimming light switches) have limited economic and environmental impact and are mainly of public relations value.

Chapter 8 Notes

[1] Kotler, P. 1994, *Marketing Management—Analysis, Planning, Implementation and Control*, 8th edn, p. 160, Prentice Hall International, Inc.: New Jersey.

[2] Menzies, D. 1990, 'From Big Mac Boxes to Yo-Yos: Group to Determine Viability of Polystyrene Recycling', *Canadian Hotel and Restaurant*, January 1990, p. 24.

[3] Stoner, J., Freeman, R. & Gilbert, D. 1995, *Management*, 6th edn, pp 85–6, Prentice Hall Inc.: New Jersey.

[4] Patroni, E. 1995, 'A Project Evaluation for an All-Suite, Environmentally Friendly Four-Star Resort Hotel in Halkidiki, Greece', MSc thesis, University of Surrey, Guildford, UK.

[5] Hartley, R. F. 1992, *Marketing Mistakes*, p. 50, John Wiley & Sons, Inc.: New York.

[6] *Business Week* 1971, 'Boise Cascade Shifts Towards Tighter Control', 15 May 1971, p. 86.

[7] *Dun's* 1974, 'Interview with Robert Vail Hansberger', September 1974, pp 12–14.

[8] Hartley, R. F. 1992, op. cit., pp 46ff.

CHAPTER 9

Financial Feasibility—Capital Costs

Synopsis of Chapter

This chapter returns to aspects of construction of the proposed develop-ment in order to prepare schedules of construction cost/cash flow, to determine borrowing requirements and to assess financial feasibility. The chapter therefore treats the capital costs of construction as a separate and important topic.

The amount of capital required and the timing of payments to suppliers and contractors will affect the financial feasibility of the project. The major categories of capital costs are considered in turn—starting with preliminary costs, then construction costs (with schedules for payments and repayments of loans), then furniture and equipment costs.

The chapter also considers some expenses that are related to the capital costs—such as depreciation (describing straight-line and declining bal-ance depreciation methods), loan repayments (principal and interest) and insurance and rates expenses. These cost categories (which are referred to as 'fixed costs' in income statements) are considered again in Chapter 10.

Preliminary Costs

The example of project capital costs presented in Figure 6.3 (p. 108) presumed that the land had to be purchased as part of the development. The cost of land might constitute approximately 10% of development disbursements.

The land might not be purchased. In some countries, under certain circum-stances, the land can be obtained on long-term lease. Depending on whether the land is purchased or leased, the cost of obtaining the site will be treated differently. If the land is purchased, it will be held in the accounts at historical value, and will not be depreciated. If the land is obtained on long-term lease (say, of forty or fifty years), that expenditure can be amortised—that is, written-off over the period of the lease. The word 'amortisation' has its root in the concept of being 'done to death'—and that is exactly what happens with the cost of the lease and other costs associated with obtaining the lease!

There might be a technical accounting argument that the building is then a leasehold improvement—and also should be written off over the period of the lease. But, for the purposes of the project evaluation, and so that the costs can be compared consistently with other developments, the cost of the building should be treated the same as if the land were purchased. This means that the construction should be depreciated—that is, the expense spread over the full period of its use. In this example, buildings will be depreciated over 25 years, and other capital expenditure (such as equipment) will be depreciated over five years. This does not mean that the value of the building is declining, or that funds are being set aside to replace it after 25 years. What it means is that the amount of money spent on this item will be spread over an estimated time that the item will be used to generate income—and so the expense of construction will be matched with the income flow.

Development costs, indeed preliminary costs such as consultants' fees and approval costs, can be capitalised—that is, rolled into the total cost of constructing the capital item and establishing it on site ready for commissioning. Some specific categories of preliminary expenditure (such as legal fees) might have to be treated in different ways according to taxation provisions. However, for the purposes of this study, all preliminary costs will be rolled into the capital cost of the new project.

For the working example of a hotel development (see Chapter 6), there were other assumptions made—namely that the developer was a partnership of an individual and two companies, each of whom would contribute just over $1 million to the project, and that this sum represented over half of the total cost. The breakdown of costs had been prepared by the developers after consultation with the architectural team.

Construction Costs Financing

The construction itself (at the cost of $3 260 000) will be partly financed by a lending authority who will advance up to $2 282 000 for a 25-year period. This represents 70% of the estimated cost of the building, secured by a first mortgage (assumed to be at 8% interest). The actual construction will take twelve months. However, the borrowing requirement will arise at stages during the construction—as the builder needs progress payments to meet suppliers' invoices and to meet payments to sub-contractors and employed staff.

Progress payments to the building contractor are as shown in Figure 9.1 (the figures are simplified).

Progress Payment	Paid	Amount
First progress payment	After 2 months	$800 000
Second progress payment	After 4 months	$400 000
Third progress payment	After 6 months	$800 000
Fourth progress payment	After 9 months	$600 000
Fifth progress payment	After 12 months	$660 000

Figure 9.1 *Progress Payments to Building Contractor*

Kevin Baker

In actual fact, the progress payments will be more frequent, and will be dependent upon the percentage of the work completed as certified by the architects, and on other contractual obligations. Also, on completion of the building, there will be an amount retained until the satisfactory rectification of any unsatisfactory work. However, for the purposes of the project evaluation— which provides for the calculation of an *estimate* of required bridging finance— a simplified schedule is acceptable.

The lending authority does not advance the amount of finance secured by the mortgage until the owner (the mortgagee) has contributed their equity—in this case 30%. Neither does the mortgage rate of 8% take effect until the building is completed. The finance is lent on an interim basis—termed 'bridging finance'. This amount is lent at a higher interest rate, taking into account the fact that lending in the course of building is more risky than lending on a completed property (because, for any number of reasons, the construction could be interrupted).

The project evaluation must take into account that the bridging finance, at say 12% (1% a month to simplify the illustration), is lent and advanced at various times as the progress payments fall due. Although construction might be completed at twelve months, an extra three months of bridging finance should be allowed for— while the building is commissioned and mortgage documents are finalised, and also as a contingency for extra interest costs. Figures 9.2 and 9.3 (p. 136) enable calculation of estimated bridging finance interest that should be budgeted.

Payment	Equity	Borrowing	Monthly Interest
Payment 1	$800 000	0	0
Payment 2	$178 000	$222 000	$2220
Payment 3	0	$800 000	$8000
Payment 4	0	$600 000	$6000
Payment 5	0	$660 000	$6600
Totals	$978 000	$2 282 000	

Figure 9.2 *Schedule of Equity/Borrowing Timing*

Kevin Baker

Month	Amount Borrow'd	Monthly Interest	Due for (Months)	Total Interest
4th month	$222 000	$2220	11 months	$24 420
6th month	$800 000	$8000	9 months	$72 000
9th month	$600 000	$6000	6 months	$36 000
12th month	$660 000	$6600	3 months	$19 800
Total				$152 220

Figure 9.3 *Schedule of Monthly Interest Due After Fifteen Months*

Kevin Baker

It can be seen that, when bridging interest on the building is up to $6600 per month, delays can be very costly indeed—especially if the bridging interest rate is higher than the 12% per annum (1% per month), used in the illustration.

For the purposes of this calculation, it is assumed that bridging interest will be payable on the furniture and fittings. A financing authority will extend funds for the purchase of equipment, furniture, and fittings—up to 75% of their cost price (which cost price includes all additional costs to transport the equipment, furniture and fittings and install them ready for use). The finance will be for a term of five years at 11%, and will be secured by the equipment. However, until the building is commissioned, the lender argues that full rights to operate the facility do not pass to the owner until the building is commissioned, and that it remains under the building contractor's control until then. The lender therefore includes funds advanced for these items of equipment and furniture under the bridging finance.

The amount of $600 000 is advanced, the equipment is paid for prior to installation in the facility, and this takes place approximately two months prior to scheduled completion. Again, an additional three months is allowed until finalisation of longer-term financing. Therefore the provision for bridging finance includes allowing for $600 000, at 1% per month for five months, which equals $30 000.

Total bridging finance provision is therefore $152 220 plus $30 000. This comes to $182 220. There is already a contingency allowance in the form of the time allowed for finalisation of commissioning and documentation, but an additional 10% should be added as a *further* contingency allowance, and a rounded total of $200 000 is thus calculated as being the amount that should be budgeted for bridging finance (interest only).

Regarding contingency allowances, authors such as Main (1988) suggest allowing 10% for working capital and a further 10% of the total investment as a contingency—despite a detailed and careful listing of specific costs.[1]

Long-Term Payments of Interest and Principal

First Mortgage

The lender requires a monthly payment of $20 000 for interest and principal. It is necessary to determine how much of this payment each month is allocated to interest (which is a tax-deductible expense) and how much to the reduction of the principal, the amount originally borrowed (which is a repayment of capital and not tax-deductible).

The annual interest due each year is calculated on the balance of the principal owing at the beginning of the period—which balance is, of course, decreasing as repayments of principal are deducted. The calculation can be made annually as shown in Figure 9.4.

Year	Annual Payment	Interest at 8%	Principal	Balance
Current	$240 000			$2 282 000
1	$240 000	$182 560	$57 440	$2 224 560
2	$240 000	$177 965	$62 035	$2 162 525
3	$240 000	$173 002	$66 998	$2 095 527
4	$240 000	$167 642	$72 358	$2 023 169
5	$240 000	$161 854	$78 146	$1 945 022

Figure 9.4 Schedule of Repayments of Principal and Interest

Kevin Baker

It is important to break up the monthly payments between principal and interest because the interest will be entered as an expense on the income statement of the new project, and interest payments over the first five years will help determine the net income, or the profit, of the development. Also, interest payments are tax-deductible, whereas repayments of principal are considered capital items (that is, repayment of the amount originally borrowed to build the capital asset).

The total amount payable in interest in principal will nevertheless be used in the projections of cash flow for the initial period of operation because, whatever the name put on the category of payment, the cash must be paid to the lending authority.

Secured Loan for Equipment, Furniture and Fittings

The secured loan for the purchase of equipment, furniture, and fittings has to be treated in the same way as the first mortgage. The monthly payments have to be separated into interest and principal. The financing authority would normally provide a prospective borrower with these figures, but the appraiser might choose to do the calculation—using the same technique as the mortgage calculation above.

Because the calculation is a long one (having to be made for each of the sixty monthly payments) the detail is included as an appendix (See Appendix A). Figure 9.5 is summarised from Appendix A.

Year	Annual Payment	Interest	Principal Owing
			$600 000
One	$13 045	$61 293	$95 253
Two	$13 045	$50 270	$106 275
Three	$13 045	$37 972	$118 573
Four	$13 045	$24 251	$132 295
Five	$13 045	$8 942	$147 604

Figure 9.5 Schedule of Repayments of Secured Loan

Kevin Baker

Depreciation

Another major expense associated with the capital development is depreciation.[2] There are various depreciation techniques. Two of the more important are *straight-line depreciation* and the *declining balance method*.

Straight-line depreciation

As the name implies, straight-line depreciation allows the capital amount, less salvage value, to be written off as an expense in equal amounts each period so that a graphical representation of the process would result in a straight line.

Declining balance method

The declining balance method of depreciation results in the capital investment being set off against income in an accelerated fashion (maximising depreciation expense and therefore paying less tax on profit in early years). This can be an advantage to a new project which is establishing itself and requires all the financial advantages it can obtain. The declining balance method of depreciation is often preferable—because it allows the investment to be written off faster.

Comparing the two methods

Assuming that the economic life of the building (the depreciable period) is 25 years, a 4% annual figure would be used for *straight-line depreciation*. Based on the assumption that, after 25 years, the building will still have resale value for its designed purpose, a residual figure would be estimated. The depreciable amount for the equipment would be 20%, (based on its estimated life being five years, after which it has some salvage value, say $200 000).[3]

The *declining balance method* (for this example) will use these figures—4% and 20% respectively. (A small balance will be left when the items have reached the end of their estimated economic life.)

The balance (that is, the recorded value of the item after depreciation for the period has been deducted) is the starting point for the calculation. Each period, the depreciation expense is calculated (and deducted from income for that year) and the balance after depreciation at the end of the period is carried over.

Development costs of $600 000 and siteworks of $290 000 have been added to the construction cost of $3 260 000 to give a total of $4 150 000 for the cost of the building.

Year	Opening Balance	Depreciation	Closing Balance
1	$4 150 000	$166 000	$3 984 000
2	$3 984 000	$159 360	$3 824 640
3	$3 824 640	$152 986	$3 671 654
4	$3 671 654	$146 866	$3 524 788
5	$3 524 788	$140 992	$3 383 797

Note: Based on 4% each year

Figure 9.6 Building Depreciation Expense (Declining Balance Method)

Kevin Baker

The depreciation expense of equipment, furniture and fittings is calculated in similar fashion.

Year	Opening Balance	Depreciation	Closing Balance
1	$800 000	$160 000	$640 000
2	$640 000	$128 000	$512 000
3	$512 000	$102 400	$409 600
4	$409 600	$81 920	$327 680
5	$327 680	$65 536	$262 144

Note: Based on 20% each year

Figure 9.7 Equipment Depreciation Expense (Declining Balance Method)

Kevin Baker

Insurance and Rates

In addition to the expenses of depreciation and interest on the loans, there are other categories of expense which are related to the capital items, and which will not generally vary—whether the hotel is full of guests, or lying empty. These costs that do not change depending upon the volume of business are termed 'fixed costs'. Fixed costs will also include some administrative charges but, in the context of this section of the project evaluation, the fixed costs to consider will be mainly insurance of the building and contents, and council rates and charges

An accurate idea of the likely cost of insurance can be obtained by approaching the developers' insurer, or insurance broker, and seeking a quote. The cost of insurance will vary according to a number of factors, including location and type of building, and the systems installed but, for the purposes of this example, assume that an insurance company has offered a set of policies that will adequately cover the building against various risks, and that the cost of that policy is $105 000 each year.

Council rates and charges can also be determined by reference to the appropriate local authority. In fact, the developer will already be paying rates and charges if the developer already owns the land. These charges come under the heading of 'holding charges', and the project evaluation has not brought them into account—because the developer will have to pay them whether the project goes ahead or not and, although they can be a factor in a decision, they do not properly belong in the project evaluation itself. They are outside the definitions of the project.

Whether the developer is already paying rates and charges, it is relatively straightforward to determine details of the amounts that would be due and payable each year by reference to the local authority. For this example under consideration, assume that rates and charges will amount to $60 000 each year.

Total Fixed Costs Relating to Capital Investment

There will be other property costs (such as those relating to maintenance) which are variable, and these are better considered under the heading of 'operating costs'. The present section of the project evaluation (relating to the financial feasibility of the capital investment) should include only interest, depreciation, and other fixed costs directly related to the building—such as insurance and rates.

If the project is part of a chain, there might also be a fixed-cost element relating to the purchase of the franchise, or the purchase of goodwill. These elements might be amortised in the same way that tangible assets are depreciated.

The example assumes that the only capital assets taken into account are those of the building and its associated infrastructure. Note, again, that the land is not depreciated, and that its value has only an indirect influence through being the basis upon which the local authority levies its rates and charges.

This analysis of the financial feasibility of the project reveals that the operation must be able to fund fixed commitments of between $542 000 and $735 000 each year after it has met all other operating costs. This will achieve just break-even (the point where all income meets all expenses), but it will not allow any return to the venture partners who will each put up over a million dollars each.

The next stage in analysing the financial feasibility of the project is to consider operating revenues and expenses.

Year	Interest (Building)	Interest (Equipm'nt)	Depreciat'n (Building)	Depreciat'n (Equipm'nt)	Other	Total
1	$182 560	$61 293	$166 000	$160 000	$165 000	$734 853
2	$177 965	$50 270	$159 360	$128 000	$165 000	$680 595
3	$173 002	$37 972	$152 986	$102 400	$165 000	$631 360
4	$167 642	$24 251	$146 866	$81 920	$165 000	$585 679
5	$161 854	$8 942	$140 992	$65 536	$165 000	$542 324

Note: Relates to each of first five years

Figure 9.8 Total Fixed Costs Relating to Capital Assets

Kevin Baker

A Last Word

Some categories of fixed charges, such as depreciation and loan interest, do not appear to be fixed at all, because they are subject to variation in certain circumstances—either as interest rates change or as assumptions regarding depreciation rates and disposal values change. However, they are referred to as 'fixed' because they do not vary with the volume of business activity.

STUDY CHECKLIST #9
FINANCIAL ASPECTS

- ● Recorded all site costs?
- ● Recorded all development costs?
- ● Recorded all holding charges?
- ● Recorded all costs/fees of connection to services?
- ● Recorded all consultant fees?
- ● Recorded all construction costs?
- ● Recorded all pre-opening and marketing costs?

Chapter 9 ■ Review and Questions

1 Indicate whether the following statements are true or false and give a reason for your answer:

   a The lending authority does not usually advance funds until the owner has put in their equity. (True/False? Why?)

   b Contingency funds are those funds set aside to pay the architect. (True/False? Why?)

   c A 'first mortgage' means that the lender of these funds has first priority on the property as a security. (True/False? Why?)

   d 'Depreciation' refers to a fund to cover the replacement of the property. (True/False? Why?)

   e It is an accounting practice not to depreciate land. (True/False? Why?)

2 Insert the word(s) that best completes each of the following, selecting your answers from the following possibilities:

   accumulated; amortised; straight-line; capitalised; written-off; principal; interest; unimportant.

   a . . . depreciation allows a capital amount to be written off as an expense in equal amounts each year.

   b Interest payments are operating expenses whereas . . . payments are not.

   c Development costs can include preliminary costs which are thereby said to be . . .

   d Capital payments in relation to leasehold property are said to be . . .

3 Discuss the following in one or two sentences (for each statement):

   a The amount written off in depreciation might not reflect the changing real value of the asset being depreciated.

   b An investor will develop a large hotel property not only for the operating profit, but also for the capital gain in the real estate.

   c It is better to buy into an existing property than to develop a new facility.

4 Analyse and discuss the following:

   Depreciation is an unrealistic expense because it is hedged about with too many uncertainties and estimates—far better to revalue properties on a regular basis, and take into account the changes in real market value.

A Sample Project

BUILDING A BETTER BARBECUE

Some pitfalls to avoid when constructing a new hospitality venture!

Figure 9.9 *Have You Over-Capitalised?*

Kevin Baker (after the style of Giles)

Chapter 9 Notes

[1] Main, B. 1988, 'Financial Feasibility', *Restaurant Business*, 10 February 1988, p. 83.

[2] Many accounting texts describe the concept and the details of depreciation. For a simple exposition, refer Coltman, M. 1990, *Understanding Financial Information—the Non-Financial Manager's Guide*, 2nd edn, pp 23 ff, International Self-Counsel Press Ltd: British Columbia.

[3] These assumptions could be challenged, but they are valid for the purposes of financial projections. The assumptions might be varied from time to time, and calculations adjusted.

Financial Feasibility—
Revenue/Expense Projections

Synopsis of Chapter

This chapter describes the projected income statement. It details methods of forecasting rooms revenue, and food and beverage revenue (including the heuristic method).

Rooms revenue depends upon rates and occupancy, and occupancy can vary for several reasons—especially during the start-up period of a new operation. There can also be seasonal variances.

Marketing strategies can affect both rates and occupancy.

Estimates of revenue/expense can be drawn up by using some information calculated in earlier chapters (such as labour costs and fixed costs), and by using statistics from comparable operations.

The bottom-line figure on the income statement is crucial for assessing the short-term and long-term viability of the project.

The Projected Income Statement

The first step in calculating projected income—that is, the net result of revenue and expenses—is to compile a schedule of these items. This schedule is referred to as an 'income statement', although other terms are sometimes used—such as 'profit-and-loss statement' or 'revenue/expense statement'. Whatever the name, the income statement is intended to show simply whether the operation makes a profit after all the costs of the operation (including taxation) are accounted for.

This projected income statement will be prepared assuming normal operations of the projected development—that is, after the start-up period when it has achieved its normal operating capacity. The statement will not consider any abnormal discounting, or the bringing to account of abnormal expenses (such as pre-opening expenses). These issues will be considered at a later stage—when cash-flow projections are compiled.

Some items on the statement have already been calculated, notably the fixed costs relating to the capital investment schedule—such as interest, depreciation, insurance on the capital assets, and rates and charges.

The main revenue item, room income, has already been considered in the chapter on competitor analysis (Chapter 4). The two most important determinants of room income—occupancy and average room rate—have already been considered in the context of market supply and demand, and reasonable estimates of both have been made. These estimates will be used to calculate annual revenue.

There are other revenue categories (such as food and beverage revenue), and other expense categories (such as marketing costs, administrative costs, and so on).

Food and Beverage Revenue

Food and beverage revenue figures have, usually, not been well calculated in feasibility studies. As Turkel observes:

> There is no serious analysis of the relative profitability of the food and beverage outlets beyond the grossly misleading departmental margins.

Turkel (1995)[1]

Payne agrees:

> F&B generally doesn't get great analysis.

Payne (1996)[2]

Food and beverage revenue can be calculated on the basis of market assumptions—such as projected seat turnover rate and the average check (the term 'check' referring to the record of food and beverage purchases by a customer). Such calculations, starting from these basics, will be as accurate as the market assumptions are accurate.

Calculating Food Revenue
If the development includes several food and beverage venues, the food revenue for each can be estimated by using a basic formula:[3]

$$R = N \times T \times C \times O$$

(where: R = revenue; N = number of seats; T = seat turnover rate;
C = average check; O = days open each year).

The number of seats in each venue and the days open each year can be readily determined but, clearly, the seat turnover rate and the average check are subject to estimate. The calculation should be repeated for each meal period, even for interim breaks, because the pattern of usage will vary.

For example, assume that the development will have a 60-seat coffee shop and an 80-seat restaurant, both open every day of the year (although limited patronage on the weekends reduces the seat turnover rate, and some bed-and-breakfast packages will reduce the average check). Employee meals are costed separately, and are included under a general heading for payroll costs.

The calculations of projected revenue for the coffee shop and the restaurant are shown in Figures 10.1 and 10.2, and the overall total projected revenue for food and beverage is shown in Figure 10.3.

Time	Calculation	Total
Breakfast	60 × 0.5 × $5.00 × 365	$54 750
Lunch	60 × 0.75 × $6.00 × 365	$98 550
Other	60 × 0.25 × $3.50 × 365	$19 162
Total Revenue		$172 462

Figure 10.1 *Coffee Shop—Projected Revenue*

Kevin Baker

Time	Calculation	Total
Lunch	80 × 0.25 × $12.00 × 365	$87 600
Dinner	80 × 0.75 × $15.00 × 365	$328 500
Total Revenue		$416 100

Figure 10.2 *Restaurant—Projected Revenue*

Kevin Baker

For the restaurant, there are assumptions that there will be significant custom from non-guests (a reasonable assumption, given the proportion of business and convention guests in the hotel), and that, on average, approximately 20% of hotel guests will use the venue.

Venue	Projected Revenue (see Figures 10.5 & 10.6)
Coffee Shop	$172 462
Restaurant	$416 100
Total Food Revenue	$588 562

Figure 10.3 *Total Food Projected Revenue*

Kevin Baker

Calculating Beverage Revenue

Beverage revenue must be calculated separately. The usual practice is to make an estimation of beverage revenue based on a percentage of food revenue for a particular venue. This percentage can be based upon prior experience. Clearly, there will be almost no beverages purchased from a bar for the breakfast, and the consumption of beverages at lunch and dinner periods will follow different patterns.

Certainly, there might be some variations to this depending upon the meal period. Breakfast covers will be more closely related to occupancy levels in most hotels, but the average check for breakfast will be lower than lunch or dinner.

For the purposes of this estimation, assume that beverage revenue is 40% of the restaurant revenue: $416\ 100 \times 40\% = \$166\ 440$.

Total Food & Beverage Revenue

From the above calculations, it is a simple matter to make a reasonable estimate of the total food and beverage revenue—as shown in Figure 10.4.

Total Food Revenue*	$588 562
Total Beverage Revenue**	$166 440
Total Food & Beverage Revenue	$755 002

* from Fig. 10.3
** assume 40% restaurant revenue

Figure 10.4 Total Food & Beverage Projected Revenue

Kevin Baker

Room Service Demand

There will be some demand for room service that might or might not be factored into the calculation of food and beverage revenue. It could be calculated by taking the room occupancy and assessing the amount of room service revenue per room occupied. For example, management estimates that 5% of guests use room service and the average check is $20. However, because this operation is a new one, the likely demand for room service, also sometimes called 'derived demand', is difficult to estimate.

Because of the degree of difficulty, it is acceptable to leave out an estimate for likely room-service revenue. This action would comply with the accounting doctrine of 'conservatism'—that is, when faced with making an estimate, it is preferable to understate a revenue figure rather than overstate it. Similarly, it is preferable to overstate an expense figure rather than understate it.

An Heuristic Method for Calculating Food and Beverage Revenue

The term *heuristic* refers to finding things out, usually by trial and error. The 'heuristic method' of calculating food and beverage income is so-called because it involves using simplified 'rules' to derive likely revenue levels. It might also be referred to as the 'rule-of-thumb' process. By this method, food and beverage revenue is calculated by using an estimate drawn from comparison with a similar operation, or by a similar rule of thumb.

Using figures from another operation, the analyst might note that food and beverage revenue is a fairly constant proportion of total revenue. This assumes that the proportion of customers (hotel guests and others) using the food and beverage venues, and their spending, will be a constant. In this case, using a comparison, food and beverage revenue is assumed to be 29% of total sales.[4,5]

The heuristic method, although it does involve estimates based on similar experiences and operations, is nevertheless comparable to the method of calculating food and beverage from basics, because the latter method must also involve estimates. The quality of the statistics derived from using the heuristic method depends upon the reality/validity of the informed guesswork involved.

Other Revenue Categories

Conference revenue

Conference revenue is a category that is linked with the analysis, and the competitor survey, that were part of the market survey. The projections of growth in demand and number of guests—the composite growth figure—will be an indicator of the likely revenue from conferences and conventions and, if not shown separately, will generally be included in food and beverage revenue.

Telephone revenue

Telephone revenue is usually a constant related to the number of guests—particularly business guests. It can be assessed by comparison with other operations. The increasing use of mobile telephones has led to a decline in the use of hotel telephone services and this item of revenue therefore does not have the significance it had in earlier times.

Merchandising revenue

Merchandising revenue, where relevant, should be subject to a separate market analysis, using figures for average tourism expenditure by visitor to the region.

Expense Categories

The largest expense category is payroll—labour charges for wages and salaries, and the associated costs (such as allowances and benefits, leave provisions, payroll taxes and superannuation). As this category (as well as others that follow) is made up of hours worked and rates of pay which are set by common awards in Australia, the overall cost is comparable with other similar operations. Hence, percentage figures from another hotel are used to draw up an income statement.

Some costs vary with the number of guests, or the volume of business. These costs are termed 'variable costs' and are calculated on the basis of total sales—which measures the economic activity of the operation. Payroll costs do not easily fit within this description because some payroll costs vary with the number of guests (such as casual cleaning hours), whereas others are fixed (for example, the enterprise must still pay full-time staff regardless of how many guests might be in the establishment). Payroll costs are best treated as 'mixed' costs—containing both variable and fixed elements.

For food and beverage, there is an item termed 'cost of sales' (also referred to as 'cost of goods sold').[6] This is the material cost of the meals and drinks services. Cost of sales can usually be estimated at approximately 30% of food and beverage revenue (allowing up to 35% as cost of sales of liquor and 25–30% as cost of sales of food). The worked examples in Figures 10.5 and 10.6 (pp 151–2) express costs (for a fictitious establishment known as 'Baker's Inn') as percentages of total sales. Thus, for consistency, cost of sales is expressed as approximately 11% of total sales.

'Other expenses' include miscellaneous costs that can be directly related to that income heading (be it rooms income, or food and beverage income etc.)—such as cleaning materials or the like.

Some expenses are not able to be directly allocated to income headings, and these expenses are therefore referred to as 'undistributed expenses'—in the sense that the amounts included there cannot be divided up among the income headings because the proportion of expense that should be divided and allocated is unclear. For example, marketing for the hotel is an expense that is clearly difficult to divide up and allocate to rooms income or food and beverage—so it is left as one total and is shown under a separate section of expenses.

In this worked example of financial feasibility, the variable expenses are estimated as a percentage of sales, using the comparable 'Baker's Inn' as a guide. Fixed costs related to the capital items (interest, depreciation etc.) are as calculated in the previous chapter. Figure 10.5 (p. 151) is the income statement of Baker's Inn that will be used as a comparison and the source of percentages for each expense category. Figure 10.6 (p. 152) is the statement for the projected operation, using the assumptions drawn from Figure 10.1 (p. 147).

1 Jul. 2001–30 Jun. 2002

Total Sales		$1 306 281	100.0%
Income by Departments:			
Rooms			
Sales	$777 792.00		59.5%
Labour Costs	-$141 571.50		-10.8%
Other Direct Costs	-$64 122.70		-4.9%
Rooms Income	$572 097.80	$572 098	43.8%
Food & Beverage			
Sales	$373 803.40		28.6%
Cost of Sales	-$121 954.20		-9.3%
Labour Costs	-$148 688.50		-11.4%
Other Direct Costs	-$34 300.04		-2.6%
Food & Beverage Income	$68 860.66	$68 860	5.3%
Conference Facility			
Sales	$87 450.00		6.7%
Labour Costs	-$58 040.00		-4.4%
Other Direct Costs	-$39 800.00		-3.0%
Conference Income	-$10 390.00	-$10 390	-0.8%
Telephone			
Sales	$38 445.88		2.9%
Cost of Sales	-$23 425.15		-1.8%
Labour Costs	-$6 519.68		-0.5%
Other Direct Costs	-$1 390.95		-0.1%
Telephone Income	$7 110.10	$7 110	0.5%
Total Departmental Income		$637 678	48.8%
Merchandising, Rentals & Other Income	$28 790.00	$28 790	2.2%
Total Operating Income		**$666 468**	**51.0%**
Undistributed Operating Expenses			
Administrative & General	$97 843.20		7.5%
Marketing	$52 477.50		4.0%
Property Mntce & Operation	$64 893.50		5.0%
Utility Costs	$78 225.60		6.0%
Total Undist. Operating Expenses	$293 439.80	$293 439	22.5%
Income Before Fixed Charges		**$373 029**	**28.6%**
Fixed Charges			
Rates & Charges	$31 633.80		2.4%
Insurance	$51 967.12		4.0%
Depreciation	$52 886.20		4.0%
Interest	$43 894.80		3.4%
Total Fixed Charges	$180 381.92	$180 381	13.8%
Income Before Taxes		**$192 648**	**14.7%**
Income Tax		$75 133	
Net Income		**$117 515**	**9.0%**

Figure 10.5 *Income Statement for 'Baker's Inn' for the Financial Year 2001/2002*

Kevin Baker

New project of 60 units total cost $3 100 000 ($800 000 equity; $2 300 000 loan)
Projected figures assuming 60 units /ADR$95/70% occupancy

	3 months	Year
Total Sales	**$611 800**	**$2 447 200**
Income by Departments:		
Rooms		
Sales	$367 080	$1 468 320
Labour Costs	–$66 074	–$264 298
Other Direct Costs	–$29 978	–$119 913
Rooms Income	$271 027	$1 084 110
Food & Beverage		
Sales	$174 975	$699 899
Cost of Sales	–$56 897	–$227 590
Labour Costs	–$69 745	–$278 981
Other Direct Costs	–$15 907	–$63 627
Food & Beverage Income	$32 425	$129 702
Conference Facility		
Sales	$45 497	$181 988
Labour Costs	–$16 919	–$67 676
Other Direct Costs	–$13 472	–$53 888
Conference Income	$15 106	$60 424
Telephone		
Sales	$24 248	$96 992
Cost of Sales	–$16 974	–$67 894
Labour Costs	–$4 059	–$16 236
Other Direct Costs	–$788	–$3 152
Telephone Income	$2 427	$9 710
Total Departmental Income	$320 986	$1 283 945
Merchandising, Rentals & Other Income	$13 460	$53 838
Total Operating Income	**$334 446**	**$1 337 783**
Undistributed Operating Expenses		
Administrative & General	$45 885	$183 540
Marketing	$40 000	$160 000
Property Mntce & Operation	$10 000	$40 000
Utility Costs	$39 500	$158 000
Total Undist. Operating Expenses	$135 385	$541 540
Income Before Fixed Charges	**$199 061**	**$796 243**
Fixed Charges		
Rates & Charges	$15 000	$60 000
Insurance	$26 250	$105 000
Depreciation	61 500	$246 000
*Interest	46 000	$184 000
Total Fixed Charges	148 750	$595 000
Income Before Taxes	**$50 311**	**$201 243**
Tax at 39%	$19 621	$78 485
Net Income	**$30 690**	**$122 758**

* Interest is 8% on $2 300 000 loan

Figure 10.6 *Projected Income for New Operation—70% Occupancy*

Kevin Baker

Room Revenue/Occupancy Variances

Start-up Period

A crucial mistake that many authors of financial feasibility projections make is to assume that the operation will achieve a satisfactory occupancy from the first day of operations. In real life, of course, any lodging property, even a franchise, will require a variable period of operation before it is well known and has developed a clientele.

It is a rule of thumb that the smaller the operation, the longer it will take to become known and to achieve a satisfactory level of operations. It is a similar truism that the smaller the property the less likely it is to have a depth of capital support—'deep pockets'—that will allow it to operate at low levels of occupancy until it is established.

Greene suggests that there is an:

> . . . old formula that you lose money in the first year of a new hotel, break even in the second and move into a surplus in the third year.
>
> Greene (1993)[7]

With regard to restaurants, they:

> . . . do well in the opening three months when a lot of people try them out and they receive opening publicity. Then they decline and steadily build up over the next year, depending on how good they are and on their marketing.
>
> Greene (1993)[7]

Those who are experienced in the particular market have to make an estimate of the time period required for a buildup to anticipated normal operating capacity. This time period might be six months, a year, or even longer. For the sake of the example, it is assumed that the new project will have, on average, 40% occupancy for the first three months, and 55% for the next six months—after which the development will have achieved its anticipated occupancy of 70%.

On the basis of these assumptions, Figure 10.7 (p. 154) indicates that the new project will make a loss for its first year—in contrast to the favourable statistics for a full year of operation at 70% occupancy presented in Figure 10.6 (p. 152).

New motel of 60 units at average room rate $92 per night
First 12 mths operation—start-up period
Projected figures for: 40% occupancy first 3 mths; 55% next 6 mths; 70% next 3 mths

	First 3 mths 40% occup.	4–9 mths 55% occup.	10–12 mths 70% occup.
Total Sales	$349 600	$945 725	$611 800
Income by Departments:			
Rooms			
Sales	$209 760	$567 435	$367 080
Labour Costs	-$37 757	-$102 138	-$66 074
Other Direct Costs	-$17 130	-$46 341	-$29 978
Rooms Income	$154 873	$418 956	$271 027
Food & Beverage			
Sales	$99 986	$270 477	$174 975
Cost of Sales	-$32 513	-$87 952	-$56 897
Labour Costs	-$39 854	-$107 813	-$69 745
Other Direct Costs	-$9 090	-$24 589	-$15 907
Food & Beverage Income	$18 529	$50 123	$32 425
Conference Facility			
Sales	$14 275	$31 222	$45 497
Labour Costs	-$7 055	-$9 864	-$16 919
Other Direct Costs	-$4 495	-$8 977	-$13 472
Conference Income	-$2 725	$12 381	$15 106
Telephone			
Sales	$13 585	$41 667	$24 248
Cost of Sales	-$9 510	-$29 167	-$16 974
Labour Costs	-$2 048	-$5 729	-$4 059
Other Direct Costs	-$680	-$1 358	-$788
Telephone Income	$1 348	$5 413	$2 427
Total Departmental Income	$177 474	$486 874	$320 986
Merchandising, Rentals & Other Income	$7 691	$20 806	$13 460
Total Operating Income	**$185 165**	**$507 680**	**$334 446**
Undistributed Operating Expenses			
Administrative & General	$26 220	$70 929	$45 885
Marketing	$75 000	$100 000	$40 000
Property Mntce & Operation	$10 000	$20 000	$10 000
Utility Costs	$39 500	$79 000	$39 500
Total Undist. Operating Expenses	$150 720	$269 929	$135 385
Income Before Fixed Charges	**$34 445**	**$237 750**	**$199 061**
Fixed Charges			
Rates & Charges	$15 000	$30 000	$15 000
Insurance	$26 250	$52 500	$26 250
Depreciation	$61 500	$123 000	$61 500
Interest	46 000	$92 000	$46 000
Total Fixed Charges	$148 750	$297 500	$148 750
Income Before Taxes	**-$114 305**	**-$59 750**	**$50 311**
Income Tax			
Net Income	**-$114 305**	**-$59 750**	**$50 311**

Figure 10.7 Projected Income for New Operation—Developing Occupancy

Kevin Baker

Seasonal Variances

The market feasibility assessment should have indicated major fluctuations in seasonal demand. For projects in resort areas, occupancy might be estimated at 80–90% at peak times, and as low as 20–30% in the off season. Occupancy varies, and usually rates vary as well.

CASE STUDY
Seasonal Variances

The small town of Kaitaia is the northernmost town in New Zealand. It is sometimes referred to as 'the winter-less north' and attracts tourists for its climate, and also because it offers motel and hotel accommodation for those proceeding on to Cape Reinga—the northern tip of New Zealand. The accommodation market is seasonal because, in winter, travelling to the far north of New Zealand is less attractive.

There is another attraction in Kaitaia and the surrounding region, and this attraction is even more seasonal in nature. There is a large shellfish (called a 'toheroa') that is found in only a few coastal areas, including Kaitaia. This shellfish can be baked or fried into a dish of unique taste. Harvesting the toheroa is strictly controlled to maintain its numbers, and a very limited quantity is canned and exported. The toheroa season extends for only a few months—beginning in September and concluding in March.

The accommodation market in Kaitaia therefore experiences high occupancies from October to March—peaking over the Christmas public holiday period. Some motels and restaurants will close for six months of the year. Any new tourism development in Kaitaia that did not take into account the toheroa season would increase the risk of inaccurate market/financial projections.

Based on Robbins & Mukerji (1994)[8]

The financial feasibility projection should be recalculated in as many time sections as necessary—when demand might vary significantly. The recalculations might include peak demand periods and off-peak demand periods, including 'shoulder periods' (that is, short periods of change between peak and off-peak). The financial projections might even be presented with occupancy figures that vary from month to month (in similar fashion to Figure 10.7, p. 154, in which occupancy was calculated at different percentages in the first four quarters of operation). In most cases in which occupancy varies, the fixed costs will remain the same, and the variable costs (the direct operating expenses) continue to be calculated as percentages of volume.

The variable costs will not always be the same percentage of revenue in dollar terms because, at peak periods, the market might support higher rates, and variable costs will therefore be a lesser percentage of revenue. For this reason, variable costs for developments subject to high-peak demand are best related to room-nights—rather than total sales or revenue dollars.

Marketing Strategies

The analysis of competitors (Chapter 4) considered the strengths and weaknesses of other players in the market place. It is likely that competitors will take action to maintain or improve their market share in the face of the new competition. The new development will have to match competitors' strategies—unless it has a clearly superior product at a better price. Most marketing strategies will have financial implications.

One strategy is to market the new development more aggressively. This will require an expanded budget for marketing/public relations/advertising. Within projections for revenue/expense, there might need to be provision for contingency marketing campaigns.

A *second strategy* is substantial discounting of the product. This can be done through the use of 'opening specials' which are marketed to attract attention, as well as to boost occupancy in the initial operating period. The revenue projections could be adjusted to account for best-case/worst-case scenarios of discounting. The average room-rate can be reworked, with an adjustment to occupancy—so that, at least, variable costs are covered (in the short term).

CASE STUDY
Discounting — the 'Novotel Phuket Resort', Thailand

The tourist accommodation market on the island of Phuket in southern Thailand is seasonal and extremely competitive—having 400 hotels and accommodation facilities. The 'Novotel Phuket Resort' is a property with 210 rooms in Patong, which has one of the more popular beaches on the island.

For five months of the year, the 'Novotel Phuket' achieves in excess of 90% occupancy over the peak season, attracting mainly international tourists. From April, however, the demand falls off as the hottest time of the year approaches. From May to September, the hotel offers discount rates of up to 50% to guests in order to maintain its market share.

Working Capital

The new venture must have sufficient funds for working capital, and this forms part of the financial feasibility study. Working capital comprises those funds needed for the property to operate—paying expenses, and purchasing assets such as stock—while waiting for revenue to be received. The need for working capital arises because, in the nature of business, stock must be purchased before it can be sold, and wages must be paid even before credit customers pay their accounts.

Working capital is defined in accounting terms as current assets less current liabilities. *Current assets* are those items purchased for use in the business and normally turned over within twelve months—such items as cash, accounts receivable, inventories and prepaid expenses. These are listed on the balance sheet of the operation. *Current liabilities* include legal obligations—such as accounts payable, accrued expenses, and the current portion of loans.[9]

Therefore, the budget for the project must include an amount to be utilised for working capital. This can be estimated by comparison with a similar operation (again, the fictitious 'Baker's Inn'). Deducting the current liabilities from the current assets of 'Baker's Inn' indicates that the development should allow at least $120 000 for working capital.

Figure 10.8 (p. 158) indicates that the proposed operation has $257 696 in current assets and $134 839 in current liabilities—a difference of $122 857. In other words, the enterprise has sufficient liquid funds on hand to meet current commitments as they fall due.

Other Tourism Ventures

Restaurants

Revenue/expense projections for restaurants can be compiled in the same way as the projections for hotel food and beverage operations detailed above in this chapter (pp 146–9).

Revenue projections are based on estimates for seat turnover and average check for each meal period, as well as on the number of seats and days of opening. Expense projections can be made by direct calculation (for example, starting from the staffing schedule), or by rule of thumb (for example using a common percentage for cost of sales for food and for beverage), or by comparison with similar operations.

Restaurant revenue/expense relativities will vary according to the range of services offered. A restaurant with a limited menu and no table service, and serving food but not alcoholic beverages (such as a burger bar or the like), will have a different cost structure from that of a restaurant offering a full menu and table service, serving food and beverages. The burger bar will seek a high turnover, offering low margins because of the nature of the competition, with a lower cost of sales than a venture offering *haute cuisine*.

Another method of compiling revenue/expense projections is to set standard costs for labour and for material costs for each meal, and to set budgets for other items—such as entertainment or marketing. However, this method is best used for budgeting for existing operations because, with a new project, there are obviously no existing benchmarks on which to base the standards.

ASSETS

Current Assets

Cash on Hand and at Bank		$17 703
Marketable Securities		$30 395
Accounts Receivable	$170 765	
Less: Provision for Bad Debts	$5 948	$164 817
Inventories		$32 799
Prepaid Expenses		$11 982

Total Current Assets	**$257 696**
Investments	**$118 231**

Fixed Assets

Tableware, Linen, Uniforms		$10 756
Furniture and Fittings	$58 568	
Less: Provision for Depreciation	$16 346	$42 222
Plant and Equipment	$83 087	
Less: Provision for Depreciation	$24 519	$58 568
Land and Buildings	$964 545	
Less: Provision for Depreciation	$230 047	$734 498
Land		$400 000

Total Fixed Assets	**$1 246 044**
TOTAL ASSETS	**$1 621 971**

LIABILITIES AND OWNERS' EQUITY

Current Liabilities

Accounts Payable	$50 395
Accrued Expenses	$18 076
Deposits in Advance	$7 800
Current Portion: Mortgage	$58 568
Total Current Liabilities	**$134 839**

Long-term Liabilities

Mortgage Payable	$348 710
TOTAL LIABILITIES	**$483 549**

Owners' Equity

Ordinary Shares	$850 000
Share Premium Reserve	$95 000
Retained Earnings	$193 423
TOTAL OWNERS' EQUITY	**$1 138 423**
TOTAL LIABILITIES AND OWNERS' EQUITY	**$1 621 971**

Figure 10.8 *Balance Sheet for 'Baker's Inn Pty Ltd' as at 1 July 2001*

Kevin Baker

Figure 10.9 is an example of a schedule for salaries and wages for a large restaurant with full menu and table service, serving food and beverages.[10] It can be used to calculate likely wages costs. Figure 10.10 (p. 160) is an example of an income statement for the same type of restaurant, dividing expenses up into categories as percentages of sales, so that new projects can estimate likely costs to be incurred for cleaning, maintenance and so on.

	Wage Costs ($)	Sub-total ($)	Total ($)	% of Total Labour Costs
Service				
Waiters	88 456.80			
Bartenders	28 745.00	117 201.80		32.9%
Food Preparation				
Chef/Cook	45 724.30			
Kitchen Assistants	67 107.20	112 831.50		31.6%
Cleaning				
Cleaners	36 194.30	36 194.30		10.1%
Total Controllable Wages Costs		**266 227.60**	**266 227.60**	**74.7%**
Employee Benefits				
Public Holiday/Leave	9 733.99			
Superannuation	15 973.66	25 707.65	25 707.65	7.2%
Marketing				
Part-time salary incl. benefits	10 965.00	10 965.00	10 965.00	3.1%
Administrative				
Clerical incl. benefits	18 230.80			
Manager/Owner	35 500.00	53 730.80	53 730.80	15.1%
TOTAL LABOUR COSTS			**356 631.05**	**100.0%**

Figure 10.9 Schedule of Labour Costs for 'Baker's Restaurant' for 1 July 2001–30 June 2002

Kevin Baker

Comparative Income Statements for the years ending 30 June 2000 and 30 June 2001

		2000	%	2001	%
Sales	Food	$572 860	66.9%	$649 750	63.6%
	Beverage	$283 500	33.1%	$371 750	36.4%
Total Sales		$856 360	100.0%	$1 021 500	100.0%
Less: Cost of Sales	Food	$276 360	32.3%	$260 950	25.5%
	Beverage	$154 065	18.0%	$166 325	16.3%
Total Cost of Sales		$430 425	50.3%	$427 275	41.8%
GROSS PROFIT		$425 935	49.7%	$594 225	58.2%
Less: Controllable Expenses	Wages & Salaries	$291 375	34.0%	$336 020	32.9%
	Administrative	$60 165	7.0%	$65 765	6.4%
	Marketing	$2 250	0.3%	$16 650	1.6%
	Other Direct Expenses	$28 800	3.4%	$33 900	3.3%
Total Controllable Expenses		$382 590	44.7%	$452 335	44.3%
INCOME BEFORE FIXED EXPENSES		$43 345	5.1%	$141 890	13.9%
Fixed Expenses	Depreciation	$7 650	0.9%	$6 930	0.7%
	Interest	$11 430	1.3%	$12 240	1.2%
Total Fixed Expenses		$19 080	2.2%	$19 170	1.9%
Income Before Tax		$24 265	2.8%	$122 720	12.0%
Tax		$9 463	1.1%	$47 861	4.7%
NET INCOME		$14 802	1.7%	$74 859	7.3%

Figure 10.10 Sample Financial Statements 'Central Tourist Restaurant'

Kevin Baker

Other Ventures

The range of tourism ventures is, of course, much larger than the lodging property sector. For non-lodging properties, the rules outlined above in this chapter still apply. If revenue and expenses can be calculated in detail in terms of the input and outputs of the specific operation, this can lead to accurate estimates—but the estimates will be only as accurate as the assumptions behind the calculations. If there are comparable operations to use as a benchmark, it is simpler and quicker to use these—although at greater risk of inaccuracy.

A Last Word

A tourism operation is not a philanthropic foundation—it exists to make a profit. If a development cannot make a profit, there is no point in going ahead.

CHECKLIST # 10
REVENUE/EXPENSE
ASPECTS

- Recorded all revenue (including one-off sales, complimentary and other income)?

- Excluded non-revenue (for example, deposits and advances)?

- Recorded all expenses (including accounting/banking, commissions, maintenance, travel, insurance etc.)?

- Excluded capital costs?

- Referred revenue/expenses to benchmarks (for example industry averages)?

Chapter 10 ■ Review and Questions

1 Indicate whether the following statements are true or false and give a reason for your answer:

a Pre-opening expenses should be accounted for during the initial operating period. (True/False? Why?)

b Average room rate cannot be estimated until the property has been operating for a period. (True/False? Why?)

c Some authors state that food and beverage outlets do not receive quality analysis of their operations. (True/False? Why?)

    d An analyst should assume that most hotel guests will use food-and-beverage outlets on the property rather than leaving the hotel to go elsewhere. (True/False? Why?)

    e 'Cost of sales' covers the material cost of meals and drinks only. (True/False? Why?)

2 Insert the word(s) that best completes each of the following, selecting your answers from the following possibilities:

variable; invariable; derived demand; elasticity of demand; conservatism; materiality; payroll; the manager.

    a The likely demand for room service is sometimes referred to as . . .

    b The accounting doctrine of . . . states that it is preferable to understate a revenue item rather than to overstate it.

    c The largest expense category in a hotel is . . .

    d The costs that vary with the number of guests or volume of business are described as . . . costs.

3 Discuss the following in one or two sentences (for each statement):

    a A hotel is in the accommodation business, so it is best for the hotelier to contract out food and beverage outlets wherever possible.

    b Calculating the total number of restaurant customers is a better measure of performance than calculating the average check.

    c It is cheaper and quicker to use 'rule-of-thumb' measures rather than go to the expense of revenue-and-expense calculations.

4 Analyse and discuss the following:

Many estimates of likely revenues, and therefore profitability, are over-optimistic because analysts are pressured to produce favourable figures so that the owners/developers can use those figures to raise finance and to muster support for the project.

A Sample Project

BUILDING A BETTER BARBECUE

Some pitfalls to avoid when constructing a new hospitality venture!

Figure 10.12 *Make Sure There Are Adequate Services*

Kevin Baker (after the style of Giles)

Chapter 10 Notes

[1] Turkel, S. 1995, 'Executive Forum', *Hotel and Motel Management*, 6 November 1995, p. 42.

[2] Payne, K. 1996, 'Executive Forum', *Hotel & Motel Management*, 18 March 1996, p. 42.

[3] This calculation is explained in various accounting texts, such as Coltman, M. 1998, *Hospitality Management Accounting*, 6th edn, pp 381ff, Van Nostrand Reinhold: New York.

[4] This percentage is drawn from sample income statements in *Bottomline*, October/November 1991, p. 16.

[5] Horwath & Horwath 1998, *Survey of Operations, Australia and New Zealand Hotel Industry*, Horwath International, Worldwide Hotel Industry: New York.

[6] The term 'cost of sales' is preferred here in order to conform to the uniform system of accounts.

[7] Greene, M. 1993, 'Let's be Feasible', *Caterer & Hotelkeeper*, 4 March 1993, p. 37.

[8] Based on a case study in Robbins, S. & Mukerji, D. 1994, *Managing Organisations—New Challenges and Perspectives*, 2nd edn, pp 131–2, Prentice Hall of Australia Pty Ltd: Sydney.

[9] For an extended treatment of working capital, refer to Coltman, M. 1998, *Hospitality Management Accounting*, 6th edn, pp 413ff, Van Nostrand Reinhold: New York.

[10] Based on an example presented in National Restaurant Association 1990, *Uniform System of Accounts for Restaurants*, 6th edn, p. 79, National Restaurant Association: Washington.

CHAPTER 11

Capital Budgeting and the Business Plan

Synopsis of Chapter

This chapter returns to aspects of capital investment in the proposed development and its initial operation—in order to prepare schedules of construction cost/cash flow, to determine borrowing requirements over time, and to assess financial feasibility in terms of return on investment and comparison with other possible investment projects.

The business draws together the financial information determined by the examination of capital costs, and projected revenue/expense statements, and adds the timing factor. The timing of cash inflows and outflows, both during construction and during operation, must be calculated so that investors can determine when funds must be injected into the venture, and when funds can be drawn out as profits.

The overall plan, including cash-flow forecasts, constitutes the business plan and indicates how the investors/owners will meet commitments as they arise.

The business plan and returns on the investment can also be analysed using evaluation tools, including 'rule-of-thumb' methods, computer analysis, formal accounting rates of return (such as the payback method), and cash-flow analysis techniques (net present value, internal rate of return). Taxes might also have an effect on the return to investors.

This analysis allows the analysts to make recommendations on the feasibility of the project—and to support those recommendations with key data.

An Extra Dimension

The final section of the project evaluation reviews much of the material that has already been collected and analysed, and places a timeline on the activities. Capital budgeting considers not only amounts to be invested, but also when they will be committed. It also considers not only how much will be returned on the investment, but also when the returns will be received.

The business plan marries this analysis with the marketing strategy—what the developers are seeking to achieve, and when and how they will implement their strategy.

Strategies work out as planned only when implemented effectively.

McCarthy et al. (1994)[1]

The capital investment analysis and the business plan (which will include aspects of the former) map out where the operation is going. The business plan will also be used by management for operational decisions—if the developer chooses to go ahead with the project on the basis of the project evaluation. It will serve as a 'blueprint' to enable decision-makers to utilise the opportunities that they believe exist in the market place.[2]

Assessing the Capital Investment—Capital Budgeting

There are many definitions of capital budgeting. Dobbins and Pike describe capital budgeting as:

The art of finding assets that are worth more than they cost.

Dobbins & Pike (1988)[3]

Horngren and Foster see it as:

. . . the making of long-term planning decisions for investments and their financing.

Horngren & Foster (1991)[4]

Investment planning is a part of the strategic planning process.

Horngren and Foster believe that there are four stages in capital budgeting, namely:[5]

1 Analysing the quantitative/financial aspects of the project, which consist of:
   a discounted cash flow (both net present value, and internal rate of return);
   b payback; and
   c accrual accounting rate of return (ROR).
2 Analysing the quantitative/non-financial, and the qualitative aspects of the project.
3 Financing the project—sources of financing include internally generated cash, the equity-security capital market, and the debt-security capital market.
4 Implementing the project and monitoring its performance—in some cases including a post-decision audit in which the predictions are compared with subsequent outcomes.

Are these tools and practices commonly used for assessments of hospitality projects? There has been a number of studies of capital budgeting in the hospitality industry—notably by Eyster and Geller (1981),[6] and by Schmidgall and Damitio (1990).[7] These studies indicated that corporations in the hospitality industry did not make proper use of capital-budgeting techniques—although Schmidgall and Damitio did find that some discounted cash-flow techniques (see below) were more commonly used in 1990 than they had been used ten years earlier. These studies suggest that there is room for improvement in the way that feasibility studies are prepared for new projects in the hospitality industry.

Capital Budgeting in the Context of Strategic Planning

Dobbins and Pike assert that:

> Investment planning is an integral part of the wider processes of strategic planning and budgetary control.
>
> Dobbins & Pike (1988)[8]

Rather than generate investment proposals on an *ad hoc* basis, companies should choose projects on the basis of how they fit in with the firm's strategic plans and corporate objectives. If there were no financial objective, there would be no criteria for choosing between alternative investment strategies and projects.

The Context of the Investment Decision

In Chapter 2, we considered the birth of a concept, and how to scan the possibilities and restraints of a new project.

The screening stage determined which opportunities were worthy of further investigation, but did not undertake a detailed analysis of individual opportunities. That is the role of the project evaluation. The types of broad assessments which have to be made include:

- whether the opportunity fits with the corporate objectives;
- whether the required resources are available;
- whether the idea is technologically possible;
- whether similar ideas have been successful (or unsuccessful) elsewhere (and why); and
- what is the likely relationship between risk and return.

At the stage when we were defining the project in some detail, both the technical aspects of the project (project life, capital required, etc.), and the cash flows, needed to be specified. Having done this, we need to be concerned with the formal evaluation of the project under consideration. The present chapter will detail the various methods of carrying out this step.

Cash Flows at Different Times

The occupancy projections for the proposed hotel included assumptions of the period required to build up the operation to full capacity. This affected the revenue/ expense projections and, clearly, it will also influence the cash flow. In addition, the cash flow will be affected by the time needed to receive payments from the first guests (this will be provided-for through the amount of working capital).

Thus, there will be four important components of the cash-flow statement:

- development costs (which were considered in Chapter 9);
- revenue projections (which, with expenses, were considered in Chapter 10);
- operating expense projections; and
- the timing and amounts of finance payments (these also were looked at in Chapter 9).

The present chapter looks at the cash flow in more detail—especially its link with the business plan. The cash flow should be presented in three versions:

- for the first three months (with cash flow presented monthly or weekly);
- for the first year (with cash flow presented monthly); and
- for the first five years of operation (with the cash-flow estimates presented quarterly—that is, each three-month period).

Figures 11.1, 11.2 (p. 169) and 11.3 (p. 170) are examples of cash-flow statements for these three time periods.

Refer also to Figure 10.7 (p. 154).

	Month 1	Month 2	Month 3	Total
Balance Brought Forward	$0	–$74 666	–$129 591	$0
Income Statement Surplus/Loss	–$50 076	–$38 963	–$25 266	–$114 305
Add back Depreciation	$20 500	$20 500	$20 500	$61 500
Increase Acct Receivable*	–$39 156	–$33 122	–$30 170	–$102 448
Increase Inventories*	–$11 170	–$8 790	–$1 820	–$21 780
Increase Prepaid Expenses*	–$7 904	–$1 160	$5 954	–$3 110
Increase Accounts Payable*	$13 140	$6 610	–$4 545	$15 205
Cash Flow from Operations	–$74 666	–$54 925	–$35 347	–$164 938
Balance Carried Forward	–$74 666	–$129 591	–$164 938	

* These figures would be drawn from the balance sheet.

Figure 11.1 *Cash Flow for the First Three Months of the Project*

Kevin Baker

	1st Qtr	2nd Qtr	3rd Qtr	4th Qtr	Total
Balance Brought Forward	0	-$164 938	-$185 222	-$173 196	0
Income Statement Surplus/Loss	-$114 305	-$41 412	-$18 338	$50 311	-$123 744
Add back Depreciation	$61 500	$61 500	$61 500	$61 500	$246 000
Increase Acct Receivable*	-$102 448	-$37 187	-$28 555	-$22 140	-$190 330
Increase Inventories*	-$21 780	-$8 920	-$6 300	-$2 367	-$39 367
Increase Prepaid Expenses*	-$3 110	-$808	$1 432	$630	-$1 856
Increase Accounts Payable*	$15 205	$6 543	$2 287	-$1 239	$22 796
Cash Flow from Operations	-$164 938	-$20 284	$12 026	$86 695	-$86 501
Balance Carried Forward	-$164 938	-$185 222	-$173 196	-$86 501	

*These figures would be drawn from the balance sheet.

Figure 11.2 Cash Flow for the First Year of the Project

Kevin Baker

It is true that there is uncertainty regarding the timing and amount of cash flow but, nevertheless, the analysis must be made. There are computer-modelling packages available that can assist with the development of cash-flow statements allowing for changes to timing and amounts received.

The cash-flow statements are crucial because they reveal that, although the cash deficit for the first year is $86 501, the cash shortfall will, in fact, peak at a higher figure. Due to commitments in the first months of the operation, the cash shortfall will reach nearly $165 000.

Note that there are some important differences between calculating profit and calculating cash surplus/deficits. Depreciation is added back to the bottom-line figure of the income statement because it is not an item relating to the actual expenditure of cash. Other items that do not feature on the income statement but appear on the balance sheet—such as the increase/decrease in accounts receivable, accounts payable and inventories—can be significant to the cash position.

Having determined the inflow and outflow of cash, the next step is to assess the need to arrange financing to cover cash deficits. This is the business plan which covers the initial periods of the operation.

Assume 5% increase in surplus each year from year 2

	1st Year	2nd Year	3rd Year	4th Year	5th Year
Income Statement					
Surplus/Loss	–$123 744	$122 758	$128 895	$135 340	$142 107
Add back					
Depreciation	$246 000	$246 000	$246 000	$246 000	$246 000
Increase Acct					
Receivable*	–$190 330	–$10 000	0	0	0
Increase					
Inventories*	–$39 367	–$5 000	0	0	0
Increase					
Prepaid Expenses*	–$1 856	0	0	0	0
Increase					
Accounts Payable*	$22 796	$5 000	0	0	0
Cash Flow					
from Operations	–$86 501	$358 758	$374 895	$381 340	$388 107
Balance Brought					
Forward	0	–$86 501	$272 257	$647 152	$1 028 492
Balance Carried					
Forward	–$86 501	$272 257	$647 152	$1 028 492	$1 416 599

* These figures would be drawn from the balance sheet.

Figure 11.3 Cash Flow for the First Five Years of the Project

Kevin Baker

The Business Plan in Detail

All the above calculations—showing capital budget, occupancy assumptions, revenue/expense statements, rate of return calculations and cash flow over three months, one year and five years—can be summarised in the business plan.

The business plan has three main purposes:

- to assist top levels of management to develop their strategy;
- to place the budgets in context; and
- to provide 'an instrument for monitoring ongoing progress and making corrections during the plan's implementation'.[9]

The business plan, as a crucial section of the project evaluation, is also important for such purposes as raising finance.

CASE STUDY
Where Timing is Crucial

The five-star 'Regent Hotel' in Sydney was closed temporarily for renovation and refurbishment. The hotel was reducing its 594 rooms to 531 in order to enlarge and upgrade its accommodation. The renovation took 90 days and cost $50 million. The timing of the renovation was crucial from three aspects.

First, the hotel sacrificed approximately 35 000 room-nights—which meant $7 million in revenue (and guests being directed towards competitors' properties).

Secondly, the 780 full-time and casual staff were not be made redundant but were maintained on full pay—being required to take training courses and utilise two weeks' annual leave. Hence, every day that the development went over schedule invoked high costs in staff pay without corresponding revenue.

Thirdly, four more five-star hotels were under construction in Sydney—the 'Westin', the 'Merchant Court Hotel', the 'Le Meridien', and the 'Radisson Plaza'.

The owners of the 'Regent' wanted to have their refurbishment completed well before new competitors opened their doors. Of the three above factors, only one (staff costs) would appear in the cash-flow projections—although the absence of revenue would have an indirect effect.

Based on *Sydney Morning Herald* (8 March 1999)[10]

The business plan will be an important document if the decision-makers decide to implement the proposed project. As a strategic plan, incorporating objectives and goals (such as desired occupancy, and required rate of return over time), it will also serve as a tool of evaluation, and an instrument for monitoring progress. The five-year plan forecasts cash flow and income for each of the five years, and provides details of the sources of finance or additional equity that will be necessary to cover the deficits of the cash flow—especially during the important establishment period. It includes the payments to investors—referred to as 'dividends' in the case of a company.

The business plan allows a reasonable period for even a unique product to prove its worth. It also provides a reasonable basis of comparison with other investment alternatives that could produce short-run returns but not long-term opportunities.[11]

Examples of statistics from business plans (incorporating cash-flow data as above) for the first year, and for the first five years, are shown in Figures 11.4 (p. 172) and 11.5 (p. 173) respectively.

	1st Qtr	2nd Qtr	3rd Qtr	4th Qtr	Total
Balance Brought Forward	0	62	–$284	$2 026	0
Income Statement Surplus/Loss	–$114 305	–$41 412	–$18 338	$50 311	–$123 744
Add back Depreciation	$61 500	$61 500	$61 500	$61 500	$246 000
Increase Acct Receivable*	–$102 448	–$37 187	–$28 555	–$22 140	–$190 330
Increase Inventories*	–$21 780	–$8 920	–$6 300	–$2 367	–$39 367
Increase Prepaid Expenses*	–$3 110	–$808	$1 432	$630	–$1 856
Increase Accounts Payable*	$15 205	$6 543	$2 287	–$1 239	$22 796
Cash Flow from Operations	–$164 938	–$20 284	$12 026	$86 695	–$86 501
Cash Flow from Financing	$165 000	$20 000	–$10 000	–$85 000	$90 000
Balance Carried Forward	$62	–$284	$2 026	$1 695	$3 499

* These figures would be drawn from the balance sheet.

Figure 11.4 *Business Plan for the First Year of the Project*

Kevin Baker

A full business plan can also include such matters as staffing, naming key executives and their roles, themes to be developed, and even the way the properties will be furnished.[12] Aspects of these topics have already been covered.

The business plan, if well designed and thought out, can take the project along the road to success, but it must have a proviso. Because the plan is a forecast, users must recognise that there is no magic crystal ball that can foresee the future with infallible accuracy. Chapter 4 considered aspects of market growth and included the worst-case/best-case scenario. This scenario could also be included in the business plan—with comment on financing implications and options to cover the alternative situations outlined in the scenario.

> Plans must take into account unforeseeable changes within the company and the environmental forces and allow for corresponding changes to occur in implementing the plans.
>
> Czinkota & Ronkainen (1995)[13]

It almost seems as if the authors of a business plan must attempt the impossible! However, with reasoned analysis and good research, the plan can go a long way towards describing what is possible and achievable.

Assume 5% increase in surplus each year from Year 2

	1st Year	2nd Year	3rd Year	4th Year	5th Year
Income Statement					
Surplus/Loss	-$123 744	$122 758	$128 895	$135 340	$142 107
Add back					
Depreciation	$246 000	$246 000	$246 000	$246 000	$246 000
Increase Acct					
Receivable*	-$190 330	-$10 000	0	0	0
Increase					
Inventories*	-$39 367	-$5 000	0	0	0
Increase Prepaid					
Expenses*	-$1 856	0	0	0	0
Increase					
Accounts Payable*	$22 796	$5 000	0	0	0
Cash Flow					
from Operations	-$86 501	$358 758	$374 895	$381 340	$388 107
Cash Flow					
from Financing	$90 000	-$90 000			
Dividends					
payable	0	-$30 000	-$130 000	-$135 000	-$140 000
Net Cash					
Inflow/(outflow)	$3 499	$238 758	$244 895	$246 340	$248 107
Balance Brought					
Forward	0	$3 499	$242 257	$487 152	$733 492
Balance Carried					
Forward	$3 499	$242 257	$487 152	$733 492	$981 599

* These figures would be drawn from the balance sheet.

Figure 11.5 *Business Plan for the First Five Years of the Project*

Kevin Baker

Methods of Capital Project Evaluation

Having presented projections of cash flow and plans for financing and dividends, the report should also include some analytical tools. Such tools allow formal comparisons between projects. There is a wide range of analytical methods available.

A 'Rule-of-Thumb' Method

A common measure of evaluation in the hospitality industry is to use what are called 'rule-of-thumb' methods. One such is the 'dollar-per-thousand' method. The analyst simply assesses whether the project will allow the management to charge one dollar of average daily rate for every one thousand dollars invested in a room.

For example, if the project has 120 rooms, and has a total cost of $18 million, the method divides the cost by the rooms—and the answer is $150 000. Charging one dollar for every thousand invested in this room gives an average daily rate of $150.

As a quick and simple method, it has some advantages, and it is based upon the experience of operators who have spent many years in the hospitality industry. However, like all methods based upon past experience rather than current market conditions, it might not always be valid.

Some writers suggest that if this rule-of-thumb method is still applied, it should be at least $1.33 per $1000 invested, and not the simple round figure of one dollar.[14]

Although such methods can provide indicators of likely returns, it is better to use more formal financial methods—especially if the project evaluation will be used for the purpose of raising finance.

Computer Packages

Formal financial modelling could be used more in the hospitality industry—given the large capital investments involved. It could be that some of the mathematics involved is daunting. However, there are computer packages that can run such things as linear-regression models to provide financial outcomes in a number of scenarios. One such computer simulation model is the 'Monte Carlo' simulation, which can estimate a range of possible outcomes for a capital investment scenario. This program can run 10 000 iterations in a few minutes on a personal computer.[15]

The computer package is not a magic answer, for the analyst must still make assessments about the information to input into the simulation, and must have the expertise to assess the resultant range of information.

Accounting Rates of Return

Accounting rates of return are quantitative measures which basically compare the accounting profit returned from an investment with various other statistics. There are several alternative terms which are in common usage, including 'return on capital employed', 'rate of return on assets', 'accounting return on investment' and 'book-value method'.

To calculate returns from the worked example of the construction of a new motel using the data from Chapter 10 in Figures 10.2 and 10.3 (p. 147), several ratios can be used. Figure 11.6 (p. 175) illustrates some of these, using measures of profitability and also solvency (that is, the ability to pay financial commitments as they fall due).

The 60-unit project presented in Chapter 10 (using Year 2 data)

Profitability Ratios

Return on Investment	Net Income ÷ Owner's Investment	$122 758 ÷ $800 000	15.3% per year
Profit Margin	Net Income ÷ Total revenue	$122 758 ÷ $2 447 200	5.0% per year
Return on Assets	Net Income ÷ Average Total Assets*	$122 758 ÷ ($3 320 000 + $3 335 000/2)	3.7% per year

*Calculate as $3 100 000 plus Acct Receivable etc., around $220 000+ $15 000 Refer to Figs 11.2 and 11.3

Solvency Ratios

Times Interest Earned	EBIT* ÷ Interest Expense	$385 243 ÷ $134 000	2.1 times
Cash Flow to Current Liabilities	Cash Flow from Operations ÷ Average Current Liabilities**	$358 758 ÷ $134 000	2.7 times

* Earnings before interest & tax. Refer Fig. 10.6—to $122 758, add $184 000 interest and $78 485 tax = $385 243.

** Around $24 000 accounts payable and $110 000 current finance

Figure 11.6 Financial Ratios of the 60-Unit Project

Kevin Baker

These accounting rates of return method have the virtues of being easy to understand, simple to calculate, and consistent with the method used to evaluate the performance of firms and divisions using accounting return on investment criteria. The major drawback of the accounting rates of return method is that it ignores the time value of money.

Main (1988) acknowledges the difficulties of evaluating financial feasibility, but insists that 'return on investment' is an indispensable measure. Main has compiled a straightforward return-on-investment model for a typical restaurant.[16]

The Payback Method

This is an alternative method of assessing investment strategies. It can be defined as:

> The period, usually expressed in years, which it takes the cash inflows from a capital investment project to equal the cash outflows.

CIMA (1990)[17]

It means, quite simply, that when a capital investment project is being considered, a frequently asked question will be: How long will it take to pay back its cost?. When the cash flows are uniform, the calculation is simple. It can be expressed as:

> Incremental amount invested (cash outflow) divided by Uniform annual incremental cash inflows from operations.

Figure 11.7 (p. 176) calculates the payback period for the hotel investment.

Payback period of the 60-unit project presented in Chapter 10 (using 5-year data)
Investment: $800 000

Cash Flow from Operations:

	Cash Flow	Cumulative Total
Year 1	–$86 501	–$86 501
Year 2	$358 758	$272 257
Year 3	$374 895	$647 152
Year 4	$381 340	*$1 028 492
Year 5	$388 107	$1 416 599

* The $800 000 payback point is reached in approximately 3.5 years

Figure 11.7 Payback Period of the 60-Unit Project

Kevin Baker

Projects with a shorter payback period will normally be preferred to those with longer payback periods—all other things being equal.

This method also has its drawbacks because its horizon is restricted to one period of time. If two projects, A and B, are being evaluated, the mere fact that A has a shorter payback period than B does not mean that A is preferable.

Assume that the developers have an alternative investment to the proposed hotel. Assume that the alternative costs only $3 000 000, has a ten-year useful life (it is a theme resort on leased land), and will also result in annual net cash flow of $300 000. The payback period of ten years will favour the alternative project. However it has a useful life of only ten years. Thus, its useful life equals its payback period. The first development yields operating income for some years beyond its payback time, and the payback method ignores this.

This example of payback is based on uniform cash flows, but this is rarely the case—particularly when many capital investment projects have a start–up period before returns are significant, or a growth period where occupancy and maximum returns do not reach their maximum for several years (such as in the example in Chapter 10). Almost by definition, capital investment projects would not be expected to produce the same cash flows in the first year of operation as in later years. When cash flows are not uniform, the payback computation takes a cumulative form. Each year's net cash inflows are accumulated until the investment has been recovered.

Discounted Cash-Flow Techniques

The remaining two methods of project evaluation take into consideration the time value of money. Both of them use the 'discounted cash–flow' technique. This is an investment appraisal technique which takes into account both the time value of money and the total profitability over the life of the project.

Discounted cash flow looks at the cash flows of the project—not at the accounting profits. Cash flows are considered because they show the costs and benefits when they occur.

The timing of the cash flows is taken into account by discounting them. The effect of discounting is to place a higher value per $1 for cash flows which occur earlier than others. One dollar received today is worth more than $1 which will not be received until next year—and the reason for this is the reverse of compound interest. (Compound interest is where the interest is calculated on the original investment plus the accumulated interest, as demonstrated below.)

If somebody invests $100 at 10% compound interest for 10 years, at the end of the first year, it will be worth $110—the initial $100 plus the $10 interest earned in year one. At the end of the second year, it will be worth $121—the value at the beginning of the year ($110), plus the interest of $11 (10% of $110). At the end of ten years, the original investment will have grown to $235.

With discounting, the question being asked is: 'How much will I have to invest today at 10% compound interest in order to have $235 in ten years' time?'. The answer is $100—as can be seen from the previous calculation.

The present value of money is the cash equivalent *now* of a sum of money to be received at a future date (discounted at a specified discount rate). These calculations can be done manually, or with calculators which have that function, or the appropriate figures can be drawn from what are called 'present value tables'. Appendix B shows present value tables.

There are two variations of assessing the capital investment using discounted cash-flow techniques—net present value, and internal rate of return.

The Net Present Value (NPV) Method

The net present value (NPV) method is a discounted cash-flow method of calculating the expected net monetary gain or loss from a project by discounting all the expected future cash inflows and outflows to the present point in time—using an estimated interest rate. The steps to calculate the net present value of a project are:

1 List the cash outflows and inflows in the years in which they occur, assuming that cash outflows occur at the beginning of a year and cash inflows are received at the end of a year.
2 From the present value table, select the discount factor for the appropriate discount rate and period of time. Multiply the cash-flow amount by the discount factor.
3 Add up the discounted cash outflows and cash inflows. If the total is zero or positive, it means that the project is returning at least the required rate, and should be accepted. If the total is negative, it indicates that the return is below the required rate, and the project should be rejected.

Continuing with the example used so far, Figure 11.8 (p. 178) indicates NPV data for the development. The present value of returns over the first five years is positive—the NPV of cash flow ($1 069 608) being greater than the NPV of the investment ($800 000). This indicates the profitability of the project and its good cash surpluses after the first year.

The 60-unit project presented in Chapter 10 (using 5-year data)

Year	Investment	Cash Flow	NPV at 8%	Net Present Value	
Year 1	-$800 000		1		$800 000
End Year 1		-$86 501	0.926	-$80 100	
End Year 2		$358 758	0.857	$307 456	
End Year 3		$374 895	0.794	$297 667	
End Year 4		$381 340	0.735	$280 285	
End Year 5		$388 107	0.681	$264 301	
Totals				**$1 069 608**	**$800 000**

Figure 11.8 Net Present Value Calculation of the 60-Unit Project

Kevin Baker

Internal Rate of Return (IRR) Method

The internal rate of return (IRR) is the management-determined rate of interest at which the present value of expected cash inflows must equal or exceed the present value of expected cash outflows of a project as a criterion for the investment to be acceptable. It could also be thought of as the maximum rate of interest which would have to be paid to a financial institution for borrowing the money invested over the life of the project in order to break even. In this context, 'break even' means arriving at a point where the net present value of the project is zero, or the IRR equals the required rate of return. Generally, projects with higher IRRs are preferred to those with lower IRRs.

The procedure for calculating the IRR is relatively simple, and really begins using a trial-and-error approach. If it is known that, at 8%, a project shows a surplus of $20 200, the actual rate is above 8%. If 12% is chosen, the project shows a deficit (that is, a negative NPV) of $71 600, so the answer is obviously somewhere between the two. Taking the mid-point, 10%, we see that this is the correct rate, since the present value of the inflows and outflows are equal. In other words, if money was borrowed at an interest rate of 10%, the cash inflows produced by the project would exactly repay the loan plus interest over the five years. If the required rate of return is less than 10%, the project will be profitable. If the rate is greater than 10%, the cash inflow will be insufficient to pay interest and repay the loan. Therefore 10% is the internal rate of return of this project.

If the internal rate is not easily found by trial and error (that is, the IRR is not an even number listed in the present value table), the IRR can be found using straight-line extension of figures given in the tables.

This method is more frequently used for comparing small projects (such as equipment purchases) where there is a choice between several alternatives. Hence, the example that follows in Figure 11.9 illustrates the technique using the example of the purchase of linen-folding equipment for $140 000—where the cash flow results from net savings in labour required to operate the equipment.

Example: Purchase of New Linen-Folding Equipment
13% Factor

Year	Net Cash Flow	Discount Factor	Present Value
Year 1	-$1 821	0.8850	-$1 612
Year 2	$48 395	0.7831	$37 898
Year 3	$48 395	0.6931	$33 543
Year 4	$48 395	0.6133	$29 681
Year 5	$74 414	0.5428	$40 392
Total Net Present Value			$139 902
Purchase Price			$140 000
Net Present Value			$98

IRR is approximately 13%. This is greater than the company IRR of 12%, so the equipment may be purchased.

Figure 11.9 Internal Rate of Return

Kevin Baker

The Effect of Income Taxes on Project Evaluation

The examples being used to illustrate the principles of project evaluation have been based on an assumption that only one rate of tax is payable, and that tax minimisation practices have not been utilised. There are, however, practices which can legitimately vary income taxes, and these will have a significant influence on decisions. For example, they can significantly reduce the net cash inflows from individual projects and change their desirability.

One factor that will affect the amount of income tax payable is the depreciation method used. The method of depreciation chosen (or allowed by taxation authorities) will affect both profit and cash flow. The straight-line method charges the same amount of depreciation each year—the assumption being that the asset earns revenue at a constant rate during its life. Accelerated depreciation is any pattern which writes off depreciable assets more quickly than does straight-line depreciation. The rationale for accelerated depreciation is that the asset will have greater revenue-generating capacity during the early years of its life when it is new—rather than in later years, when it is becoming less efficient and outmoded.

One example of accelerated depreciation is the diminishing balance method. In this method, a constant percentage is written off each year, based on the written-down value of the asset—rather than the original cost, as used in the straight-line method. Accelerated depreciation means that more depreciation occurs in the earlier years of a project when the tax savings from tax deductions are in dollars with a relatively high present value. An example is given in Figure 11.10.

Sales		$100 000
Less expenses:		
General	$62 000	
Depreciation	$18 000	
	$80 000	$80 000
Net income before taxes		$20 000
Income taxes at 40%		$8 000
Net income after taxes		$12 000

Taking the above figures, the cash flow from operations is:
sales ($100 000) – cash expenses ($62 000) – tax paid ($8000) = cash flow ($30 000).

Figure 11.10 A General Example of Income Tax/Depreciation

Kevin Baker

From this it can be seen that the tax effect of depreciation can affect the cash flow. In more complex examples the magnitude of this factor can influence the decision of whether or not to proceed with the project

Risk Analysis

All financial analysis and calculation is made on the basis of assumptions concerning a set of variables. Conditions might change, and the assumptions that underpinned the analysis might no longer hold good. For this reason, it can be advisable to carry out what is called 'sensitivity analysis'.[18] This recalculates financial aspects on the basis of changes in the variables upon which that calculation was made.

In the financial modelling of revenue and expense, there was some sensitivity analysis—when the surplus/deficit was recalculated on the basis of changing occupancy, and it was also suggested that changes in rates due to discounting or competitor's challenge should be taken into account when preparing income projections. Besides occupancy and rates, the project evaluation could remodel financial projections allowing for changes in interest rates, changes in financing (between fixed and variable interest finance), increased cost of construction, or delays in construction that exceed contingency periods in the timeline.

External factors which could impact upon the development—such as changes to government policy or local opposition—should have been identified in the review of general market factors, but it might be useful to take them into account when making a financial analysis.

If the project is a very large one, any of these factors could be significant, and the study should identify those factors which will be 'sensitive' to change and could affect the bottom line of the project.

A Word on 'Expert Systems'

There is a number of computer packages which can assist with the compilation of cash–flow statements as part of business plans. However, the task is a complex one, and computer packages remain limited by the quality of input of the analyst.

A higher level of computer usage has supported the concept of artificial intelligence and the development of 'expert systems' to assist the process of feasibility analysis. They are especially useful in the hospitality industry in order to handle the complexities of reservation projections and capacity management.

Conclusion

The above discussion concerned financial tools of analysis of a project. There are certainly other ways of measuring the desirability of a project besides financial ones—although in the private sector, where it is essential for the long-run survival of a corporation to make a profit, the financial imperative is paramount. However, there are other measures that impact indirectly on an enterprise's profitability.

Some writers suggest that objectives such as 'maintaining customer satisfaction and good image' should be part of management targets for any new hotel.[19]

Another opinion is that most of today's feasibility studies do not include research on what potential hotel guests actually want. According to this opinion, the emphasis is on financial measures and competitors, and more time should be spent considering the desires of the consumer.[20]

Essentially, a good project evaluation will be one that meets the needs of the decision-makers, and provides them with the quality information and analysis that they need to make the best possible decision on the information available at the time.

A Last Word

A well-prepared and conducted project evaluation can assist decision-makers on the advisability of a project. However, in Berg's words:

> Explore the when, why and how of getting a study—and then how to use it.
>
> Berg (1988)[21]

It is as important to know how to use the completed study as it is to know how to conduct the analysis.

CHECKLIST # 11
BUDGETING/PLANNING

- Construction/completion estimates accurate?
- Timing contingencies allowed in timelines?
- Financing drawdowns linked to critical path of construction?
- Timing of costs and revenues accurately recorded?
- Realistic operating levels allowed for initial operation?
- Details of debt repayments recorded—including fees and charges?
- Overdrafts arranged and financing budgeted?

Chapter 11 ■ Review and Questions

1 Indicate whether the following statements are true or false and give a
   reason for your answer:
   a Accounting rate of return is an accounting measure which basically
      considers the timing of profit. (True/False? Why?)
   b Firms sometimes ignore the increased level of working capital
      necessary to support increased levels of activity. (True/False? Why?)
   c Accelerated depreciation methods result in maximum tax advantage.
      (True/False? Why?)
   d Projects with a longer payback period will normally be preferred to
      those with shorter payback periods. (True/False? Why?)

2 Insert the word(s) that best completes each of the following, selecting
   your answers from the following possibilities:
   asset valuation; investment; capital budgeting; corporate objectives; variable;
   invariable; SWOT analysis; important.
   a . . . considers not only amounts to be invested, but also when they
      will be committed.
   b . . . planning is a part of the strategic planning process.
   c Costs which are fixed for short time periods are frequently . . . over
      longer time periods.
   d The types of broad assessments which have to be made include
      whether the opportunity fits with the . . .

3 Discuss the following in one or two sentences (for each statement):
   a A dollar is a dollar is a dollar—better to count actual dollars and be
      accurate than to make adjustments for inflation etc. and risk making
      errors through inaccurate estimates.
   b The use of accounting rates of return encourages managers to take a
      short-term view of operations, whereas they should have a long-term
      view and be guided more by strategies such as gaining market share.
   c The problem with using complex measures of performance is that
      investors do not use that sort of information—they are only
      interested in the bottom line (that is, the profit figure).

4 Analyse and discuss the following:
   The business plan depends upon a number of assumptions and, if one of
   those assumptions is proved false, the whole plan falls apart.

Chapter 11 Notes

[1] McCarthy, E., Perreault, W., Quester, P., Wilkinson, J. & Lee, K. 1994, *Basic Marketing—a Managerial Approach*, p. 26, Richard D. Irwin, Inc.: Sydney.

[2] Czinkota, M. & Ronkainen, I. 1995, *International Marketing*, 4th edn, p. 21, Harcourt Brace & Company/The Dryden Press: Fort Worth.

[3] Dobbins, R. & Pike, R. 1988, 'Capital Budgeting', In Cowe, R. (ed.) *Handbook of Management Accounting*, 2nd edn, p. 38, Gower Publishing: Aldershot.

[4] Horngren, C. & Foster, G. 1991, *Cost Accounting—a Managerial Emphasis*, 7th edn, p. 673, Prentice-Hall: New Jersey.

[5] Ibid. pp 674–5.

[6] Eyster, J. & Geller, A. N., 'The Capital Investment Decision: Techniques Used in the Hospitality Industry', *Cornell Hotel and Restaurant Administration Quarterly*, vol. 22., no.1, May 1981, pp 69–73.

[7] Schmidgall, R. & Damition, J., 'Current Capital-Budgeting Practices of Major Lodging Chains', *Real Estate Review*, Fall 1990, pp 40–5.

[8] Dobbins, R. & Pike, R. 1988, op. cit., p. 38.

[9] Kotler, P., *Marketing Management—Analysis, Planning, Implementation and Control*, 8th edn, p. 92, Prentice-Hall International, Inc.: New Jersey.

[10] Reported by Dennis, A., in the *Sydney Morning Herald*, 8 March 1999, p. 3.

[11] McCarthy, E., Perreault, W., & Quester, P. 1997, *Basic Marketing—a Managerial Approach*, 2nd Australasian edn, p. 93, McGraw-Hill Australia/Richard D. Irwin, Inc.: Sydney.

[12] Coltman, M. 1998, *Hospitality Management Accounting*, 6th edn, p. 539, Van Nostrand Reinhold: New York.

[13] Czinkota & Ronkainen 1995, op. cit., p. 21.

[14] Staley, H., 'Project Evaluation's Rule-of-Thumb Withstands Test of Time', *Hotel & Motel Management*, vol. 214, no. 3, February 1999, p. 10.

[15] Atkinson, S., Kelliher, C. & LeBruto, S. 1997, 'Capital Budgeting Decisions Using Crystal Ball', *Cornell Hotel and Restaurant Administration Quarterly*, October 1997, p. 26.

[16] Main, B., 'Financial Feasibility', *Restaurant Business*, 10 February 1988, pp 82–6.

[17] CIMA Study Text 1990, *Management Accounting Techniques*, p. 584, BPP Publishing: London.

[18] Noted in Tourism South Australia 1993, *Development Guide for the Preparation of Feasibility Studies for Tourism Projects*, Adelaide, 1993, p. 16.

[19] Pyo, S., Chang, H. & Chon, K. 1995, 'Considerations of Management Objectives by Target Markets in Hotel Feasibility Studies', *International Journal of Hospitality Management*, vol. 14, no. 2, June 1995, pp 151–6.

[20] Zodrow, G. 1989, 'Supplement: A New Look at Feasibility Studies', *Lodging Hospitality*, vol. 45, no. 5, May 1989, pp 19–20.

[21] Berg, P. 1988, 'Project Evaluation: Make it Work for You', *Hotel and Resort Industry*, vol. 11, no. 9, September 1988, pp 44–6.

CHAPTER 12

Franchises

Synopsis of Chapter

This chapter discusses aspects of franchising in relation to the setting up a new tourism/hospitality operation.
The advantages for the franchiser include financial benefits from the sale of the right to use the brand, and economies of scale in the provision of supplies and marketing. The main disadvantage is maintaining a consistency of quality of franchised services/products.

The franchisee benefits through utilising the expertise and marketing of the franchiser, but the disadvantages include the cost of the franchise, and limitations on the operation of the project.

There are nine criteria for assessing the cost/benefit of a franchise, and there are also measures that should be taken to confirm the value of the services and support that are being offered.

What is a Franchise?

Franchising can be defined as:

> . . . the authorising of an individual by a company to sell certain products or services in a particular area.
>
> New SOED (1997)[1]

Franchising is a rapidly expanding concept. It covers tourism and hospitality operations including:

- restaurants (for example, 'Pizza Hut' and 'McDonalds');
- motels (for example, 'Travelodge' in the United States, and the 'Quest' group in Australia); and
- theme parks.

In the United Kingdom, there has been a particular expansion of budget hotel chains. The 'Travel Inn' chain increased total rooms to 20 000 in the late 1990s/early 2000s, and 'Travelodge' took its total to 10 500.[2]

Typically, franchisers have established a quality product, have marketed the product so that it is widely known, and have then demonstrated their expertise in their field by a lengthy period of profitable operation. The franchisers are then able to market their format, their brand name, and their skilled support through a franchise package. Those who purchase the franchise, the franchisees, are able to enter the market place with a reasonable hope of success because they are backed by specific expertise and market exposure.

Franchising is especially attractive to small investors. The support of the franchiser often makes it easier for the small investor to obtain financing because banks and finance institutions usually take account of the strength of the franchiser in assessing the franchisee's application for finance.

The franchise offers the franchisee:

- an efficient, profitable and proven format of service;
- affiliation with an organisation that can offer support and assistance; and
- marketing of a brand and logo that already have good recognition in a segment of the market.

The Format of the Franchise

The format of the franchise can be replicated through the use of established procedures. These will commonly be available in procedures manuals for the main aspects of the operation. These procedures cover operational aspects (such as food-service presentation and layout), and purchasing/stores functions.

The franchiser will usually also offer the services of skilled staff who can train new personnel in operating procedures.

There should be ongoing support through site visits and inspections by senior executives of the franchiser, who will check procedures and advise on problems that arise.

Support and Assistance

The support services noted above would usually be covered in the franchise fee. In addition, the franchiser can be a source of technical support and assistance in other aspects of the new operation—such as site selection and suitability, the design of the building, and the arranging of finance. Other additional services could include branded consumables—such as paper supplies and guest supplies.

Marketing

Marketing is likely to be the most important aspect of the franchise. Marketing will include the branding of the service, as well as ongoing marketing campaigns. Usually, the franchiser will be able to demonstrate a successful marketing track record, and well-developed plans for future marketing.

The franchisee can expect to be required to contribute to ongoing advertising that publicises the brand in general, and regional/individual properties in particular. The franchisees benefit from a common reservations system that effectively markets all the properties in the chain through what is called a 'referral' process. The franchisees also usually benefit through the franchiser's existing sales network—particularly in the group and conference traveller markets.

Advantages and Disadvantages of Franchising

There are advantages and disadvantages in franchising—for both the franchiser and the franchisee. A project evaluation of a project that involves a franchise has unique features.

For the Franchiser

Advantages
There is the obvious benefit of being able to sell the franchise for a financial return. In addition, the franchiser can achieve economies of scale in the provision of branded supplies—as well as receiving a margin on their sale to franchisees.

The franchiser can expand the brand into new territories without the risk of overcapitalisation or overstretching its own resources. There are major marketing advantages in advertising, and in developing reservation and sales networks in expanding the number of properties under the umbrella of the brand.

Disadvantages
Ensuring an ongoing consistency of quality in all the franchisees is a problem—one 'bad apple' can contaminate a whole barrel.

Poor service in one property of a chain can influence the public perception of all of them. The greater the number of franchises, the more difficult it is to ensure quality. The franchiser also might face the problem of stretching skilled staff too thinly.

For the Franchisee

Advantages
Some of the advantages of purchasing a franchise have been noted above. Advantages include marketing and technical support, as well as assistance in obtaining finance.

The franchiser commonly has global expertise and, in the tourism and hospitality industry, such expertise is crucial to an efficient and modern operation. There is an important advantage in that the initial pick-up period of the new operation is usually reduced when it is franchised. There is existing advertising, promotional and reservations support that can bring early financial benefits to a new venture.

Disadvantages

The franchisee assumes a number of obligations in a franchise agreement—just as the franchiser does.

The first and most pertinent obligation is financial. The franchisee must meet certain costs and fees. These can include fixed monthly fees and percentages (based on occupancy or available room, food and beverage sales etc.), as well as upfront payments. These payments can be a heavy financial burden for a new operation—especially if the value of the brand does not bring in anticipated levels of business.

The second area of potential disadvantage is that the franchiser usually stipulates the standards of the property, and a new franchisee thus loses a degree of independence. These standards can relate to staffing practice and hours of operation, and also to physical standards (such as the size and quality of rooms, and the provision of facilities such as a swimming pool and spas).

A third area of potential difficulty is that there can be problems in relation to agreed territories.

Summary of Advantages/Disadvantages

It will be apparent from the above that a project evaluation of a franchised project is not as straightforward as an evaluation of a stand-alone property. There are difficulties in assessing the value of the franchise, as well as the appropriateness of the ongoing costs and obligations. One such difficulty is that the franchiser might be a very large corporation, with complex global operations that are not easy to evaluate in the context of establishing a new franchise. However, the evaluation must be done—no matter how large or prestigious the franchiser might be.

A full feasibility study should be completed before any commitment to the purchase of a franchise. If this is done, the franchiser/franchisee partners should be able to avoid an unhappy relationship. Unfortunately, many franchised ventures end in disappointment. Rowe writes:

> . . . these are not happy times for franchisees . . . franchisees increasingly feel subject to the whims of their partners.

Rowe (1997)[3]

Criteria for Assessing the Franchise

1. Resale

It is important to consider whether the franchisee would be able to recover their investment by reselling the franchise. It must be established whether the franchise can be onsold, with the approval of the franchiser. Besides being able to recover the initial investment, there should be some provision for the franchisee to benefit from a capital gain from the venture—which the franchisee will have achieved through his/her own hard work.

2. Exclusivity

The franchisee should have a degree of exclusivity in the use of the brand name within a territory or region. The last thing that a franchisee would want would be another property of that name operating in the same area. For the protection of his/her investment, the franchisee is entitled to seek limits to competition.

3. Project Compatibility

The franchisee's plans for the site and market, and the franchiser's expertise and image, should match the proposed venture. For example, it would be unusual for some of the major hotel chains to operate in a small regional city.

4. Tenure

Some franchise agreements operate on the basis of the franchiser renting signage to the franchisee on a monthly basis—making the tenure of the franchise agreement tenuous. The franchise agreement should be for a fixed period that is sufficient for the franchisee to recover the initial investment and to earn an appropriate return on that investment.

5. Branded Supplies

The franchisee should have some guarantees about the cost and availability of branded equipment and supplies—including the markup that the franchiser can take.

6. Track Record of the Franchiser

A franchisee is entitled to have information on the franchiser's experience and future plans, and to confirm the franchiser's history of continuous and stable growth in a market similar to that of the proposed venture.

7. Reputation

Linked to an examination of the franchiser's track record is a critical analysis of their reputation—especially their relationships with other franchisees. Have they been honest and fair? Have they been responsive to problems? Do they have a good record of dealing with their financiers and with government authorities? Is the franchiser a corporation that is expanding or declining?

8. Skills and Expertise

The franchiser should have:
- a number of executives with skills and good reputations in the industry;
- a good national and international sales network;
- an efficient and up-to-date reservations system;
- a good control system;
- imaginative and vigorous marketing and advertising plans; and
- experienced operational managers.

9. A Sound Financial Position

The franchiser will seek to examine the financial affairs of a prospective franchisee. The franchisee should also examine the affairs of the franchiser—because the relationship will be one of mutual benefit.

Gathering the Information

It might not be easy to ascertain all the above in order to assess the value of the franchise. Some prudent measures that a prospective franchisee could take include:
- check the franchiser's latest annual reports if available;
- check the résumés of individuals in the franchiser's management;
- visit some existing franchises to check the quality and apparent morale of the property;
- interview the franchisers' operators;
- try to contact and interview previous owners of the franchise;
- visit sales and marketing representatives of the franchiser; and
- visit and interview other industry executives or travel companies about the franchiser's reputation.

Usefulness of Franchises

There are certainly areas of operation where franchises could offer no benefits. For example, an operation serving a niche market, or a boutique hotel, would be better off standing alone. It is even likely that small operators know speciality markets better than large operators and there is no advantage to be gained by purchasing a franchiser's expertise.

There is one further proviso to consider under this topic of purchasing a franchise—always conduct an independent project evaluation, even for a purchase of a franchise, and do not rely on the franchiser's own material alone.

CASE STUDY
Branding a New Purchase

In 1998, the US-based 'CapStar' hotel group paid $150 million for the six 'Medallion' hotels, and planned a $3.5 million renovation of the 'Medallion Hotel' in Dallas.[4] Although the hotel had had a 1997 occupancy of 70%, the sales manager commented: 'It's been harder to go after business with an independent name . . . It is a real disadvantage because if someone wants to book a room from 300 miles away, they've probably never heard of it'.[4] In the opinion of the sales manager, a brand name can increase sales by 15–20%. According to a hotel investment adviser, there had also been a problem in competing with the nationwide, convenient, reservation services offered by major brands.[4] A change to a brand name could also give the 'Medallion Hotel' the opportunity to compete in a higher-quality market. Hence, the new owners of the Dallas 'Medallion' examined the feasibility of rebranding the hotel to one of the major brands that CapStar already managed—including Hilton, Sheraton, Marriott, Westin or Crowne Plaza.

A Last Word

There are three crucial things for a potential franchisee to do in a project evaluation for a franchise:

- plan what the potential franchisee wants to do;
- ascertain whether those plans are compatible with the franchise; and
- get advice from every possible quarter.

CHECKLIST # 12 FEASIBILITY OF FRANCHISES

- Can the franchise be resold?

- Is the territory protected?

- Is the franchise concept compatible with the desired project?

- What is the tenure of the franchise?

- What are the arrangements for branded products?

- What is the track record of the franchiser?

- What is the reputation/financial situation of the franchiser?

Chapter 12 ■ Review and Questions

1 Indicate whether the following statements are true or false and give a reason for your answer:

   a A franchise purchase includes the use of a brand name. (True/False? Why?)

   b A franchisee offers a franchiser affiliation with a proven profitable operation. (True/False? Why?)

   c A franchiser offers a franchisee specially designed procedures for their operation. (True/False? Why?)

   d A franchiser can use an existing sales network to assist the franchisee. (True/False? Why?)

2 Insert the word(s) that best completes each of the following, selecting your answers from the following possibilities:
merchandising; independent; franchise signage; franchise fees; referral process; exclusivity; value; retrospective.
  a . . . is a term used for marketing one property through all others in the chain.
  b . . . can be calculated on a number of bases.
  c A franchiser should guarantee a franchisee . . . of use of the brand within a given territory.
  d You should not merely accept a franchiser's data, but should always conduct an . . . project evaluation.
3 Discuss the following in one or two sentences (for each statement):
  a There are no big profits to be made in purchasing franchises because the franchiser has already skimmed off the best part of the profit.
  b There is no point purchasing a franchise unless the franchiser is a global operation and has become a household name, and therefore can generate high levels of custom for the franchisee.
  c Many franchisees think that purchasing a franchise entitles them to sit back and make their profit from the hard work of the franchiser.
4 Analyse and discuss the following:
  When a franchisee purchases a franchise, he/she should ensure that it is for as long a period as possible—such that the franchisee will have an adequate time frame to achieve a return on the investment.

Chapter 12 Notes

[1] *New Shorter Oxford English Dictionary* (New SOED) 1997, CD Version 1.0.03, OUP: Oxford.
[2] Jolley, R. 1999, 'Kings of the Road', *Caterer & Hotelkeeper*, 28 January, p. 25.
[3] Rowe, M. 1997, 'Franchisee versus Franchisor', *Lodging Hospitality*, July 1997, p. 22.
[4] Sayewitz, R. 1997, 'Medallion Name May Change After Acquisition by CapStar', *Dallas Business Journal*, 15 December 1997, reported at
<http://www.amcity.com/dallas/stories/121597/story5.html>.

CHAPTER 13

Presentation of the Project Evaluation

Synopsis of Chapter

This chapter summarises the main sections of the project evaluation and draws them together, describing how the report should be prepared and presented—including visual presentation techniques.

Essentially, the report should be concise, clear and adequate for its purpose—which is to analyse and present aspects related to a major investment project so that parties involved can make the best possible decisions in regard to that project.

The Decision-Makers

First and foremost, the authors and presenters of a project evaluation must keep in mind the decision-makers who will use the study—for these are the people who will base investment decisions upon the material compiled by the study team. The study report should be addressed to the commissioning individuals on the first page, as if it were correspondence, and should refer to the specifics of the task that the study team was required to examine and analyse.

The main aim of the analyst in presenting the results of his/her work must be to make it as easy as possible for the decision-makers to understand and use the information put before them.

Clarity and simplicity of information help with comprehension. In particular, the conclusions must be clear and simple. They must also be pragmatic. In other words, the project evaluation must produce recommendations that are simple, clear and feasible.

The intent of the study must be to communicate information in a form that is accessible, easily understood, and conducive to achieving the objectives—which usually entail making a pragmatic decision or decisions. To those ends, the study team must know something of the background of those who commissioned the report. For example, if the commissioning individual is an architect, architectural terms and concepts can be used freely. If the decision-maker is an accountant, financial terms need not be interpreted, but other issues of design and construction should be clarified.

However, the question of the use of technical terms is subject to a proviso. Terminology can be a device that acts as a form of shorthand language, but it can also be a cause of obfuscation. Any terminology used in a study must be defined in the introductory section. The use of arcane language, or jargon, is a device that exclusive groups use to preserve the borders between their knowledge and the world at large. There is no place for jargon in compiling a project evaluation. The rule of thumb should be—if a particular word will be well understood and express the concept better, use it; but if a word does not make the picture clearer for all, do not use it.

The Timing of the Project Evaluation

A project-evaluation report must never be late.

The intention of a project evaluation is to produce accurate and timely information for the decision-maker. If the study report is delayed, there is a risk that the information might not be as relevant as it could be. Investment decisions will depend upon the production of the document. It reflects badly upon the professionalism of the feasibility team if it is unable to organise itself sufficiently to meet the deadlines for the presentation of the fruits of its work. Lateness suggests that those who cannot work to a deadline might not be able to work to a high standard in other aspects of their task.

A schedule for the writing, the production and the delivery of the project evaluation must be compiled at an early stage of the study process. That schedule must then be adhered to. The schedule might include a contingency period to allow for delays in research, and to allow for delays in supporting material being made available, and so on. But the final date must be fixed as a pillar of iron. The team leader/coordinator must be alert to keeping all the team members up with the schedule.

The Value of Simplicity

The description of the research, and the conclusions of the project evaluation, are best presented in as simple a fashion as possible. The objective of the study is to present a recommendation or set of recommendations so that those who commissioned the study can make a decision. The most important part of the study, therefore, will be the few pages (perhaps even a single page) that presents the recommendations. It can be a measure of the clarity and simplicity of the report if the recommendations can be described on a single page.

The recommendation might be presented twice—first in the context of an executive summary and, secondly, in the final section of the study report itself (where they can include full and detailed backing by facts and statistics or implications drawn from research material).

The recommendations need to be fully supported with facts and information. The introduction to the study should outline what the objectives of the work are, and the path that will be followed to reach them. The body of the study will be taken up with the information and selection of data under the various headings used in this book. There are two broad areas to consider—a market project evaluation and a financial project evaluation. Recommendations will probably flow from both these areas, and therefore can usefully be grouped under the two headings.

It is important to list limitations of the study, and assumptions made in compiling the data and making the recommendations—for the quality of a structure is dependent upon the quality of the foundations.

Where data must be included to support recommendations, it is better to use graphs where possible, instead of lengthy tables. A diagram or diagrams might also be useful. A clear and simple picture conveys more information than columns and pages of statistics. However, it must be remembered that a picture must *illustrate* something. That is, it must have a purpose, and should not be included merely for the sake of having a picture.

The addition of extraneous material obscures the data. For example, the addition of material such as tourism brochures, or advertising material expounding the virtues of a region, have only limited relevance to the study and distract from the flow of information.

Including too much material in addenda also detracts from the real value of the study and its presentation. Adding whole reports, for example, to 'beef up' the study and make it appear much larger than it is, is not a good practice. Where data have been published in other reports, they should be selectively quoted, or sections reproduced (with permission)—but there is almost never sufficient reason to include whole reports. Where the work of another author or publication is used, the source must be acknowledged.

A thick tome that an analyst can thump down on the boardroom table might seem dramatic, but few executives make decisions on the *quantity* of material, preferring instead the *quality* of the information. One important use of the project evaluation—in raising venture finance—is also not assisted by making the report as thick as a telephone book.

Presentation in Detail

The detail of the presentation is also important. Again, there is a value in simplicity. The style of writing should be clear and straightforward. A simple word is better than a word with many syllables—it is easier to get a golf ball (rather than a tennis ball) through a pipe! If a sentence can be broken up into shorter sentences, do so. Keep paragraphs short, with titles and headings that let the reader's eye follow the train of the discussion. Start each section on a new page.

Some parts of the study can be improved by the use of numbering for the various sections and supporting diagrams.

Keep the typeface clear and the background uncluttered. A simple and clear presentation is easier to read and comprehend than a document that is over-produced—that is, with decoration on every page and background pictures intended to have aesthetic appeal and impress readers—but which seldom achieve either.

Tonge provides a comprehensive listing of the areas to be considered in the presentation of a project evaluation, the writing of it, and having it designed and printed.[1] Tonge emphasises the importance of simplicity in the report, and especially the need for proofreading—to pick up the small but embarrassing errors that can mar an otherwise professional report. The most embarrassing glitches (such as the incorrect spelling of the names of significant people in the process[2]) should be simple to resolve at the writing stage.

To achieve the overall aims of simplicity of expression, absence of errors and generally impressive presentation, it is sensible to seek professional editorial advice before sending the report for final publication. The analysts who are preparing the report will be surprised to find that a professional editor will dis-cover all manner of errors that have been overlooked by the authors. These might be errors of fact, errors of logic, errors of proper grammar and spelling, and so on. Despite the authors' own best efforts to check their own material, it is extremely difficult to edit and proofread one's own work, and professional assis-tance in this regard is essential.

Visual Presentation

There is always value in having a supporting visual presentation to back up a written report. Clear and relevant photographs, or short videos, can impart a sense of what the development is all about, and the theme that underpins it. Overhead transparencies or 'PowerPoint' presentations can support and outline a case for or against development—provided that the summaries are succinct and clear.

For larger developments, investment in such formats as 3-D modelling and computer imagery can also be useful—provided that such presentations are supplementary, and that the evaluation team does not attempt to use them in the place of a full and detailed report. The risk in overemphasising visual presenta-tions is that slickness and style might overshadow the substance of facts.

Conclusion

The changing economic circumstances of the times, and the increased competi-tion in the hospitality industry, have helped to emphasise the need for accurate and timely feasibility studies to assist investment decisions.

The project evaluation will never eliminate the risk involved in investment decisions, but it can reduce the level of risk. The risk of a failed development project can be reduced in proportion to the quality of analysis, and the accuracy and reliability of information on which the analysis is based.

But the risk will always remain—because a new project looks to the future, and there is never a guarantee that the future will be the same as the present or the past. The risk remains, but the possible financial return should be commensurate with the risk.

To quote Greene:

> Many hotels and restaurants have gone bust because their owners failed to carry out feasibility studies to determine long-term profits prior to acquisition. ... A project evaluation does not ensure success, nothing can do that. But it can back up an instinctive feeling, or identify snags no one else has thought of.
>
> Greene (1993)[3]

It all comes back to the entrepreneur, and the original idea. That was where this book started. It would be a sad day, and the beginning of our decline as a society, if there were no entrepreneurs coming forward with new ideas. In the project evaluation, if it is done well, the entrepreneur can find a tool to examine whether the idea might work and produce a return. Then the entrepreneur might be encouraged to put the idea into action, and on such actions the progress and wellbeing of humanity depends. And, of course, hospitality project development can also be exciting.

A Very Last Word

The Greek philosopher Socrates taught that the way of wisdom was to be found in following the *medius res* ('middle way') in all things—rather than going to extremes. In report presentation, the 'middle way' is to be found in presenting the information and conclusion clearly and precisely—without going to extremes of inadequacy or complexity of message.

CHECKLIST # 13
COMPLETING THE REPORT

- Spelling (including names) correct?

- Sentences and structure concise and clear?

- Sections clearly numbered?

- Is it understandable to an uninformed reader?

- Are facts and graphs supported by evidence where
  necessary?

- Are sources acknowledged?

- Has the draft report been professionally edited?

- Is the report well printed?

Chapter 13 ■ Review and Questions

1 Indicate whether the following statements are true or false and give a reason for your answer:
   a A project evaluation must be kept very short. (True/False? Why?)
   b Care must be taken in using technical terms. (True/False? Why?)
   c It is better to ignore a deadline and be late rather than rush the work. (True/False? Why?)
   d Present recommendations in as simple a form as possible. (True/False? Why?)
   e The recommendations of a study might be presented more than once in the body of the report. (True/False? Why?)

2 Insert the word(s) that best completes each of the following, selecting your answers from the following possibilities:
   excluded; jargon; material; detail; extraneous; relevant;extemporise; provisions.
   a There is no place for . . . in a project evaluation.
   b The addition of . . . material can obscure the data.
   c Material that is not essential to the background and explanation of recommendations should be . . .
   d The . . . of the presentation is also important.

3 Discuss the following in one or two sentences (for each statement):
   a The style of the presentation is more important than the substance of the report.
   b A good report on a promising project should sell itself.
   c The most important purpose of the evaluation report is telling the investors what they already know.

4 Analyse and discuss the following:
   The presentation of the project evaluation should include as much material as possible, with appropriate scientific language—the more complex the better—because report will be judged on its length, not on its detail.

Chapter 13 Notes

[1] Tonge, R. 1997, *How to Conduct Feasibility Studies for Tourism Projects*, 6th edn, pp 54ff, R. Tonge & Associates, Gull Publishing: Queensland (available from Australian Bankers' Association, Melbourne).
[2] Ibid. p. 57.
[3] Greene, M. 1993, 'Let's be Feasible', *Caterer & Hotelkeeper*, 4 March 1993, p. 38.

CHAPTER 14

Example—The Manhattan Beach Project

Synopsis of Chapter

The following study is a fictitious example, and the country of Bluedonia is not meant to parallel any existing country.

Although the example is fictitious, it is inspired by, and has similarities to, a study conducted by Purdon Associates for Zenith of Canberra. The author acknowledges the work of Purdon Associates, and is especially grateful to Rob Purdon of Purdon Associates and Phil Whitelock of Zenith.

Manhattan Beach Motel for People with Special Needs

A Feasibility Study

Prepared by Chickenwire Overburg & Co.,
2/63 Morton Avenue, Yasston, Bluedonia

For Dr K. Baker
Managing Director Mirovic Investment Pty Ltd

July 2003

The Feasibility Study Team

J. Chickenwire is the principal author of the study, with assistance from B. Billtonbarbie and C. Sideswiper.

Acknowledgments

The assistance of the Ruby Coast Tourism Authority and the Manhattan Beach Council is gratefully acknowledged.

Disclaimer

Chickenwire Overburg & Co., their agents and employees, will not be liable for any damages or loss resultant from the actions of any person in response to the information, assertions, representations or recommendations contained in this study document.

Executive Summary

Chickenwire Overburg & Co. (hereinafter called 'the consultants') were instructed by Dr K. Baker of Mirovic Investment Pty Ltd to examine and report upon the feasibility of a project to construct a 40-unit motel with associated amenities, specifically designed to cater for the special needs of infirm aged people and people with disabilities, in the coastal town of Manhattan Beach, situated in the Ruby Coast region of Bluedonia.

Consequent to those instructions, the consultants carried out preliminary market studies of supply and demand, environmental research, and regional and site inspections to determine factors that would affect the viability of the proposal.

The consultants found that, in the area of Manhattan Beach, there is a limited number of accommodation properties that have appropriate access and facilities suitable for the comfort of people with special needs. All hospitality properties in the Ruby Coast region were examined. The average occupancy of those properties ranges from 82% in peak season (November to April) to 57% (in the off season).

Market research indicates that the area attracts local visitors from the capital city of Bluedonia as well as international visitors. More than 40 000 local and international visitors tour the region. Each of these people stays, on average, for six days. Of those visitors, based on general population statistics, approximately 15% would be expected to have a disability or mobility difficulty.

The findings of the feasibility study are:

▼ The construction of a property of 40 units, designed specifically for people with special needs, offers the probability of positive returns on investment (before tax and interest) of the order of 10–11% after three years.
▼ The property should be of at least 3-star quality, aimed at attracting the family tourism market.
▼ Council and regional tourism authorities are supportive of the concept proposal.
▼ The proposed site offers sound marketing possibilities without obvious building or zoning problems.

After consideration of the marketing, legal, design and financial aspects of the proposal, the consultants recommend that the project be commenced.

J. Chickenwire
Chickenwire Overburg & Co.
26 May 2003

Contents

1 Introduction
Purpose of the Study
Background
Methodology
Site Description

2 SWOT Analysis
Strengths
Weaknesses
Opportunities
Threats

3 Tourist Market
Trends
Accommodation and Activity
Accommodation Price Range
Potential Market Sectors

4 Physical Development Concept
Indicative Development Concept
Development Costs
Approval Process

5 Financial Assessment
Project Budget
Cash Flow

6 Summary and Conclusions

Attachments

1 Introduction

1.1 Purpose of the Study

This feasibility study has been prepared by Chickenwire Overburg & Company to comply with a brief issued by Dr K. Baker of Mirovic Investment Pty Ltd, seeking an analysis of a new project which would involve accommodation for people with special needs at Manhattan Beach, Bluedonia.

The study addresses the issues surrounding the development of the project, and identifies the steps which should be taken to guide the project to satisfactory completion.

1.2 Background to the Study

1.2.1 Initiation of the Concept

In 2002, Mirovic Investments Pty Ltd purchased a 4-hectare oceanside block of land on Manhattan Beach, approximately one kilometre from the town, and has sought investment possibilities for the site. In January 2003, principal of the company, Dr K. Baker, first proposed the construction of a motel and units for people with special needs, perceiving that there were few such properties on the Manhattan Peninsula or, indeed, in the rest of the nation. An initial enquiry concerning lines of finance indicated that funds would be available to construct a facility of approximately forty units.

Likely guests/clients of the facility and its benefits would include:

▼ people with disabilities seeking opportunities/facilities for training in sporting activities, and so on; and

▼ people with disabilities seeking purpose-designed recreation, accommodation or rehabilitation.

1.2.2 Support from Local Community

The region has had limited economic development in recent years and, therefore, projects such as this would be well received. Informal discussions with local authority councillors and regional tourism advocates indicated that there would be broad support for the development.

Evidence for this would include:

▼ advocacy for the project in local media;

▼ prompt processing of the development plans by council; and

▼ assistance with the preparation of development and building plans by local authority officers.

1.3 The Methodology of the Study

The evaluation of the project was made after independent research and assessment, including the following elements:

▼ meetings with a range of prominent members of the Manhattan Beach community—including staff of council and elected councillors;

▼ a site inspection of the main features of Manhattan Beach and the surrounding region;

▼ discussions with government agencies—including the Bluedonia Tourism Ministry—regarding various aspects of the project (including visitor numbers and availability of project funding);

▼ analysis of the latest available national census data;

▼ a telephone survey of local transport agencies; and

▼ a review of literature on assisted accommodation.

1.4 Site Description

Manhattan Beach is located on the south coast of Bluedonia on the Hinchbook Highway approximately midway between Cousins Point and Medway Bay (see Figure 1).

The proposed development is located at the northern gateway to Manhattan Beach approximately 2 km from Manhattan Beach town centre (see Figure 2). The site has extensive frontage and existing access to the Hinchbook Highway and Drumbeat Avenue.

The land is flat to gently undulating. It has a good coverage of mature native trees. Several water storage ponds have been established nearby on a council park to reticulate irrigation water provided by treated effluent from the sewage treatment works for Manhattan Beach.

The development site available for motel accommodation comprises an area of approximately 3.08 ha (220 m × 140 m) in the north-east corner of the site bounded by Hinchbook Highway and Drumbeat Avenue. This site is relatively flat, with a small cross-fall of approximately two metres. It is separated from the council park by a shallow drain (which could be used as a water feature).

The motel site has no apparent development constraints and no known land title claims by indigenous people—although written confirmation from the Bluedonia Government Land Titles Registry will be required to confirm this.

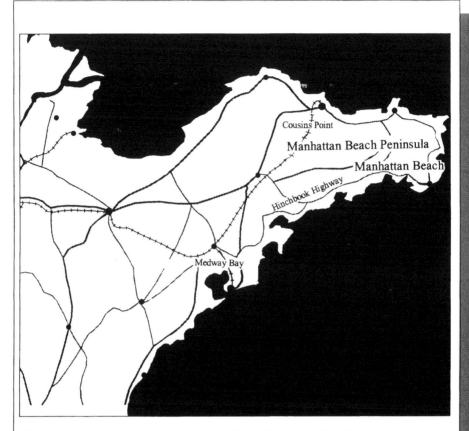

Figure Manhattan 1: Manhattan Beach Township and Location of Development

Kevin Baker

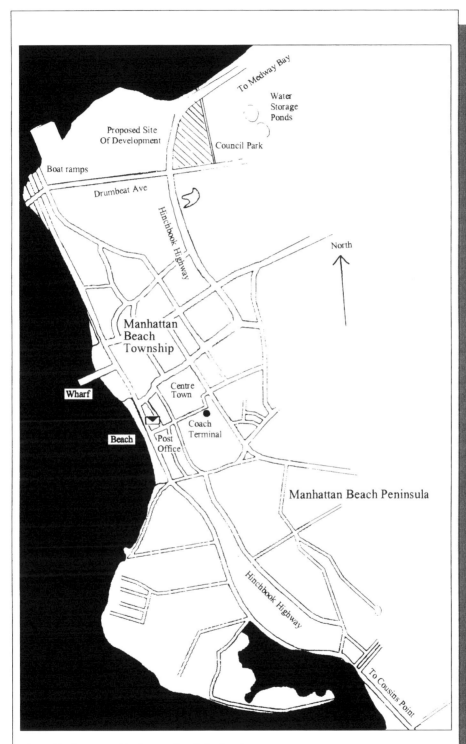

Figure Manhattan 2: Manhattan Beach Peninsula

Kevin Baker

2 SWOT Analysis

A preliminary SWOT analysis was undertaken by the study team as a means of assessing the main elements in the project. The outcome of this analysis is provided below.

Items under each heading have been listed in descending order of importance. As with all such assessments, implementation of the project needs to emphasise its strengths and opportunities, as well as working to eliminate weaknesses and threats.

2.1 Strengths

▼ uniqueness of the project in terms of accommodation for people with disabilities;
▼ strong local community support;
▼ letters of support for the project from groups involved with disability;
▼ support from local council;
▼ support from local politicians;
▼ flat, attractive and accessible site within Manhattan Beach;
▼ Manhattan Beach has many attractive qualities, including scenic beauty, dolphins, sports fishing, a 'village atmosphere', and an interesting history;
▼ site has no major development constraints;
▼ site has good exposure to highway;
▼ good existing highway access; and
▼ no apparent indigenous land title claims on site.

2.2 Weaknesses

▼ location of Manhattan Beach (relative distance from Bluedonia capital compared with other intervening holiday opportunities);
▼ adverse local economic conditions and limited growth prospects ;
▼ reliance on relatively narrow market base (disabled groups) for core business;
▼ project might have to rely heavily on broader tourist market to survive (limited market perception of Manhattan Beach as a major tourist destination for domestic and international visitors);
▼ lack of disabled access within Manhattan Beach (especially to/in the town centre);
▼ substantial marketing budget required to attract visitors to Manhattan Beach;
▼ different designs required to accommodate duality of market;
▼ development site has limited views if designed to maximise northerly winter aspect; and
▼ relative distance of site to Manhattan Beach town centre (also an opportunity—guests stay on site and use motel facilities).

2.3 Opportunities

- ▼ ongoing marketing and promotional campaign to boost awareness of project and advantages of Manhattan Beach;
- ▼ a number of potential government funding sources for capital development in this region;
- ▼ Medway Bay Motel and Units appears to have reasonably good occupancy rates and above-average room tariffs for disabled facilities suggesting good market demand;
- ▼ prospects for expansion of wharf and associated business activities at Manhattan Beach;
- ▼ growth of mature-age visitor travel market and specialist seasonal sports markets (for example lawn bowls, golf, fishing);
- ▼ lack of many other facilities (for people with disabilities) in region; and
- ▼ daily transport services to/from Manhattan Beach to the capital, and its links with international travel hubs.

2.4 Threats

- ▼ competition from existing motels for non-disability market; and
- ▼ slow down of tourist numbers from metropolitan areas as a result of local economic circumstances.

2.5 Summary

The major conclusions to be drawn from this SWOT analysis are:

- ▼ The project has substantial strengths and opportunities that can be used to generate a viable project outcome.
- ▼ There are a few threats to the project, but these are not of sufficient importance to recommend cancellation of the project.

3 Tourist Market

3.1 Tourism Trends

The Bluedonia National Tourism Strategy includes plans for the Ruby Coast region and identifies tourism as a major contributor to the regional economy. During 2001/2002, tourism expenditure for the region was estimated at 125.5 million Bluedonia dollars (B$), and 13% of the labour force (1998) was engaged in recreation and personal services. Tourist accommodation provided 480 jobs.

Although there has been a trend towards declining levels of visitation to the area over recent years, a gradual increase is now evident, and numbers are returning to levels experienced during 1997–98 as depicted in Table 1.

Table 1 Total Visits and Nights by Region

	Year	Manhattan	Lookabout Bay
	Peninsula	District	District
Total visits	1997–1998	786	645
	1998–1999	723	602
	1999–2000	687	577
	2000–2001	694	589
	2001–2002	770	634
Total nights	1997–1998	3 456	3 022
	1998–1999	3 182	2 860
	1999–2000	2 876	2 634
	2000–2001	2 995	2 722
	2001–2002	3 309	2 955
Total visitors (incl. day tours) to Ruby Coast region	2001–2002		40 890

Source: Visitors to Regions of Bluedonia, Bureau of Tourism Information, 2001.

The regional Tourism Strategy is focused on the promotion and product development of:

▼ nature-based attractions;
▼ farm stay and rural accommodation;
▼ special interest events and products;
▼ a small number of executive conference facilities (within 30 minutes airport);
▼ a backpacker network; and
▼ packages reflecting themes relating to the regional attributes of natural assets, location, lifestyle, rural industry, and heritage—these packages being aimed at the low- to mid-price budget.

The strategy is not strongly focused on Manhattan Beach and there will be a need to offset this factor by a more localised promotions campaign that differentiates this market and emphasises the varied attractions of this local area including dolphins, beaches, scenic views, low-cost accommodation, village (non-tourist) atmosphere and interesting history.

3.2 Tourist Accommodation and Activity

Table 2 summarises tourist accommodation establishments in Manhattan Beach and other main tourism centres in the Ruby Coast region and adjacent areas including Dogwatch (22 km north), Perridullah (17 km north), Hoops Landing (58 km north), and Lookabout Bay (137 km south).

Table 2 Existing Tourist Accommodation

Manhattan Beach	4	hotels (total of 27 rooms)
	9	motels (total of 176 units/rooms)
	2	caravan parks (total of 38 cabins/caravans onsite)
Dogwatch	3	hotels (total of 22 rooms)
	6	motels (total of 115 units/rooms)
	1	caravan park (total of 16 cabins/caravans onsite)
Perridullah	6	hotels (total of 82 rooms)
	11	motels (total of 201 units/rooms)
	3	caravan parks (total of 76 cabins/caravans onsite)
	22	holiday apartments (total of 186 units)
Hoops Landing	2	hotels (total of 18 rooms)
	3	motels (total of 72 units/rooms)
	1	holiday B&B (total of 6 rooms)
Lookabout Bay	7	hotels (total of 65 rooms)
	14	motels (total of 302 units/rooms)
	4	caravan parks (total of 88 cabins/caravans onsite)
	28	holiday flats (total of 260 units)

Source: Bluedonia Motorists' Holiday Guide 2001–02

There is a high level of seasonal variation with most activity occurring during the summer vacation break. Tourists are typically seeking low-budget to mid-budget accommodation/holiday packages aimed at families—hence the prevalence of caravan parks and holiday units.

Room occupancy rates for hotels and motels in the Ruby Coast Statistical Region (incorporating the area from Manhattan Beach to Lookabout Bay) in the March Quarter 2001 was at 81.8%, which was a slight rise over the corresponding period of 2000. The average length of stay was 4.2 nights. Occupancy in the September Quarter 2001 was at 56.7%.

There were 32 hospitality properties surveyed by the Bluedonia Department of Statistics. These properties had a total of 634 guest rooms. The properties surveyed had total guest revenue of B$2 632 500—which constituted average takings of B$4155 per guest room or B$82 200 per property for the March 1997 Quarter. *(Data Source: BDS Catalogue No. X3000—Visitor Accommodation, March Quarter 2001)*

Most tourists visit the region by road, and approximately 91% of visitors travel to the region in a private vehicle. Other transport options are available through the daily bus services to the capital with Blueboy Express. Daily plane flights are available from Lookabout Bay to metropolitan centres with Swooper Airlines.

Coach Tours visit the area regularly. Overnight stops in Manhattan Beach vary between one and five nights. Bus tour companies travel from a wide source area. Discussions with motel owners indicate that visitors on tour usually remain on the motel premises and dine at the motel facilities. There are more tours scheduled in October, November, March and April outside school holiday times as tour passengers are generally aged persons.

3.3 Accommodation Price Range

Prices for motel units vary according to rating and season. Local examples include:

Dolphin Spray Motor Inn
Main street, central location, Manhattan Beach; 3.5-star rating
Rates B$58–90 (single); B$68–105 (double)

Jingle Motel
On the highway, 1.5 kilometres from the post office; 2.5-star rating
Rates B$32–65 (single), B$37–70 (double)

3.4 Potential Market Sectors

3.4.1 People With Disabilities

The Office of Tourism Opportunities has developed a strategy for tourism by people with disability as part of its national program—'The Tourism Reward: A Good Holiday For All Bluedonians and Visitors'—which identifies some specific needs:

▼ to increase awareness among tourism service providers of the needs of tourists with disabilities; and
▼ to highlight the opportunities presented by this market.

The strategy provides detailed information on the travel patterns, needs and experiences of people with a physical or intellectual disability. The strategy material presents some key facts.

1 Most disabled travellers require the assistance of a companion.
2 Most respondents travel with 2–5 people (typically friends or family members) in their group.
3 The generally low level of employment of people with disabilities constrains regular travel (even where moderate costs are involved) because their average income is less than B$10 000 per year.
4 Most people with disability take at least one trip in the year, with the majority of stays within the 1–5 nights' range, and the main reason for travel is for holiday/pleasure, and visiting friends and relatives.
5 The most common accommodation used is homes of friends/relatives, followed by motels and rented flats/houses.

6 The main mode of travel to destinations, and at the destination, is private vehicles.

7 The annual volume and value of the domestic tourism market for people with a physical disability is substantial (there are more than 200 000 people with disability in Bluedonia) with an estimated market-generated expenditure of B$60 million Bluedonia-wide.

Accommodation suitable for disabled persons is limited in the Manhattan Beach area. A summary of the number and types of accommodation offered on the Ruby Coast, as provided through the central tourism data base, is given in Attachment A.

There are only two premises in the region providing recognised facilities for disabled persons. The nearest of these to Manhattan Beach is located on the Hitchawhile Creek near Hoops Landing, 62 km north of Manhattan Beach. It has been specifically designed to accommodate people with disabilities, their carers and families. It offers beach-leisure activities in eight cabin-type units. It is fully booked for the 2003/2004 holiday period.

3.4.2 Aged Tourism

The population of Bluedonia is ageing. The populations of many countries from which visitors come are also ageing. Of 1.6 million visitors to Bluedonia in 2001, more than 20% were aged 55 years or over. Accommodation suitable for people with disability might also be considered as an attraction to aged visitors—both domestic and international.

A survey of international visitors by the Office of Tourism Information identified the most popular activity for older international visitors as being visits to national parks or reserves. Older visitors are more likely to visit botanical gardens and craft workshops/studios, and they go to the beach as much as other visitors (but are less likely to swim).

The proposed site at Manhattan Beach offers potential for aged persons' enjoyment of a number of active and passive outdoor recreational and sporting facilities. There are existing facilities close to the proposed motel site including facilities for swimming and basketball, and the use of ovals for various activities.

3.4.3 Other Tourist Groups

Organised bus tours and private parties of sporting groups (fishing, golf, lawn bowls) occur on a regular and frequent basis, and use facilities in Manhattan Beach as well as other parts of the Ruby Coast. Participants in these tours comprise a range of ages, although they are often aged people without children. There is an opportunity to actively market to these groups by promoting Manhattan Beach generally, as well as the proposed development specifically.

3.4 Conclusion

The development at the Manhattan Beach site of motel accommodation designed for disabled persons and aged people, would:

▼ be in keeping with the region's tourism strategy to develop special-interest events and products;
▼ supplement a shortage of disabled accommodation in an area that attracts tourists from large population centres of Bluedonia and neighbouring countries;
▼ be attractive to an ageing tourist population—particularly with the location of natural attractions, and the bowling greens and golf course, adjacent to the accommodation; and
▼ attract disabled travellers as a recognised growth market.

4 Physical Development Concept

This section provides an indicative development concept and estimates of capital costs associated with construction of new onsite works—including motel-style accommodation and ancillary services.

The accommodation will be designed to incorporate such features as wide doorways and ramp access in order to ensure that the units are comfortable for guests with a disability. The costings are compiled on that basis.

The capital costs identified in this section are also used in subsequent sections of this report. It should be emphasised, however, that all costings are indicative only at this stage.

4.1 Development Concept

For the purpose of this study, a number of assumptions have been made about the type and standard of development required to establish the first stage of the project.

Key assumptions used in the initial costing of this project are as follows:

▼ the project will comprise a 40-unit single-storey motel with access off the existing highway (each unit being designed to latest architectural standards for people with disabilities);
▼ a strong emphasis on site landscaping to create a point-of-difference design concept; and
▼ active and passive solar design to reduce energy costs.

4.2 Development Costs

Table 3 details development costs associated with establishment of the proposed 40-unit motel, associated infrastructure, and possible onsite recreation facilities.

The Table shows that the development would cost approximately B$2.6 million—including short-term interest-only commercial funding.

Building costs in the local area should be very competitive for a project of the size. The estimates are therefore conservative. The Table assumes an interest rate of 9% for bridging finance and a construction time of nine months.

Table 3 Development Costs

SITE COSTS		
Land—existing block of 2 hectares		
Legal costs	B$2 000	
Site testing and surveys	B$6 000	
Total Site Costs	**B$8 000**	**B$8 000**
CONSTRUCTION		
Construction (1000 sq.m @ B$850/sq.m)	B$1 700 000	
Parking & landscaping	B$60 000	
Connection to services	B$200 000	
Unit furniture & fixtures (B$4000 per unit	B$160 000	
Contingency (10% of B$2 120 000)	B$212 000	
Total Construction Costs	**B$2 332 000**	**B$2 332 000**
FEES		
Architect's fees (5% of total constr. costs)	B$116 600	
Other fees (engineer etc.; 2.5% of tot. constr. costs)	B$58 300	
Council fees/rates/charges	B$10 000	
Total Fees	**B$184 900**	**B$184 900**
INTEREST		
Interest (9% pa on B$2 524 900 for 9 months)	B$85 215	
Total Interest	**B$85 215**	**B$85 215**
TOTAL PROJECT COST (Exc. Land)		**B$2 610 115**

In addition, B$80 000 will be required for prepaid expenses (such as initial marketing and opening expenses).

4.3 Development Approval Process

The local government authority, the Manhattan Beach County Council, has advised that it will 'fast-track' any approval process for this site in light of the potential benefits to Manhattan Beach and local employment, and it has stated support for the project.

A project of the scale envisaged for Stage 1 would normally take a minimum of 2–3 months from lodgement to approval. It would require public notification and consideration by the local traffic committee including the Bluedonia Ministry of Transport (BMT) because of its highway location. The number of units, use of existing access, and good sight lines associated with this entrance work should be favourably considered by BMT, and substantial expenditure on new road works would appear to be unlikely. Minor widening of slip lanes at the entrance could be required. It is unlikely that a detailed traffic study would be required.

5 Financial Assessment

5.1 Project Budget

Table 4 Projected Revenue/Expenses

	Option 1 (55–80% Occupation)		Option 2 (60–85% Occupation)	
Revenue	B$748 250		B$803 000	
Total Revenue		B$748 250		B$803 000
Less expenses:				
Operating expenses	B$299 300		B$321 200	
Indirect expenses	B$77 500		B$77 500	
Depreciation	B$70 250		B$70 250	
Total expenses	B$447 050	B$447 050	B$468 950	B$468 950
Surplus		B$301 200		B$334 050

Revenue Assumptions:
 (i) The advertised rate for units will range from B$95 to B$115 per unit (single and double occupancy) and, allowing for discounting, this will result in an average daily rate of B$80 in the peak season (November–April) and B$70 in the off season (May–October).
 (ii) The occupancy in the peak season will range between 80% and 85%; the occupancy in the off season will range from 55% to 60%.
 (iii) These operating figures will be reached after three years (bearing in mind the marketing required for the project and the circumstances of the Ruby Coast).

Expense assumptions:
 (i) Operating costs are 40% of revenue.
 (ii) Indirect expenses are fixed.
 (iii) Depreciation expense is B$70 250.
 (iv) Prepaid expenses of B$80 000 have been written-off over the first two years of operation.

Total capital investment is:
   B$2 610 115 plus estimated land value of B$350 000 = B$2 960 115.
Projected returns after three years are:
   B$300 000 to B$335 000

This means a return on investment (before tax and interest) of 10–11%. Additional facilities such as a restaurant could be considered as future additions to the motel.

5.2 Cash Flow

Table 5 Projected Cash Flow

	Year 1 (Construction 9 months)	Year 2	Year 3	Year 4
Opening Balance	0.00	–B$24 377	B$38 532	B$229 443
Revenue	B$87 600 (3 months)	B$467 200	B$700 800	B$748 250
Less:				
Operating Expenses	B$35 040	B$186 880	B$280 320	B$299 300
Indirect Expenses	B$19 375	B$77 500	B$77 500	B$77 500
Depreciation	B$17 562	B$70 250	B$70 250	B$70 250
Prepaid Expenses	B$40 000	B$40 000		
Deficit Interest	B$2 700			
Surplus/(Deficit)	–B$24 377	B$89 870	B$272 730	B$301 200
Taxation		B$26 961	B$81 819	B$90 360
Closing Balance	**–B$24 377**	**B$38 532**	**B$229 443**	**B$440 283**

Assumptions:
  (i) Operation at average 30% occupancy for three months in first year, then average 40%, 60% and 67.5% (that is, 55%–80%) in subsequent years.
 (ii) Prepaid expenses of B$80 000 written off over first two financial years.
(iii) Ongoing interest payments not included, except for overdraft interest (11%) on initial deficit.
(iv) Taxation calculated at 30% of surplus.

6 Summary and Conclusions

In the Manhattan Beach district and in the Ruby Coast region generally, there is a limited number of accommodation properties that have appropriate access and facilities suitable for the comfort of people with special needs. The average occupancy of all hospitality properties in the Ruby Coast region ranges from 82% in peak season (November–April) to 57% in the off season.

Market research indicates that the area attracts visitors from Bluedonia as well as overseas. More than 40 000 local and interstate visitors tour the region, and each stays, on average, six days. Of those visitors, based on national statistics, approximately 15% would have a disability or mobility difficulty, and the evidence also indicates that most people with disability who travel do so with one or more companions, which suggests a significant and growing demand for purpose-built facilities.

Despite the seasonal nature of occupancy generally, there was evidence that there were tour visits by aged people, and a number of these could be attracted by a facility especially built to cater for those with access difficulties. Of course, not all people who are aged have a disability, and not all people with disability are aged, and these constitute two clear market segments.

The findings of the feasibility study are that:

1 The construction of a property of 40 units, designed specifically for people with special needs, offers the probability of positive returns on investment (before tax and interest charges) of the order of 10–11% after three years.
2 The property should be of at least 3-star quality, aimed at attracting the family tourism market.
3 Council and regional tourism authorities are supportive of the concept proposal.
4 The proposed site offers sound marketing possibilities without obvious building or zoning problems.

After consideration of marketing, legal, design and financial aspects of the proposal, the consultants recommend commencing the project and preparing development and building plans for council.

[Appendices and Attachments as noted would follow in an actual report. They are not included here.]

APPENDIX A

Extended Principal/Interest Calculation

ASSUMPTIONS
1 All payments are equal amounts of $13 045.45.
2 Interest is 11% compounded monthly (approximately 0.9167% per month).

	Beginning Principal	Payment of Interest	Repayment of Principal	Ending Principal	Annual Interest	Annual Principal
1	$600 000.00	$5500.00	$7545.45	$592 454.55	$61 292.60	$95 252.80
2	$592 454.55	$5430.83	$7614.62	$584 839.93		
3	$584 839.93	$5361.03	$7684.42	$577 155.52		
4	$577 155.52	$5290.59	$7754.86	$569 400.66		
5	$569 400.66	$5219.51	$7825.94	$561 574.71		
6	$561 574.71	$5147.77	$7897.68	$553 677.03		
7	$553 677.03	$5075.37	$7970.08	$545 706.96		
8	$545 706.96	$5002.31	$8043.14	$537 663.82		
9	$537 663.82	$4928.59	$8116.86	$529 546.95		
10	$529 546.95	$4854.18	$8191.27	$521 355.68		
11	$521 355.68	$4779.09	$8266.36	$513 089.33		
12	$513 089.33	$4703.32	$8342.13	$504 747.20		
13	$504 747.20	$4626.85	$8418.60	$496 328.60	$50 270.05	$106 275.35
14	$496 328.60	$4549.68	$8495.77	$487 832.83		
15	$487 832.83	$4471.80	$8573.65	$479 259.18		
16	$479 259.18	$4393.21	$8652.24	$470 606.94		
17	$470 606.94	$4313.90	$8731.55	$461 875.38		
18	$461 875.38	$4233.86	$8811.59	$453 063.79		
19	$453 063.79	$4153.08	$8892.37	$444 171.42		
20	$444 171.42	$4071.57	$8973.88	$435 197.55		
21	$435 197.55	$3989.31	$9056.14	$426 141.41		
22	$426 141.41	$3906.30	$9139.15	$417 002.25		
23	$417 002.25	$3822.52	$9222.93	$407 779.32		
24	$407 779.32	$3737.98	$9307.47	$398 471.85		
25	$398 471.85	$3652.66	$9392.79	$389 079.06	$37 971.99	$118 573.41
26	$389 079.06	$3566.56	$9478.89	$379 600.17		
27	$379 600.17	$3479.67	$9565.78	$370 034.39		
28	$370 034.39	$3391.98	$9653.47	$360 380.92		
29	$360 380.92	$3303.49	$9741.96	$350 638.96		
30	$350 638.96	$3214.19	$9831.26	$340 807.70		
31	$340 807.70	$3124.07	$9921.38	$330 886.32		
32	$330 886.32	$3033.12	$10 012.33	$320 874.00		

Beginning	Beginning Principal	Payment of Interest	Repayment of Principal	Ending Principal	Annual Interest	Annual Principal
33	$320 874.00	$2941.34	$10 104.11	$310 769.89		
34	$310 769.89	$2848.72	$10 196.73	$300 573.16		
35	$300 573.16	$2755.25	$10 290.20	$290 282.97		
36	$290 282.97	$2660.93	$10 384.52	$279 898.45		
37	$279 898.45	$2565.74	$10 479.71	$269 418.73	$24 250.82	$132 294.58
38	$269 418.73	$2469.67	$10 575.78	$258 842.95		
39	$258 842.95	$2372.73	$10 672.72	$248 170.23		
40	$248 170.23	$2274.89	$10 770.56	$237 399.67		
41	$237 399.67	$2176.16	$10 869.29	$226 530.39		
42	$226 530.39	$2076.53	$10 968.92	$215 561.47		
43	$215 561.47	$1975.98	$11 069.47	$204 492.00		
44	$204 492.00	$1874.51	$11 170.94	$193 321.06		
45	$193 321.06	$1772.11	$11 273.34	$182 047.72		
46	$182 047.72	$1668.77	$11 376.68	$170 671.04		
47	$170 671.04	$1564.48	$11 480.97	$159 190.07		
48	$159 190.07	$1459.24	$11 586.21	$147 603.86		
49	$147 603.86	$1353.04	$11 692.41	$135 911.45	$8941.84	$147 603.56
50	$135 911.45	$1245.85	$11 799.60	$124 111.85		
51	$124 111.85	$1137.69	$11 907.76	$112 204.10		
52	$112 204.10	$1028.54	$12 016.91	$100 187.18		
53	$100 187.18	$918.38	$12 127.07	$88 060.12		
54	$88 060.12	$807.22	$12 238.23	$75 821.88		
55	$75 821.88	$695.03	$12 350.42	$63 471.47		
56	$63 471.47	$581.82	$12 463.63	$51 007.84		
57	$51 007.84	$467.57	$12 577.88	$38 429.96		
58	$38 429.96	$352.27	$12 693.18	$25 736.79		
59	$25 736.79	$235.92	$12 809.53	$12 927.26		
60	$12 927.26	$118.50	$12 926.95	$0.31		
					$182 727.31	$599 999.69

APPENDIX B

Present Value Table

Present Value of $1 Received in the Future

Rate per Compounding Period

Periods Hence	2%	3%	4%	5%	6%	8%	10%	12%	15%	20%
1	0.980	0.971	0.962	0.952	0.943	0.926	0.909	0.893	0.870	0.833
2	0.961	0.943	0.925	0.907	0.890	0.857	0.826	0.797	0.756	0.694
3	0.942	0.915	0.889	0.864	0.840	0.794	0.751	0.712	0.658	0.579
4	0.924	0.889	0.855	0.823	0.792	0.735	0.683	0.636	0.572	0.482
5	0.906	0.863	0.822	0.784	0.747	0.681	0.621	0.567	0.497	0.402
6	0.888	0.838	0.790	0.746	0.705	0.630	0.564	0.507	0.432	0.335
7	0.871	0.813	0.760	0.711	0.665	0.583	0.513	0.452	0.376	0.279
8	0.854	0.789	0.731	0.677	0.627	0.540	0.467	0.404	0.327	0.233
9	0.837	0.766	0.703	0.645	0.592	0.500	0.424	0.361	0.284	0.194
10	0.821	0.744	0.676	0.614	0.558	0.463	0.386	0.322	0.247	0.162
11	0.800	0.722	0.650	0.585	0.527	0.429	0.350	0.287	0.215	0.135
12	0.789	0.701	0.625	0.557	0.497	0.397	0.319	0.257	0.187	0.112
13	0.773	0.681	0.601	0.530	0.469	0.368	0.290	0.229	0.163	0.093
14	0.758	0.661	0.577	0.505	0.442	0.340	0.263	0.205	0.141	0.078
15	0.743	0.642	0.555	0.481	0.417	0.315	0.239	0.183	0.123	0.065
16	0.728	0.623	0.534	0.458	0.394	0.292	0.218	0.163	0.107	0.054
17	0.714	0.605	0.513	0.436	0.371	0.270	0.198	0.146	0.093	0.005
18	0.700	0.587	0.494	0.416	0.350	0.250	0.180	0.130	0.081	0.038
19	0.686	0.570	0.475	0.396	0.331	0.232	0.164	0.116	0.070	0.031
20	0.673	0.554	0.456	0.377	0.312	0.215	0.149	0.104	0.061	0.026
30	0.552	0.412	0.308	0.231	0.174	0.099	0.057	0.033	0.015	0.000
40	0.453	0.307	0.208	0.142	0.097	0.046	0.022	0.011	0.004	0.001
50	0.372	0.228	0.141	0.087	0.054	0.021	0.009	0.003	0.001	–

Answers to Questions

Chapter 1

1 Only short answers (True/False) are provided here. The reasons that are offered require assessment on an individual basis.

  a **False**

  b **False**

  c **True**

  d **False**

  e **False**

  f **True**

  g **False**

  h **False**.

2 **a** Besides determining how well the proposed operation can meet the owner's objectives, a project evaluation can be used for attracting venture finance, formulating ongoing plans and **supporting development applications**.

  b Large hotel operators use linked reservation systems that are also known as **global distribution systems**.

  c Recent surveys have generally found that projected occupancy and net income figures in feasibility studies are **overestimated**.

  d The crucial role in the project evaluation team is that of **team leader**.

  e A **negative** report in the project evaluation might be difficult to present but might be in the best long-term interests of the parties.

  f The structure of the project evaluation should be kept as **simple** as possible.

3 Answers to Question 3 are not proffered because of the wide variety of possible answers.

4 The answer should include:

- discussion of the importance of a detailed plan for the study;
- the coordination and review of the work of the study team;
- the financial goals of the study;
- a schedule for the work;
- communication between the team and the commissioning body; and
- contingency plans for delays or problems.

Chapter 2

1 Only short answers (True/False) are provided here. The reasons that are offered require assessment on an individual basis.
   a **False**
   b **True**
   c **False**
   d **False**
   e **True**
   f **True**

2 a A trend can be described as a sequence of events with **momentum** and durability.
   b We might expect consumers who are 'stressed out' to give themselves rewards such as **weekend** skiing trips or holidays.
   c Entrepreneurs have **ideas** and want to do something about them.
   d In the view of McCarthy et al., a business should be socially and economically useful, should develop an organisation, and should **earn a profit in the long run**.
   e The mission statement of the business is both philosophical and **qualitative**.
   f 'Environmental scanning' is an **initial** assessment of the market.

3 Answers to Question 3 are not proffered because of the wide variety of possible answers.

4 The answer should include:
   ■ discussion of models of development; and
   ■ the specific purpose of a project evaluation as an analytical report;
   (There might be duplication, but that is not necessarily a bad thing.)

Chapter 3

1 Only short answers (True/False) are provided here. The reasons that are offered require assessment on an individual basis.
   a **True**
   b **False**
   c **False**
   d **False**
   e **False**
   f **True**

2 a The characteristics of a market can be assessed through **quantitative** and qualitative analysis.
   b 'A problem **well-defined** is half-solved.'

    c Primary information is that gathered **first-hand** by the evaluation team.

    d Interest rates and energy prices are examples of **external** factors that might affect the feasibility of a project.

    e In order to assess the general hospitality and tourism characteristics of a specific region, it is useful to compile a visitor **profile**.

    f Culture includes tangible and intangible factors, and examples of intangible factors are **attitudes, beliefs and languages**.

3 Answers to Question 3 are not proffered because of the wide variety of possible answers.

4 The answer should include a discussion of how analysts should:

- be critical in using information from secondary and tertiary sources;
- be able to interpret the data from secondary and tertiary sources where necessary (noting the distinction between statistical material and extrapolations from that material); and
- refer to source data (and where that data is properly used, how this remains a cost-effective and efficient way of obtaining statistical and other information).

Chapter 4

1 Only short answers (True/False) are provided here. The reasons that are offered require assessment on an individual basis.

    a **False**

    b **True**

    c **True**

    d **False**

    e **False**

    f **False**

2 **a** A project evaluation should have three dimensions—a review of the present situation and an **analysis of past operations**, as well as a **projection of future operations**.

    b There are **three** options for analysing the market for a new product.

    c Information on probable competitors is presented in an **inventory** of those competitors and their services.

    d Guest categories/segments of higher growth might be termed '**high-priority segments**' for new projects.

    e The **fair-share** method of assessing market demand totals the number of rooms in the target market place, and calculates what proportion to that total the new project will contribute.

    f Supply/demand assessments can be distorted by **external, non-market** factors.

3 Answers to Question 3 are not proffered because of the wide variety of possible answers.

4 The answer should include:
- the advantages and disadvantages of using projections;
- the uses of the study; and
- the required degree of accuracy of estimates of occupancy and net income.

Chapter 5

1 Only short answers (True/False) are provided here. The reasons that are offered require assessment on an individual basis.

  a True
  b False
  c False
  d False
  e True
  f False

2 **a** The aim of a developer should be to compile an '**optimum site-use**' concept.

  b Although wishing to utilise the site properly, a developer should nevertheless allow for the possibility of **future expansion**.

  c A rehabilitated site might have site **risks**.

  d After assessing aspects of the building, a study will consider other factors such as **property identification**, **landscaping** and **parking**.

  e Size and quality of the development are **physical** characteristics.

  f Poor siting of entrances can lead to a lack of **manoeuvring room**.

3 Answers to Question 3 are not proffered because of the wide variety of possible answers.

4 The answer should include discussion of the following:
- that a hospitality development is generally too large to be altered cheaply;
- whether a hospitality or tourism operation is too site-specific to be relocated;
- whether physical characteristics can be altered (particularly for future demand or demand changes); and
- the large capital-intensive investment in a hotel.

Chapter 6

1 Only short answers (True/False) are provided here. The reasons that are offered require assessment on an individual basis.
   a **False**
   b **False**
   c **True**
   d **False**
   e **False**
   f **True**

2 a A hotel must respond to market needs, but must also **function** adequately.
   b **Business travellers** would value telecommunications and secretarial services.
   c A **time-and-materials** contract means the owner incurs the risk of cost overruns.
   d 'Value engineering' is a **systematic** method of analysing needs versus costs versus resources.
   e A construction timeline can be presented as a '**critical-path**' diagram.
   f Protection clauses should include a **disputes-settling** procedure.

3 Answers to Question 3 are not proffered because of the wide variety of possible answers.

4 Answers could include comment on:
   ■ whether projects have a lifespan, or whether fashions and trends are cyclical;
   ■ whether there are aspects of hospitality operations that are universal and timeless (for example, accommodation services), and whether large projects can be said to have a number of lifespans, in that they can be altered and even change their nature (for example, one generation's modern style becomes the heritage style of the next); and
   ■ constraints on returns, such as market factors.

Chapter 7

1 Only short answers (True/False) are provided here. The reasons that are offered require assessment on an individual basis.
   a **False**
   b **False**
   c **True**
   d **False**
   e **True**
   f **True**

2 a **Technology** might change the nature of the check-in process.
  b **Wages and salaries** comprise approximately 35% of the revenue of some properties.
  c Linked properties carrying out the same business in different locations can be referred to as **franchises**.
3 Answers to Question 3 are not proffered because of the wide variety of possible answers.
4 Answers can make reference to:
  ■ the benefits of flatter structures in providing timely decision-making (and, hence, better service to guests);
  ■ motivation for base-level staff to accept greater responsibility—including extrinsic rewards (for example, increased wages), and intrinsic rewards (for example, greater job satisfaction).

Chapter 8

1 Only short answers (True/False) are provided here. The reasons that are offered require assessment on an individual basis.
  a **True**
  b **False**
  c **True**
  d **True**
  e **True**
2 a There are **four** levels of support for environmental issues.
  b Organisations should encourage their stakeholders to develop environmentally appropriate **ways of operating**.
  c **All** developments must comply with environmental laws and regulations.
  d Usually, an environmental impact study (EIS) will be required on sites of **heritage value**.
3 Answers to Question 3 are not proffered because of the wide variety of possible answers.
4 Answers could describe:
  ■ examples of energy reduction measures that incur significant savings (such as insulation measures);
  ■ how, even if the savings of individual measures are limited, the cumulative savings can be extensive and there are benefits in establishing an 'environmentally conscious' regime.

Chapter 9

1 Only short answers (True/False) are provided here. The reasons that are offered require assessment on an individual basis.
   a **True**
   b **False**
   c **True**
   d **False**
   e **True**

2 a **Straight-line** depreciation allows a capital amount to be written off as an expense in equal amounts each year.
   b Interest payments are operating expenses whereas **principal** payments are not.
   c Development costs can include preliminary costs which are thereby said to be **capitalised**.
   d Capital payments in relation to leasehold property are said to be **amortised**.

3 Answers to Question 3 are not proffered because of the wide variety of possible answers.

4 Answers should include:
   ■ the taxation and cash-flow implications of depreciation;
   ■ some different methods of calculating the expense;
   ■ the fact that the option of revaluing frequently has the drawback of being expensive (and is also subject to estimates).

Chapter 10

1 Only short answers (True/False) are provided here. The reasons that are offered require assessment on an individual basis.
   a **True**
   b **False**
   c **True**
   d **False**
   e **True**

2 a The likely demand for room service is sometimes referred to as **derived demand**.
   b The accounting doctrine of **conservatism** states that it is preferable to understate a revenue item rather than to overstate it.
   c The largest expense category in a hotel is **payroll**.
   d The costs that vary with the number of guests or volume of business are described as **variable** costs.

3 Answers to Question 3 are not proffered because of the wide variety of possible answers.

4 This statement might indeed be true, but answers should discuss the consequences for the owners/developers if they become overcommitted in a project that does not prove to be as profitable as they anticipate.

Chapter 11

1 Only short answers (True/False) are provided here. The reasons that are offered require assessment on an individual basis.

   a False
   b True
   c True
   d False

2 **a Capital budgeting** considers not only amounts to be invested, but also when they will be committed.

   b Investment planning is a part of the strategic planning process.

   c Costs which are fixed for short time periods are frequently **variable** over longer time periods.

   d The types of broad assessments which have to be made include whether the opportunity fits with the **corporate objectives**.

3 Answers to Question 3 are not proffered because of the wide variety of possible answers.

4 The discussion should include:

   ■ a review of how assumptions are made;
   ■ the facts that underpin them;
   ■ the degree to which they will affect operations; and
   ■ the fact that, if circumstances change, the business plan itself can be subject to review.

Chapter 12

1 Only short answers (True/False) are provided here. The reasons that are offered require assessment on an individual basis.

   a True
   b False
   c False
   d True

2 **a** '**Referral process**' is a term used for marketing one property through all others in the chain.

   b Franchise fees can be calculated on a number of bases.

    c A franchiser should guarantee a franchisee **exclusivity** of use of the brand within a given territory.

    d You should not merely accept a franchiser's data, but should always conduct an **independent** project evaluation.

3 Answers to Question 3 are not proffered because of the wide variety of possible answers.

4 Answer should include:

- reference to the return on investment;
- an assessment of the advantages and disadvantages of being locked into a long period of operating a franchise which might or might not meet the targets determined at the time of making the agreement; and
- reference to franchise agreements that run month to month.

Chapter 13

1 Only short answers (True/False) are provided here. The reasons that are offered require assessment on an individual basis.

    a **False**

    b **True**

    c **False**

    d **True**

    e **True**

2 **a** There is no place for **jargon** in a project evaluation.

    b The addition of **extraneous** material can obscure the data.

    c Material that is not essential to the background and explanation of recommendations should be **excluded**.

    d The **detail** of the presentation is also important.

3 Answers to Question 3 are not proffered because of the wide variety of possible answers.

4 Answer should include:

- the different users of the project evaluation;
- the information they will look for;
- the fact that, although it is true that not everyone will read every word of the study, all the sections will be read in detail by someone;
- if the reader cannot find what they want quickly and clearly, there is every chance that the project will not be fairly assessed; and
- reference to the return on investment.

Glossary of Tourism/Hospitality Associations

Australian Federation of Travel Agents (AFTA)

AFTA is a trade association formed in 1957 to represent the interests of retail travel agents. Since its formation, it has established a code of ethics, stimulated, encouraged and promoted the desire to travel, and discouraged unfair competition without interfering with initiative and enterprise. Membership consists of 1500 travel agents and representatives from other sectors including hotels, wholesalers and tour operators.

Australian Liquor, Hospitality and Miscellaneous Workers Union

This union covers employees in businesses in the hospitality and tourism industries— including hotels, motels, restaurants, cafés, and general tourism enterprises. The union provides financial services, a legal advisory service, assists with establishing enterprise agreements, and provides access to a superannuation fund. It has approximately 220 000 members nationally.

Australian Automobile Association

This organisation is a peak industry body made up of state and territory motor associations. It acts to coordinate the activities of its members on matters of mutual interest, and links Australia with similar overseas bodies. It is based in Canberra.

Australian Hotels Association (AHA)

The AHA represents the interests of over 6100 hotels and resorts around Australia— ranging from suburban pubs to five-star properties. Its main roles include: (1) the representation of members on matters of common interest (including taxation, excise duty and industrial relations); (2) the provision of information to members regarding industry issues and trends; (3) the provision of networking opportunities for members; and (4) the facilitation of human resource development within the hotel sector. The AHA has state and territory branches which are responsible for electing a national executive. The executive, in turn, oversees the management the AHA's national office in Canberra.

Australian Tourist Commission

The main objectives of the commission are to increase the number of visitors to Australia from overseas, and to maximise the benefits that overseas visitors bring to Australia.

CHRIE (Council on Hotel, Restaurant & Institutional Education)

CHRIE was founded in 1946 as a non-profit association for schools, colleges and universities, offering programs in hotel and restaurant management, food services management, and culinary arts. In recent years its focus has expanded, and its mission statement has evolved, making it a market place facilitating exchanges of information, ideas, research, products and services related to education, training and resources development for the hospitality industry.

Green Globe

Green Globe is a world travel and tourism council initiative to help environmental awareness and management in the tourism industry. Its prime objective is to provide low-cost practical means for all travel and tourism industry businesses to achieve environmental improvements.

International Air Transport Association (IATA)

IATA is an international organisation established to represent and to serve the airline industry, and to help develop cost-effective, environmentally friendly standards and procedures to facilitate the operation of international air transport

International Des Skal Clubs Association

This is an organisation that aims to develop friendship and common purpose among members of the tourism industry, and to foster goodwill between the people of the world through tourism. Membership is open to people who have a position of responsibility in the industry for more than five years.

Meetings Industry Association of Australia

The association is a national, independent, non-profit body dedicated to fostering professionalism and excellence in all aspects of meeting managements.

Restaurant and Catering Association

This association supports and aids individual restaurants and catering services.

Tourism Council of Australia

The council was established in 1967 as a non-commercial statutory corporation. It is a committee made up of government, industry and union representatives that seek to maintain a high level of skills and training for the workers in the tourism industry

Tourism Training Australia

This is a non-profit organisation established by the tourism industry. Its primary function is to identify the training needs of the industry, and to take action to meet those needs.

World Tourism Organisation (WTO)

The WTO is the principal collator and publisher of global statistics on tourist activities. Most countries use the WTO standard definitions. The WTO also monitors international trends in tourism, provides assistance to national governments or their organisations (in the area of tourism planning and management), collects and disseminates information, and publishes reports on various matters (such as the protection of natural and cultural resources).

Glossary of Tourism/Hospitality Terms

Bistro

A place which serves food and beverages, together with some sort of entertainment; an informal restaurant; might be either an independent business or part of a larger business (such as a hotel or club).

Café

A room or building where light refreshments are served.

Cafeteria

An inexpensive restaurant or snack bar—usually self-service.

Caravan Park

Commercial open-air accommodation establishment at which caravans can be rented by travellers, or sites can be hired on which travellers might place their own caravans; hiring fee frequently includes use of electricity and access to shower, toilet and laundry facilities.

Casino

Area within a ship, hotel, resort, which is licensed for gambling activities.

Club

Normally an establishment providing food drink, sometimes entertainment, overnight accommodation and other facilities and services for members (but not for the general public).

Coach

A bus (single-decker or double-decker) used for long-distance travel, or for sightseeing.

Coachline

A company that runs coach services; often runs chartered tours as well.

Convention Centre

A specialised facility designed to accommodate large gatherings of people for a range of purposes including conferences, events and exhibitions.

Cruise Ship

A vessel built and designed with onboard accommodation, restaurants, gym, swimming pool and other recreational activities.

Duty-Free Shop

A building or area (usually within a ship, resorts, or hotel airports; or as a separate establishment in a city) where goods are purchased without tax by international visitors and residents travelling to international destinations.

Escorted Tour

A tour which uses the services of a tour manager or tour escort; or a tour package that include the services of a tour escort for its entire duration.

Fast-Food Outlet

A limited-menu retail outlet offering quick counter service and take-away service; usually based on systems with standard recipes, procedures and products; often chain-operated with brand names.

Guest House

A small owner-managed establishment normally providing accommodation, food and beverage to residents only.

Hotel

This word is used to describe a range of accommodation properties. In the traditional usage 'hotels' were defined as places offering sleeping accommodation for hire to travellers and transients, and including services such as food, beverage and entertainment along with other facilities and services. There is a great variety in hotels—ranging from large, high-quality properties with numerous additional services (such as business centres and health clubs), to small basic properties providing few services beyond operating a bar.

Inbound Tour Operator
An individual or firm that acts to organise tourism industry services into packages that are commonly put together at the request of travel agents.

Motel
A commercial accommodation property providing accommodation for motorists. Originating in North America as a response to growth in motor travel, early motels were distinguished by low-rise buildings with rooms normally accessible from outside, adjacent to a car park. There are various grades of motels with many properties offering additional services and facilities (such as restaurant, pool and in-house movies). Facilities are often limited, as guests tend to arrive late in the afternoon and leave early in the morning. Motels are sometimes known as motor hotels, motor inns, and motor lodges.

Nature Attraction
A natural, recurring structure, plant or animal that attracts tourists.

Pub
A term commonly used in Australia for a small hotel where socialising and consuming beverages provides the main source of revenue.

Resort
An accommodation property that provides leisure opportunities

Resort Area
A district frequented by tourists and excursionists, which provides a range of leisure opportunities and accommodation types.

Restaurant
An establishment at which meals are served to the general public.

Tavern
Licensed premises having no accommodation but providing bottle sales, bar service and counter meals.

Theme Park
A purpose-built complex designed with the intention of providing visitors with an atmosphere of another place and time—usually concentrating on one dominant theme around which architecture, landscaping, costumed personnel, rides, shows, food services and merchandises are coordinated (an example being 'Disneyland' in Florida, USA).

Tour Wholesaler
A firm which combines tourism services produced by other businesses into a single service offering; these services including air travel, accommodation and local sightseeing.

Tourist Information Centre
A centre where locals and travellers might find information on events and attractions that are going on in the local community and district.

Travel Agent
An intermediary who derives financial gain (in the form of a commission) by linking suppliers of tourism services with consumers through the provision of reservations, ticketing and other services.

Youth Hostel
A type of budget accommodation, at which bathroom/toilet facilities are often shared, and where only basic services are provided.

Bibliography

Articles and Theses

Cahill, M. 1988, 'Hoteliers Can Reap Rewards by Welcoming Appraisers', *Hotel and Motel Management*, vol. 203, no.12, pp 18ff.

Dickey, C. 1996, 'Niche for the Night, *Newsweek*, 9 December 1996, p. 71.

Greenfield, M. 1986, 'Who Put the Lake in the Lobby?', *Newsweek*, 13 January 1986, p. 76.

Hart, C. 1986, 'Product Development: How Marriott Created Courtyard', *The Cornell Hotel and Restaurant Quarterly*, November 1986, p. 68.

Hensdill, C. 1996, 'Partnerships in Dining', *Hotels*, February 1996, p. 57.

Liatsos, G. 1996, 'A Project Evaluation for the Renovation of a Four-Star Hotel in Nicosia, Cyprus', MSc thesis (unpublished), University of Surrey, Guildford, UK.

Macomber, J. 1989, 'You Can Manage Construction Risks', *Harvard Business Review*, March–April 1989, p. 158.

Mankarious, R. & Nehmer, J. 1992, 'Structuring the Contractual Relationship in a Hotel Renovation Project', *The Real Estate Finance Journal*, Winter 1992, p. 91.

No Author Noted, 'Sample Inn Accounts', *Bottomline*, October/November 1991.

Ohlin, J. 1993, 'Creative Approaches to the Americans with Disabilities Act, *The Cornell Hotel and Restaurant Administration Quarterly*, October 1993, pp 19ff.

Overstreet, G. 1989, 'Profiles in Hotel Feasibility', *Cornell Hotel and Restaurant Administration Quarterly*, February 1989, pp 8–19.

Overstreet, G. 1989, 'Profiles in Hotel Feasibility: the Consequences of Overbuilding', *Cornell Hotel and Restaurant Administration Quarterly*, May 1989, pp 10–18.

Patroni, E. 1995, 'A Project Evaluation for an All-suite, Environmentally Friendly Four-Star Resort Hotel in Halkidiki, Greece', MSc thesis, University of Surrey, Guildford, UK.

Petit, R. 1985, 'Integrated Planning: The Experts Interact', *Lodging*, November 1985.

Pyo, Sung-Soo, Chang, Hye-Sook & Chon, Kye-Sung 1995, 'Considerations of Management Objectives by Target Markets in Hotel Feasibility Studies', *International Journal of Hospitality Management*, vol. 14, no. 2, pp 151–6.

Robichaux, M., 'Competitor Intelligence—A Grapevine to Rivals' Secrets', *Wall Street Journal*, 12 April 1989, p B2.

Rowe, M. 1997, 'The New F&B Rules', *Lodging Hospitality*, March 1997, p. 20.

Russell, J. 1991, 'Value Engineering the Disney Way', *Architectural Record*, December, 1991, p. 24.

Scoviak, M. 1996, 'The Full Service Business Room of the Future, *Interior Design*, June 1996, p. 154. [Note that this author sometimes publishes as 'Scoviak' and sometimes publishes as 'Scoviak-Lerner'.]

Scoviak-Lerner, M. 1994, 'The New Look of Hotels—Twelve Trends Influencing Today's Design', *Hotels*, May 1994, p. 52. [Note that this author sometimes publishes as 'Scoviak' and sometimes publishes as 'Scoviak-Lerner'.]

Scoviak-Lerner, M. 1995, 'One of a Kind Design', *Hotels*, May 1995, p. 30. [Note that this author sometimes publishes as 'Scoviak' and sometimes publishes as 'Scoviak-Lerner'.]

Scoviak-Lerner, M. 1996, 'Market-Driven Design Trends for the Millennium', *Hotels*, May 1996, p. 58. [Note that this author sometimes publishes as 'Scoviak' and sometimes publishes as 'Scoviak-Lerner'.]

Suntornpong, Busarakorn 1996, 'Master Plan and Project Evaluation Tourism Development of Phuket Thailand', MSc thesis, University of Surrey, Guildford, UK.

Szivas, E. & Riley, M. 1996, 'The Role of the Hotel Project Evaluation in the Development Process: Putting Utility into Perspective', *International Journal of Contemporary Hospitality Management*, vol. 8, part 6, pp 29–30.

Tarras, J. 1990, 'Accuracy of Hotel Project Evaluation Projections', *FIU Hospitality Review*, vol. 8, part 1, pp 53–9.

Taylor, S. 1997, 'Food for Thought', *Lodging Hospitality*, March 1997, p. 27.

Terpak, M. 1989 'The Fast-Track Construction Alternative', *The Real Estate Finance Journal*, Winter 1989, p. 75.

Wagner, G. 1995, 'ADA: A Look Back, *Lodging Hospitality*, October 1995, p. 47.

Yesawich, P. 1988, 'Planning: The Second Step in Market Development', *The Cornell Hotel and Restaurant Administration Quarterly*, February, 1988, p. 72.

Books

CIMA Study Text 1990, *Management Accounting Techniques*, BPP Publishing: London.

Coltman, M. 1998, *Hospitality Management Accounting*, 6th edn, Van Nostrand Reinhold: New York.

Czinkota, M. & Ronkainen, I. 1990, *International Marketing*, 4th edn, The Dryden Press (Harcourt Brace College Publishers): Fort Worth, Texas.

Daniels, J. & Radebaugh, L. 1995, *International Business—Environments and Operations*, 7th edn, Addison-Wesley Publishing Company: Massachusetts.

Dobbins, R. & Pike, R. 1988, 'Capital Budgeting, In Cowe, R. (ed.) *Handbook of Management Accounting*, 2nd edn, Gower Publishing: Aldershot.

Hartley, R.F. 1992, *Marketing Mistakes*, John Wiley & Sons Inc.: New York.

Horngren, C. & Foster, G. 1991, *Cost Accounting—A Managerial Emphasis*, 7th edn, Prentice Hall: New Jersey.

Kemper, A., 1979, *Architectural Handbook*, Wiley: New York.

Kotler, P. 1994, *Marketing Management—Analysis, Planning, Implementation and Control*, 8th edn, Prentice-Hall International, Inc.: New Jersey.

Lewis, G., Morkel, A. & Hubbard, G. 1993, *Australian Strategic Management—Concepts, Context and Cases*, Prentice Hall of Australia P/L: Sydney.

McCarthy, E., Perreault, W., Quester, P., Wilkinson, J. & Lee, K. 1994, *Basis Marketing—A Managerial Approach*, Richard D. Irwin Inc., Sydney.

McDonald, M. 1995, *Marketing Plans—How to Prepare Them and How to Use Them*, 3rd edn, Butterworth-Heinemann Ltd: Oxford.

Mile, M., Haney, R. (Jnr) & Berens, G. 1996, *Real Estate Development Principles and Process*, The Urban Land Institute: New York.

National Restaurant Association 1990, *Uniform System of Accounts for Restaurants*, 6th edn, National Restaurant Association: Washington.

Robbins, S. & Mukerji, D. 1994, *Managing Organisations—New Challenges and Perspectives*, 2nd edn, Prentice Hall of Australia P/L: Sydney.

Rushmore, S. 1988, *How to Perform an Economic Feasibility Study of a Proposed Hotel/Motel*, American Society of Real Estate Counselors: Chicago.

Stanton, W., Miller, K., & Layton, R. 1994, *Fundamentals of Marketing*, 3rd edn, McGraw-Hill Book Company: Sydney.

Stoner, J., 1995, *Management*, 6th edn, Prentice Hall, Inc.: New Jersey.

Tonge, R. 1997, *How to Conduct Feasibility Studies for Tourism Projects*, 6th edn, Gull Publishing: Queensland.

Index

Notes:

1. In this index, the abbreviation proj.ev. stands for project evaluation.
2. Because virtually all entries apply to hotels, no separate subject entry for hotels is listed in this index. Separate entries are made for other types of hospitality operations.